FROMMER'S

COMPREHENSIVE TRAVEL GUIDE

BERLIN '91-'92

by Beth Reiber

D1386598

PRENTICE
HALL
PRESS

NEW YORK • LONDON • TORONTO • SYDNEY • TOKYO • SINGAPORE

FROMMER BOOKS

Published by Prentice Hall Press
A division of Simon & Schuster Inc.
15 Columbus Circle
New York, NY 10023

ISBN 0-13-337858-6
ISSN 1048-2660

Design by Robert Bull Design
Maps by Geografix Inc.

Manufactured in the United States of America

FROMMER'S BERLIN '91-'92
Editor-in-Chief: Marilyn Wood
Senior Editors: Judith de Rubini, Pamela Marshall, Amit Shah
Editors: Alice Fellows, Paige Hughes
Assistant Editors: Suzanne Arkin, Ellen Zucker
Contributing Editor: Robert Daniels

CONTENTS

1 INTRODUCING BERLIN 1

SPECIAL FEATURES
- *What's Sepcial About Berlin 2*
- *Dateline 3*

2 PLANNING A TRIP TO BERLIN 21

SPECIAL FEATURES
- *Berlin Calendar of Events 24*
- *Frommer's Smart Traveler—Airfares 27*

3 GETTING TO KNOW BERLIN 30

SPECIAL FEATURES
- *What Things Cost in Berlin 33*
- *Fast Facts: Berlin 45*

4 BERLIN ACCOMMODATIONS 53

SPECIAL FEATURES
- *Frommer's Smart Traveler—Hotels 54*
- *Cool for Kids: Hotels 69*

5 BERLIN DINING 89

SPECIAL FEATURES
- *Frommer's Smart Traveler—Restaurants 93*
- *Cool for Kids: Restaurants 126*
- *Restaurants by Cuisine 134*

APPENDIX 230

INDEX 237

LIST OF MAPS

ABOUT THIS FROMMER GUIDE

What Is a Frommer City Guide? It's a comprehensive, easy-to-use guide to the best travel values in all price ranges—from very expensive to budget. The one guidebook to take along with you on any trip.

WHAT THE SYMBOLS MEAN

 FROMMER'S FAVORITES—hotels, restaurants, attractions, and entertainments you should not miss

 SUPER-SPECIAL VALUES—really exceptional values

 FROMMER'S SMART TRAVELER TIPS—hints on how to secure the best value for your money

IN HOTEL AND OTHER LISTINGS

The following symbols refer to the standard amenities available in all rooms:

    A/C air conditioning   TEL telephone   TV television
    MINIBAR refrigerator stocked with beverages and snacks

The following abbreviations are used for credit cards:

AE American Express	DISC Discover	EU Eurocard
CB Carte Blanche	ER enRoute	MC MasterCard
DC Diners Club		V VISA

TRIP PLANNING WITH THIS GUIDE

Use the following features:

What Things Cost In . . . to help your daily budget

Calendar of Events . . . to plan for or to avoid

Suggested Itineraries . . . for seeing the city and environs

What's Special About Checklist . . . a summary of the city's highlights—which lets you check off those that appeal most to you

Easy-to-Read Maps . . . showing walking tours; city sights; hotels and restaurant locations—all referring to or keyed to the text

Fast Facts . . . all the essentials at a glance: climate, currency, embassies, emergencies, information, safety, taxes, tipping, and more

OTHER SPECIAL FROMMER FEATURES

Cool for Kids—hotels, restaurants, and attractions

Did You Know?—offbeat, fun facts

Famous People—the city's greats

Impressions—what others have said

INVITATION TO THE READERS

In researching this book I have come across many wonderful establishments, the best of which are included here. However, I'm sure that many of you will come across other wonderful hotels, inns, restaurants, guest houses, shops, and attractions. Please don't keep them to yourself. Share your experiences, especially if you want to comment on places that I have covered in this edition that have changed for the worse. You can address your letters to:

Beth Reiber c/o Prentice Hall Press, Travel Books
15 Columbus Circle, New York, NY 10023

A DISCLAIMER

Readers are advised that prices fluctuate in the course of time and travel information changes under the impact of the varied and volatile factors that affect the travel industry. The author and publisher cannot be held responsible for the experiences of the reader while traveling. Readers are invited to write the publisher with ideas, comments, and suggestions for future editions.

A NOTE TO THE READER

As we go to press, the reader should note that prices for restaurants, museums, and entertainments in East Berlin will probably change during the next few months.

Zip codes in reunified Berlin will also change slightly. Instead of the prefixes D and DDR, zip codes will now carry a prefix of W for West and O for East: for example, W-1000 Berlin 30.

CHAPTER 1

INTRODUCING BERLIN

1. GEOGRAPHY, HISTORY & POLITICS
2. THE PEOPLE
3. ART, ARCHITECTURE & CULTURAL LIFE
4. FOOD & DRINK
5. FAMOUS BERLINERS
6. RECOMMENDED BOOKS & FILMS

In history books to come, 1989 will shine like a star as a year that ushered in a new era. No one could have predicted that within a period of a few weeks the Eastern European system would crumble and the Berlin Wall come tumbling down, leaving the way open for the two Germanys to reunite. Rarely has there been a revolution of such magnitude without widespread bloodshed and war. East Germany's revolution of November 9, 1989, was completely free of violence. It was also one of the most joyous revolutions of our time.

The focus of East Germany's revolution was, of course, Berlin, former German national capital and both a symbol and a victim of the Cold War. For more than 40 years Berlin was a divided city buried deep within East Germany, a division made even more poignant after the erection of the Wall. More than 100 miles long and 13 feet high, the Berlin Wall was built in 1961 to stop the mass exodus of East Germans into West Berlin that was draining East Germany of its youngest, best-educated, and brightest citizens. How ironic that in 1989 another exodus from the East to the West triggered the Wall's sudden demise.

Today Germany is wrestling with challenges posed by reunification, and no city is more affected than Berlin. If you visited Berlin before the Wall came down, you know how shockingly different were the two sides of the city. Now the city must physically integrate two separate systems that had 40 years to develop, each with its own political, social, economic, cultural, and ideological values. Everything—from bus lines to telephone lines—has had to be coordinated and extended. Even similar museum systems grew out of collections divided between

○ **Berlin has always been liberal, tolerant, and open-minded, with a "live for today" attitude**

East and West after the war, so that today Berlin has two Egyptian museums, two historical museums, two museums of modern art, and two museums of European masterpieces. And that's only the tip of the iceberg.

But Berlin has learned to adapt quickly, and the metamorphosis of the city is taking place even as I write this—and will continue to take place in the years to come, especially in the eastern part. Visitors from around the globe are flocking to see Berlin without the Wall, and the

WHAT'S SPECIAL ABOUT . . . BERLIN

History in the Making
- [ ] No more Wall—Germany's showcase of reunification

Museums
- [ ] The Pergamon Museum in East Berlin, with the Pergamon Altar, Market Gate of Miletus, Babylonian Processional Street, and other architectural wonders
- [ ] The Gemäldegalerie in Dahlem, with 20+ Rembrandts among other masterpieces
- [ ] The Ägyptisches Museum, with the bust of Nefertiti
- [ ] The Neue Nationalgalerie and Nationalgalerie, for outstanding collections of Berliner impressionist and expressionist artists
- [ ] Museum Haus am Checkpoint Charlie, a small but important museum documenting the history of the Wall and nonviolent revolutions around the world

Nightlife
- [ ] Famous opera houses and concert halls, including the Deutsche Oper Berlin and the Philharmonie
- [ ] Cabarets, a Berlin tradition
- [ ] Live-music houses, featuring jazz, rock, folk, and international stars on tour
- [ ] Bars and pubs that stay open all night long
- [ ] Discos and dance halls for all ages

Shopping
- [ ] KaDeWe, the largest department store on the European continent; famous for its food floor
- [ ] Ku'damm, one of Europe's most fashionable streets; great for window-shopping
- [ ] Europa-Center, a large mall with 70 shops, restaurants, and bars
- [ ] More than 100 art galleries
- [ ] Outdoor and indoor markets, a treasure trove for antiques, junk, and crafts

Festivals
- [ ] International Film Festival, held every February
- [ ] Jazz-Fest Berlin in autumn, a colorful mix of avant-garde and classical jazz, with musicians from around the world
- [ ] Weihnachtsmarkt, an annual Christmas market, held around the Ku'damm

Diversity
- [ ] A large ethnic population, including Turks and Greeks
- [ ] Colorful neighborhoods, including Kreuzberg with its Turkish population, working-class Köpenick, and Dahlem with its middle-class homes
- [ ] Restaurants featuring cuisines from around the world: Greek, Turkish, Italian, Japanese, Chinese, Indian, and Thai

entire city is once again the lively, crowded, and vibrant place it used to be. Berlin has always been Germany's least provincial city, liberal, tolerant, and open-minded, with a distinct "live for today" attitude only partly created by years of living with the Wall. No wonder it's always been a magnet for Germans seeking alternative lifestyles, as well as for young Europeans, who generally skip Germany in preference to the more easygoing atmosphere of Paris, Amsterdam, or Copenhagen or the warm beaches of Greece. Of course, it doesn't hurt that the bars of Berlin stay open all night long. Its nightlife is one of the best in Europe.

But more than anything else, Berlin has inherited a rich cultural legacy. Not only does it have some of the best museums in the world—with treasures such as the bust of Nefertiti and the magnificent Pergamon Altar—but also opera, theater, symphony, jazz, international film premieres, and much, much more. And with the opening up of Eastern Europe, it also serves as a perfect gateway to other destinations, especially the eastern half of Germany, Poland, and Czechoslovakia.

In short, this is a great time to be visiting Berlin, as it forges ahead to a new beginning. It gives me indescribable pleasure to write about a Berlin that is whole again, about a Wall that is now history. Years from now, the wonder of future generations will be that there ever was a Wall at all.

1. GEOGRAPHY, HISTORY & POLITICS

Berlin lies in the geographical center of Europe, about halfway between Moscow and Lisbon. It shares the same latitude with London and Vancouver, the same longitude with Naples. With almost 3.5 million people and a total area of 340 square miles, it is Germany's largest city. In fact, it's larger than New York City, and could easily accommodate the cities of Atlanta, Boston, Cleveland, and San Francisco within its boundaries. West Berlin alone has 190 square miles of woods, lakes, rivers, and parks, which served as an important breathing space for its dwellers during the decades of the Wall. Berlin is 184 miles from Hamburg, 343 miles from Frankfurt, and 363 miles from Munich. After the division of Germany following World War II, Berlin was more than 100 miles inside East Germany, closer to Poland than to West Germany.

FROM MEDIEVAL TRADING TOWN TO ROYAL CAPITAL

As ironic as it now seems, Berlin started out as a divided city back in the 12th century, when two settlements were founded on opposite sides of the Spree River. Located about halfway between the fortresses of Spandau and Köpenick, Berlin and Cölln developed as trading towns, spreading along the banks of the Spree in what is now Berlin-Mitte. Although they were not particularly interested in unification, it became

DATELINE

- **1200** Two settlements, Berlin and Cölln, grow up along the Spree River
- **1237** Cölln first mentioned in documents
- **1244** Berlin first mentioned in documents

(continues)

inevitable as they grew, and in 1307 they merged under the name of Berlin and built a joint town hall.

In the next few centuries the people of Berlin fell under the rule of various dynasties and suffered repeated attacks by robber barons. In 1414, Count Friedrich Wilhelm of the house of Hohenzollern came to the rescue and defeated the most notorious of the robber barons. Soon thereafter Count Friedrich proclaimed himself the prince elector of Brandenburg. Although the people of Berlin revolted against the Hohenzollern takeover, the rebellion was easily quashed. In 1470 Berlin became the official residence of the electors of Brandenburg. (The German word for "elector," by the way, is *Kurfürst,* which literally means "chosen prince.")

Under the Hohenzollerns, who ruled for the next 500 years, Berlin changed from a town of merchants, whose guilds set the tone of urban life, to a town of civil servants and government administrators, courtiers, and officials. Noblemen and jurists moved to this new city of opportunity, and the subsequent clamor for necessities and luxury goods also drew many craftsmen to Berlin. From 1450 to 1600 the population grew from 6,000 to 12,000. But then came the plague, smallpox, and the destructive Thirty Years War (1614–48). Fought between Protestants and Catholics, the war destroyed half of the city's population. Luckily for Berlin, however, Friedrich Wilhelm I came to power in 1640; one of the city's most able rulers, he gained great popularity after defeating the Swedes in the decisive battle of Fehrbellin in the Thirty Years War. To this day he is still known as the Great Elector. To bolster the town's economy, in 1685 he invited 6,000 Huguenots—French Protestants, who were forced to flee religious persecution—to settle in Berlin. By 1700 nearly one Berliner in five was of French extraction.

In 1701 the Great Elector's son, Elector Friedrich III, crowned himself the first king of Prussia and became Friedrich I. Up until then, Prussia had been only a duchy under the rule of electors. In 1709 the Prussian king merged Berlin and several surrounding towns into one community, declared Berlin his royal residence, and made it the royal capital of Brandenburg-Prussia. The way was now paved for Berlin to become the most important political, economic, and cultural center of the area. The town, which blossomed under the skillful talents of such well-known architects as Andreas Schlüter, Karl Friedrich Schinkel, and Georg Wenzeslaus von Knobelsdorff, grew by leaps and bounds. In a flurry of activity, the royal palace (destroyed in World War II) was enlarged, the boulevard of Unter den Linden was laid out, the Brandenburger Tor (Brandenburg Gate) and 12 other city gates were built, and such buildings as the Supreme Court (now the Berlin Museum), the Opera, and the Arsenal were completed.

But the man credited with elevating Berlin to one of Europe's premier capitals was Friedrich II, better known as Frederick the Great, who reigned from 1740 to 1786. During his reign he doubled the size of the Prussian army and made Prussia the greatest military power in Europe. An enlightened administrator, he instituted many social reforms and encouraged improvements in industry and agriculture. He also built a charming summer residence in nearby Potsdam, where he could escape from time to time.

Under Frederick the Great, Berlin became a mecca for the Enlightenment, attracting the philosopher Moses Mendelssohn, the author Gotthold Ephraim Lessing, the publisher Friedrich Nicolai, and Voltaire, who came to Potsdam as the king's guest and stayed three years. In 1763 Frederick took over a failing porcelain company, and gave it a production monopoly, banning all foreign imports. The company, the Königliche Porzellan-Manufaktur (KPM), is still well known today. By 1800 Berlin boasted 200,000 inhabitants, making it the third-largest city in Europe after London and Paris.

On October 27, 1806, Napoleon marched into the capital of Prussia, entering triumphantly through the Brandenburger Tor. As part of the spoils from his victory over Prussia, he removed the Quadriga—a chariot drawn by four horses, and the symbol of Berlin—from atop the gate and carted it off to Paris. This struck at the very

DATELINE

- **1740** Reign of Friedrich II (the Great), who elevates Berlin into a European capital city
- **1791** Brandenburger Tor (Brandenburg Gate) built
- **1806** Napoleon enters Berlin, signaling two years of French occupation
- **1862** Otto von Bismarck becomes chancellor of Prussia
- **1871** Berlin becomes capital of the German Reich
- **1918** End of World War I; Kaiser Wilhelm II abdicates
- **1919** Weimar constitution adopted, making Germany a republic
- **1920** Greater Berlin is formed and subdivided into 20 precincts
- **1933** Hitler and the National Socialists come into power; the Third Reich begins
- **1936** Jesse Owens, an American black athlete, wins in the 11th Summer Olympics held in Berlin
- **1939** Hitler invades Poland, beginning World War II
- **1945** The German army surrenders. Berlin is divided into four zones occupied by the Four Powers
- **1948** Eleven-month Berlin

(continues)

DATELINE

Blockade. Berlin Airlift supplies West Berlin

- **1949** Founding of the German Democratic Republic (DDR), with East Berlin as its capital
- **1961** Construction of the Wall begins on August 13, sealing off the Western Sector
- **1963** President John F. Kennedy visits Berlin, pledging support of a free West Berlin
- **1971** Allies sign the Four-Power Agreement on Berlin, confirming political and legal ties between West Berlin and West Germany
- **1972** West Berliners are allowed to visit East Germany
- **1987** 750th anniversary of Berlin, celebrated in both parts of the city
- **1988** Berlin is declared the Cultural City of Europe
- **1989** Hungary opens its borders to allow East Germans to go to the West. Nov. 9 the Wall is opened by the East German government. The Wall itself is dismantled
- **1990** East Germany adopts West German currency, drops all visa re-

(continues)

heart of the proud Prussians, who finally managed to rout the French a couple of years later. They recovered their Quadriga, added an Iron Cross and a Prussian Eagle, and replaced it atop the Brandenburger Tor.

In the 1800s, as the tidal wave of the Industrial Revolution overtook Berlin, many of the city's working people found themselves left behind in a wake of poverty. Although educational reform and abolition of serfdom helped to alleviate the poor person's lot, life for a majority of the people became more and more difficult. Peasants flocked into Berlin hoping to find work, and women and children were exploited in dismal factories. The middle class, meanwhile, demanded political power in keeping with their newly acquired social status. Although there were several revolts, notably the March Revolution of 1848, few concessions were gained. By the 1870s, 70,000 out of a population of 826,000 were homeless. Even those with a roof over their head often lived in gloomy and depressing flats that never saw the light of day. Berlin had the dubious distinction of being the world's largest tenement city.

FROM CAPITAL OF THE GERMAN REICH TO CAPITAL OF THE THIRD REICH

In 1871 Otto von Bismarck, the Prussian chancellor, succeeded in uniting all of Germany with a nationalist policy under the slogan "iron and blood." Berlin became capital of this new German Empire, attracting even more industry and settlers; by 1906 the city had two million inhabitants. After the turn of the century Berlin began to challenge Munich as the country's cultural capital, attracting such artists as Max Liebermann, Lovis Corinth, and Max Slevogt. Ornate apartment dwellings sprang up, sprouting the intricate lines of art nouveau. Max Reinhardt came to Berlin to take over as director of the Deutsches Theater, and Richard Strauss became conductor of the Royal Opera.

In 1920 Berlin incorporated 7 formerly autonomous towns, 59 rural communities, and 27 landed estates to form a Greater Berlin, which was then divided into 20 precincts. This made Berlin the Continent's industrial giant, the nucleus of the North German railway network, and a major commercial, banking, and stock-exchange center. Through the golden twenties, Berlin continued to flourish as an avant-garde intellectual and cultural center, and such archi-

DATELINE

quirements for entering East Berlin
• **1990** Reunification takes place on October 3

tectural greats as Walter Gropius and Hans Scharoun left their marks upon the city. In 1926 a young playwright named Bertolt Brecht scored a huge success with the premiere of his *Dreigroschenoper* (*Threepenny Opera*). Altogether there were 35 theaters, several opera houses, and more than 20 concert halls. Berlin's university gained a reputation as one of the best in the country, and Albert Einstein, who was director of physics at what would later become the Max-Planck Institute, received the Nobel Prize in 1921. As many as 150 daily and weekly newspapers were published in Berlin.

But underneath the glittering facade, trouble was brewing. The woes of the working class had become increasingly acute, and the general feeling of despair and hopelessness was captured by such artists as Käthe Kollwitz and Heinrich Zille and writer Kurt Tucholsky. Like the rest of Germany, Berlin had suffered hardships during World War I, including a weekly rationing of one egg, 20 grams of butter, and 80 grams of meat per person. Heating fuel, lighting, and clothing were rationed as well. But the end of the war brought little relief, even though the emperor had abdicated and Germany was proclaimed a republic. Parts of the country were sliced off and given to the victors, and Germany was saddled with huge war reparations. In the winter of 1918–19 there were 300,000 people out of work in Berlin alone. To make matters worse, inflation had reached such grotesque proportions that money was virtually worthless: it took barrelfuls just to buy a loaf of bread. When new banknotes were finally issued, one new banknote equaled 1,000 billion of the worthless old paper marks.

In the crisis, sections of the middle class were wiped out, and extremist factions were strengthened. There were struggles between extreme rightists and leftists, often resulting in street fights, brawls, militant strikes, and bloody riots. As Germany began to move toward recovery, the Great Depression hit in 1929. The economic crisis went from bad to worse, with 636,000 unemployed in Berlin by the end of 1932. Many families lost their jobs and their homes; some people committed suicide.

Little wonder that an obscure political party called the National Socialists arose from the ashes of World War I and gained followers with promises of making Germany great again. On January 30, 1933, Adolf Hitler became chancellor of Germany, and one of his first moves was to rid "Red Berlin" of its leftist majority. First, Berlin's Communist Party headquarters were raided by police on the pretense that the party had planned a coup d'état. Then, on the night of February 27, 1933, the Reichstag building was mysteriously set on fire. Although no one ever proved who set the fire—indeed, some people think it was the Nazis themselves—hundreds of Communists,

Social Democrats, trade unionists, and intellectuals were rounded up, imprisoned, tortured, and even murdered.

But the reign of terror had only just begun, and after 20,000 books by German authors were publicly burned in a Berlin square in May 1933, the country's best writers left the country. Scientists soon followed. On November 9, 1938, Berlin was the scene of the so-called Kristallnacht (the night of broken glass), a wave of terror directed against Jews. Synagogues and Jewish businesses were burned to the ground. During the next years, as many as 50,000 Berliners of Jewish faith died in concentration camps. By the time Germany invaded Poland in 1939 and catapulted Europe into another world war, it had rid itself of virtually all opposition.

BERLIN AFTER 1945

Berlin suffered heavy casualties and was virtually destroyed in World War II. The legacy of the "Thousand-Year Reich" left behind a wasteland of ruin. Of the 245,000 buildings in Berlin before the war, 50,000 were destroyed. As many as 80,000 Berliners had lost their lives. At first peace brought little relief. There were food shortages and fuel shortages, and anyone who had anything to sell resorted to the black market. Berliners laden with furs and jewelry headed for farms in the country, trying to barter luxuries for food. Even drinking water had to be brought in from the country. Fuel was so scarce that all the trees were cut down along the streets and in city parks so people wouldn't freeze to death.

But soon Berliners were at work clearing away the rubble, too busy trying to survive and create a liveable world to worry about tomorrow. But their fate had been sealed even before the end of the war—the Allies had divided Germany and Berlin into occupation zones to be governed by Great Britain, the United States, the Soviet Union, and later, France. Although each Allied Power had supreme authority in its own zone in Germany, Berlin was to be ruled jointly. This proved easier said than done, however.

In the summer of 1945 Churchill, Truman, and Stalin converged on Potsdam, where they agreed to disarm and demilitarize Germany. There was never any intention to split the country in half or change Berlin's role as capital. Rather, they agreed that Nazism must be abolished and that local self-government should be set up on a democratic basis. But they had no plans for how things should proceed and differing ideas of what constituted a democracy. And as time went on, political aims and ideological differences between the Soviet and Western powers became more evident.

When elections were held for Berlin's Municipal Assembly in October 1946, the Social Democrats (SPD) won almost half of the votes, while the Socialist Unity party, the Soviet-sponsored Communist party, garnered only 19.8% of the votes, clearly a rejection by the majority.

In 1948 the introduction of the Deutsche Mark (DM) by the Western Powers delineated a financial separation between their zones and East Germany, strengthening West Berlin's ties with West Germany.

As far as the Soviets were concerned, Berlin, with a growing democratic following, was becoming a dangerous thorn in the Soviet side. In retaliation, they introduced their own currency and declared it legal tender throughout all Berlin. They then imposed a road blockade of Berlin. Since food, raw materials, and necessities for two million people came from West Germany, the only alternative was to fly in supplies. Gen. Lucius D. Clay, who organized the Berlin Airlift, called the blockade "one of the most brutal attempts in recent history to use mass starvation as a means of applying political pressure."

Although some Berliners did respond to offers of food from the East, the majority preferred to bear hardship rather than come under Soviet influence. On June 26, 1948, the largest airlift in history began, and within weeks 4,000 tons of supplies were being flown into Berlin daily; Tegel Airport was built in only three months. At the peak of the airlift, a plane was landing every one to two minutes, and in April 1949 a record was set when nearly 13,000 tons of supplies were flown in on a single day. During the eleven months that the airlift lasted, more than 200,000 flights had brought in 1.7 million tons of supplies.

The Soviets had hoped that the blockade would prove the end of Western influence in Berlin, but instead, it drew the Western Powers together, formed a bond of friendship between Berliners and the West, and convinced the Western Powers that they must remain in Berlin to defend their concept of freedom. Soon thereafter, the Municipal Assembly and the City Council, which had had their seats in the Eastern Sector, moved to the Western Sector. The Communists responded by appointing their own City Council. The city was now divided, politically and ideologically. From then on, each part of the city followed its own course of development. In 1949 East Berlin became capital of the German Democratic Republic (DDR). In 1952 telephone communications between the two cities were cut off, tram and bus lines were severed, and West Berliners were no longer allowed into the surrounding East German countryside, although there was still unrestricted movement throughout Berlin. In 1955 West Germany became a member of NATO; East Germany, a member of the Warsaw Pact. The Cold War was on.

And yet, hardly anyone could imagine that a divided Germany was anything but temporary. As far as West Germany was concerned, its goal was reunification and the reestablishment of Berlin as capital. An uprising of East German workers on June 17, 1953, which was brutally quashed by Soviet soldiers, only reconfirmed West Germany's commitment.

Meanwhile, Berlin began to grow and prosper. Whereas 300,000 Berliners were unemployed in 1950, the number decreased to 90,000 just seven years later. Berliners could travel freely throughout the city, with the result that many East Berliners flocked to factories in West Berlin. Housing estates mushroomed, replacing homes that had been destroyed in the war. In 1957 West Berlin hosted a competition that brought 50 leading architects from around the world to design housing for the Hansaviertel (Hansa Quarter). Clearly, West Berlin was recovering much more rapidly than East Germany, and it soon became an attraction for East Germans eager for a look at the new Berlin. Many of them decided to stay, including skilled specialists. In fact, East Germany was losing people to the West not only in unprecedented numbers but also those it sorely needed if it was ever to get its feet back on the ground. From 1949 to 1961, approximately three million East Germans left their country.

In November 1958 Nikita Khrushchev issued the Berlin Ultimatum, demanding that the Western Powers withdraw from West Berlin. Since Berlin was seen as an important player in the "domino theory" of Communist takeovers, the Western Powers refused.

On August 13, 1961, East Germany began erecting a wall between East and West Berlin by tearing up streets and putting up posts and barbed wire. A few days later the wall was reinforced with concrete and brick. Movement between the two Berlins was now forbidden, leaving families and friends separated by what soon became known around the world simply as the Wall. Measuring 13 feet high and approximately 100 miles long, the Wall was backed up by hundreds of guardhouses, 293 sentry towers, patrol dogs, and a vast swath of brightly illuminated no-man's-land. However, that didn't completely stop the East German exodus; approximately 5,000 of them managed to escape to West Berlin, most during the early years, when the Wall was not yet perfected; 78 people lost their lives trying to do so.

For 28 years the Wall stood as a constant reminder of Germany's forced division. Even for visitors, the shock of seeing the Wall for the first time was chilling, a feeling that intensified at border control points such as Checkpoint Charlie. Mirrors were shoved under cars to make sure no one was hiding underneath; travelers on foot were shuttled through doors that clanged shut behind them, as though they were entering a high-security prison. The difference between the two Berlins became more radical over time. West Berlin was a capitalist's dream—intense, aggressive, and chaotic, a whirling blend of traffic, people, neon, and noise. East Berlin, on the other hand, was conservative and subdued, sterile and quiet, with soldiers everywhere. The contrast was like night and day.

In 1971 the Four Powers signed an agreement that confirmed political and legal ties between West Berlin and West Germany. Telephone communications between the two Berlins were restored, and West Berliners were allowed to visit East Germany. For the next 18 years, conditions between East and West improved steadily. However, Westerners traveling into East Germany were required to exchange a minimum amount of Western currency into East German marks, and travel was still complicated and difficult for non-Germans.

In autumn of 1989 Hungary dismantled its borders to the West and allowed East Germans to pass through. This prompted a full-scale exodus, as tens of thousands of East Germans poured into

---

IMPRESSIONS

All free men, wherever they live, are citizens of Berlin, and therefore, as a free man, I take pride in the words, "Ich bin ein Berliner."
—JOHN F. KENNEDY, 1963

Hungary on their way to the West. Pro-reform demonstrations began throughout East Germany, resulting in the ouster of hard-line East German leader Erich Honecker on October 18. By November 1989 approximately 175,000 East German refugees had fled their homeland, almost 1% of the country's total population. It was clear that something had to be done to staunch the flow. But no one dreamed that the Wall itself would fall.

On the evening of November 9, 1989, East Germany announced that it was permanently lifting travel restrictions on its citizens, giving them freedom to travel for the first time since the Wall was erected in 1961. That evening 50,000 East Berliners streamed into West Berlin and were welcomed on the other side with embraces and tears. Many Berliners climbed on top of the Wall to dance and celebrate.

A teacher working in West Berlin recalled what it was like in those first heady days of the Wall's opening: "On Friday [November 10] I went to the school where I work, but the director decided to cancel all classes, because history was being made in the streets and the children should see it. So I went to Potsdamer Square, and the whole experience was so emotional, so strange, that I had goosebumps several times that day. We watched the East Berliners come through the opening in the Wall. The first ones seemed very unsure of themselves, as though they still didn't believe they could. They came slowly, with big eyes. Some of them, especially the older ones, wept. It was as if they were being let out of prison after so many years."

Soon thereafter West Germany announced its dedication to reunification, and East German elections held March 18, 1990, signaled the official demise of the Communist regime.

But as the months wore on and the newness wore off, new problems began to surface, and there were fears about the future in both East and West. By March 1990, as many as 500,000 East Germans had settled in the West, entitling them to "adjustment money," household compensation, housing subsidies, and job retraining. In keeping with a policy that had been established years before, any East German coming into West Germany for the first time, even for a day, was entitled to a welcoming token of 100 DM ($60), but the West German government had never dreamed that virtually the entire country would come over to get it. Many West Germans began worrying about the financial burdens of reunification, especially the cost of East German economic development.

East Germans, on the other hand, were concerned about what the sudden influx of goods and show of material wealth might do to the values of the nation's youth, not to mention fears aroused by a previously unheard-of influx of drugs. Furthermore, East Germans worried about being treated as second-class citizens, economically and culturally; loss of benefits they had under the old regime; and unemployment that must result from the closing of non-competitive, formerly subsidized enterprises.

Berlin faces not only the physical challenges of integrating two systems that have existed side by side for decades. Pitied for years as a victim of the Cold War, it must now deal with ghosts from the past, as neighbors of a reunified Germany remember it as capital of the Third Reich.

And the future? One of change, certainly, especially in East Berlin as investors move in and open hotels, restaurants, shops, and factories. Berlin may again be capital of reunified Germany. Considering what's happened during the past half century, and especially during the past few years, no one would be surprised. The story of Berlin, one of the most compelling and riveting stories of our time, is still being written.

2. THE PEOPLE

No one could ever accuse the Germans of being too lighthearted or frivolous. Indeed, they rank as among the most reserved in Europe. They take pleasure in neatness, in precision, in the established order of things, and even their language has changed little over the centuries. Instead of creating new words for new concepts or objects, for example, the Germans are more apt to string together words they already know.

There's little doubt that Berliners are Germans through and through, and are even Prussian on top of that, but they are also known for their dry wit and humor. They have what's called *Schnauze,* a Texas-like attitude that says everything in Berlin is bigger and better—a trait they share with the Bavarians. According to one joke that recently made the rounds, a Bavarian boasted that Bavaria was better than Berlin because it had the Alps. He then smugly asked a Berliner whether Berlin had any mountains that compared.

"No," answered the Berliner calmly, looking his rival squarely in the eyes. "But if we did, you can be sure they'd be higher than yours."

With a population of almost 3.5 million people, Berlin is the most densely populated city in Germany. It also has the largest non-German population of any German city, with foreign nationals making up more than 10% of the total residents in West Berlin. One of the first and biggest tides of immigration brought the Huguenots in the 17th century. With them came their language and food, still evident in Berlin today—a *Boulette,* for example, is a meatball that can be traced to the Huguenots and is today considered a Berlin specialty.

In more recent times, newcomers to Berlin have included large numbers of Turkish, Yugoslavian, Greek, and Polish immigrants. Turks are the largest minority in Berlin, numbering more than

IMPRESSIONS

Take, for instance, the Prussians: they are saints when compared with the French. They have every sort of excellence; they are honest, sober, hardworking, well instructed, brave, good sons, husbands, and fathers and yet. . . . all with whom I have been thrown were proud as Scotchmen, cold as New Englanders, and touchy as only Prussians can be.
—HENRY LABOUCHERE, 1871

100,000. They live mainly in the West Berlin precincts of Kreuzberg, Neukölln, and Wedding. Although problems occasionally arise because of differences in cultural backgrounds, Berlin on the whole enjoys a greater harmony than elsewhere in Germany. Decades of isolation have helped forge a sense of community spirit. Years of living with the Wall have bred tolerance and determination.

As for the Berliner wit, it's most evident in a penchant to nickname everything in sight. The Kongresshalle, for example, built as the American contribution in a 1957 architectural competition, is irreverently called the "pregnant oyster," while the new church next to the Gedächtniskirche is known as the "lipstick and powder puff," and a large global fountain in front of the Europa-Center is the "wet dumpling."

3. ART, ARCHITECTURE & CULTURAL LIFE

Home of the Deutsche Oper and the Staatsoper, the Berlin Philharmonic Orchestra, and more than 100 museums, Berlin is Germany's cultural capital. But it's a new city, with little remaining after the destruction of World War II. Its oldest buildings, for example, are actually reconstructions. Thus, even the Nikolaikirche and the Marienkirche (both in East Berlin), which are considered the city's oldest structures, have been either rebuilt or renovated. The Berlin Palace, a sumptuous Renaissance residence for the Prussian kings, was deemed by the East German government to be irreparably damaged and was torn down to make way for East Berlin's modern Palace of the Republic.

Some buildings, however, remain from the 1700s, including the Arsenal on Unter den Linden, a fine baroque building now housing the Museum für Deutsche Geschichte (Museum of German History), and the nearby Opera House, built by Georg Wenzeslaus von Knobbelsdorff in the mid-1700s. And of course, no Berlin structure is better known around the world than the Brandenburger Tor (Brandenburg Gate), completed in 1786 and one of 13 gates that used to mark the entrance to the city. There are also some fine turn-of-the century patrician homes, especially on Fasanenstrasse and other side streets off the Kurfürstendamm, known as the Ku'damm. As for modern architecture, there's the Bauhaus-Archiv by Walter Gropius and the Hansaviertel (Hansa Quarter), a residential area designed by 50 leading architects from around the world, each of whom was asked to design one building.

✪ **Charlottenburg Palace is considered Berlin's most beautiful baroque building**

But for the most part, Berlin's artistic heritage lives on in its museums. Berlin's love affair with museums can be traced back to the

1820s, when construction of a museum complex was begun by King Friedrich Wilhelm III, who wished to make his collection of masterpieces available to the viewing public. Located on Museumsinsel (Museum Island) in East Berlin, the complex grew through the next century, as German archeologists searched the world for treasures from Egypt, Persia, and Greece. Berlin today is home of the famous bust of Nefertiti, the incredible Pergamon Altar, and the breathtaking Gate of Ishtar. It boasts not only a wide array of art museums but also history museums, collections of applied arts, and special-interest museums. Luckily for tourists, most are concentrated in four areas of Berlin—Dahlem, Tiergarten, Charlottenburg, and Museumsinsel.

Of course, it would be wrong to assume that all Berlin's treasures originated someplace else, for the city was home to a great many artists during the past century. One of the earliest to gain fame was Adolph von Menzel (1815–1905), a largely self-taught painter who became known for his portraits. A man who sought company in Berlin's many coffeehouses, he is considered a forerunner of the impressionists. He was followed by a group of artists who in 1892 founded the Secession movement, headed by Max Liebermann, which was concerned with developing its own stylistic approach to impressionism. Liebermann, Lovis Corinth, and Max Slevogt are considered the foremost German impressionists.

But the real shot in the arm for Berlin's artistic circles was the new generation of painters who flocked to Berlin after the turn of the century. Foremost among them was a group that came from Dresden during 1910 and 1911, known as Die Brücke (The Bridge). What they found was the fastest-growing city in Europe, with villas, tenements, and factories springing forth at an amazing tempo. Many of the new crop of artists viewed this industrial giant as something of a nightmare, a place that inspired fear, longing, unrest, and expectation of impending doom. Rather than simply imitating nature or photographing people, these painters felt their work should reflect inner feelings and conflicts. Thus was born German expressionism. Ernst Ludwig Kirchner, Emil Nolde, Max Pechstein, and Oskar Kokoschka were important artists of the time, as were Käthe Kollwitz and Heinrich Zille, both Berliners dedicated to portraying the city's growing army of the poor.

> ✪ **The new generation of painters, who viewed industrial Berlin as something of a nightmare, felt their work should reflect their inner feelings—thus was German expressionism born**

Berlin's artists are richly represented in the city's many museums, including the Brücke-Museum in Dahlem, with works of Die Brücke artists; the Käthe-Kollwitz-Museum near the Ku'damm; and the Neue Nationalgalerie (New National Gallery), in the Tiergarten museum complex. The Neue Nationalgalerie, in particular, has an outstanding collection of works by Berlin's artists, including Menzel, Max Beckmann, Corinth, Kokoschka, and Kirchner. Another great museum for Berliner art is the Nationalgalerie (National Gallery) on

Museumsinsel in East Berlin, with works by Liebermann, Slevogt, Kirchner, Nolde, Kokoschka, and Kollwitz. In addition, works by contemporary artists of Berlin are shown regularly in special exhibitions in the Neue Nationalgalerie and the Berlinische Galerie.

As for the rest of Berlin's cultural scene, it boasts a rich tradition of the stage. Much of Germany's theatrical history stems from Berlin, for it was here that playwrights Gerhart Hauptmann and Bertolt Brecht, as well as Henrik Ibsen and August Strindberg, made their first major breakthroughs. Max Reinhardt, recognized as the man who introduced German theater to the world, was director of Berlin's Deutsches Theater from 1905 to 1920 and again from 1924 to 1932 (he was also the mastermind behind the world-famous Salzburg Festival). In the 1920s Berlin had approximately 35 theaters, several opera houses, and more than 20 concert halls.

Today Berlin is still famous for its theater, including the Schiller-Theater and the Berliner Ensemble. In addition, it also has cabaret, albeit not in the same form or intensity as before the Hitler era. In addition, Berlin is home to two well-known opera houses, the International Film Festival, the Philharmonic Orchestra, and a number of concert halls and live-music houses. Little wonder Berlin has a reputation as the city that never sleeps. There's so much to do and see, who would want to?

4. FOOD & DRINK

The Germans may have found more ways to use pork than any other people on earth. If you don't believe me, just go to the food floor of Berlin's KaDeWe department store, where you'll find 1,000 different kinds of sausage alone, most of them made with pork. Portions in a German restaurant are huge, consisting of a main entrée plus a couple of side dishes heaped onto the plate, not to mention the almost obligatory rounds of beer. In other words, German food is not a weight-reducing cuisine; and no one would dream of asking for a "doggie bag." But few seem to worry about calories in Germany—witness the coffee shops packed at 4pm, the unofficial coffee break around the country, when everyone downs cups of coffee and mountains of tortes and cakes as though it were his or her last meal.

BREAKFAST

The typical German breakfast consists of bread or rolls topped with marmalade, cheese, or—you guessed it—sausage. Unlike American sandwiches, which are stuffed with as many ingredients as they can hold, in Germany it's customary to place only a single ingredient upon each roll or slice of bread. If it's a slice of bread, a German is apt to eat it with a knife and fork, the fork turned upside down. Along with the bread is a soft-boiled egg in an eggcup. If it's a buffet breakfast in a hotel, other items may include cereals such as Muesli (a grain cereal similar to granola) and cornflakes, fruit, juices, and coffee. German coffee is much stronger than American coffee—and there's rarely a bottomless cup in Germany, though some hotels give extra servings to guests during breakfast. In higher-class hotels, breakfast buffets will also include scrambled eggs, bacon, and hash-brown potatoes. At the other extreme is a Continental breakfast, consisting simply of coffee or tea and rolls with marmalade.

If your hotel doesn't serve breakfast, you have a choice of many famous coffeehouses, most of them up and down the Ku'damm. An alternative is one of the many breakfast cafés, which are open not only early in the morning but much of the night as well—to serve the needs of hungry night crawlers, most of them young people.

LUNCH & DINNER

For lunch or dinner, your choice of venue ranges from expensive restaurants serving Continental cuisine (a mixture of German, French, and Italian ingredients and dishes) to the neighborhood *Gaststätte,* simple German restaurants that often serve as the local pubs as well. Traditionally, most Germans eat their big meal of the day at lunch.

In a German restaurant, start your meal with a hearty bowl of soup—which may end up being all you can consume. One of my favorites is Linsensuppe (lentil soup, often with pieces of sausage). Leberknödelsuppe (a dumpling soup made with beef liver, onions, and garlic) and Kartoffelsuppe (potato soup) are other common choices. Gulaschsuppe, borrowed from Hungary, is a spicy soup featuring beef, paprika, and potatoes. Appetizers include Hackepeter (raw minced meat or steak tartare) and Soleier (pickled eggs). Breads are almost endless in variety, from rye or Pumpernickel to various kinds of hard rolls called Brötchen.

For the main dish, one of Berlin's best-known specialties is Eisbein (pig's knuckle), usually served with Sauerkraut and potatoes or puréed peas. Kasseler Rippenspeer is smoked pork chops, created long ago by a butcher in Berlin named Kassel. A Boulette is a type of meatball served with mustard. Other pork items you might find on a German menu include Schweinebraten (pot-roasted pork) and Spanferkel (suckling pig). If you come across a Schweinshaxen, it's grilled knuckle of pork. A Schlachtplatte (roughly translated, it means a butcher's platter) is only for the adventuresome, consisting as it does of fresh blood sausage, Leberwurst (liverwurst), pig's kidneys, and boiled pork.

As for those Würste, or sausages, you'll encounter them on almost every menu, as well as at stand-up food stalls, where they're served with a hard roll and mustard. Every region of Germany has its own specialties. In Berlin it's Bockwurst, a superlong sausage, often served with Erbsensuppe (split-pea soup). Another favorite is Bratwurst from Nürnberg, often prepared with beer, and the Wiener.

If you want something other than pork, choices readily available may include Sauerbraten (marinated beef in a thick sauce), Schnitzel (breaded veal cutlet), Brathering (grilled herring), Brathuhn (roast chicken), Aal grün (boiled eel in a dill sauce), and gebratene Leber (sautéed liver with onions and apples). Other main courses include Tafelspitz (boiled beef with vegetables), Leberkäs (a type of German meatloaf, common to southern Germany), and Sülze (jellied meat). The vegetarian, in almost any restaurant, can order a Gemuseplatte, or dish of assorted vegetables.

DRINKS

Germany is known for its wines and its beers, both of which are in plentiful supply in Berlin. Berlin, however, is not a wine-producing region. Frederick the Great tried it at his summer residence at Potsdam—but the rows of grape vines at Schloss Sanssouci are all that remain of his efforts. Berlin does, however, offer wines from other German regions, including the Rhine region (Rheingau, Rheinhesse, and Rheinpfalz), Baden-Württemberg, and Franken. Wines range from the Riesling to Sekt (a sparkling wine), from dry (*Trocken*) to sweet (*Süss*). Unless you know your German wines or simply want to experiment, ask your sommelier or waiter for a recommendation.

As for beer, Berlin's most famous brew is called *Berliner Weisse,* a draft wheat beer served with a shot of raspberry or a green woodruff syrup and usually drunk in summer. If you simply order *ein Bier,* you'll get either a draft beer (*vom Fass*) or bottled beer (*eine Flasche*). An Export is slightly stronger but is still considered light; a Bock beer is dark and rich. A Pils or Pilsener is light and slightly bitter.

5. FAMOUS BERLINERS

Otto von Bismarck   (1815–98) Known as the Iron Chancellor, Bismarck was a brilliant politician who succeeded in uniting all of Germany in 1871 and became the empire's first chancellor. Although he was dismissed from office by Kaiser Wilhelm II in 1890, Bismarck remained a popular figure in Berlin.

Willy Brandt   (b. 1913) A prominent and popular member of the Social Democratic Party (SPD), Brandt served as mayor of Berlin from 1957 to 1966, weathering such critical events as the construction of the Wall. In 1969 he became chancellor of West Germany and received the Nobel Peace Prize in 1971; in 1974, however, he stepped down after the uncovering of an espionage ring caused as much uproar in Germany as Watergate did in the United States.

Bertolt Brecht (1898–1956) One of Germany's best-known playwrights, Brecht came to Berlin in 1920, working with Max Reinhardt at the Deutsches Theater. An ardent Marxist, Brecht wrote epic dramas that scorned the materialistic self-absorption of the upper class and underscored the plight of the poor and the working class. In 1928 he achieved fame with the success of his *Dreigroschenoper (Threepenny Opera)*. Other well-known plays include *Mother Courage and Her Children* and *The Good Woman of Szechuan*. In 1933 Brecht left the city, but after the war he returned to East Berlin, where he founded his own theater, the famous Berliner Ensemble, which continues to stage his works.

Walter Gropius (1883–1969) Born in Berlin, Gropius studied architecture not only there but in Munich. In 1919 he became director of the Weimar School of Art, which he reorganized into the legendary Bauhaus. From 1928 to 1934 he worked as an architect in Berlin, immigrating in 1934 to England and then in 1937 to the United States, where he worked as a professor at Harvard University until 1952. Among his accomplishments in Berlin, there's an apartment building he designed in the Hansaviertel as part of a 1957 international competition, as well as the Bauhaus-Archiv, which was built after his death according to his designs.

Heinrich von Kleist (1777–1811) Kleist, who served for a time in the Prussian army, wrote a number of short stories and plays, including *Der Zerbrochene Krug (The Broken Pitcher)* and *Prinz Friedrich von Homburg*. Throughout his life, however, Kleist was plagued with depression and restlessness, leaving and returning to Berlin many times. He ended up taking his own life on the shores of Wannsee lake on the outskirts of Berlin.

Georg Wenzeslaus von Knobelsdorff (1699–1753) After studying in Italy, Paris, Spain, and Dresden, Knobelsdorff went on to become one of Germany's leading rococo architects. A friend of Frederick the Great's, he actualized sketches drawn by Frederick for Schloss Sanssouci in Potsdam, which today remains Knobelsdorff's greatest achievement. He also designed the Deutsche Staatsoper (destroyed by fire in 1843) on Unter den Linden in East Berlin. A noted landscape architect, he laid out the Sanssouci park.

Käthe Kollwitz (1867–1945) A Berliner, Kollwitz was a gifted graphic artist, painter, and sculptress who sought to capture such emotions as tenderness, despair, grief, and happiness in her studies of common Berliners, particularly those of the working class. See her works at the Käthe-Kollwitz Museum on Fasanenstrasse near the Ku'damm.

Max Liebermann (1847–1935) Liebermann, a painter and graphic artist who was born and died in Berlin, is considered the main representative of impressionism in Germany. He was founder and president of the Secession movement, a group of artists concerned with developing their own impressionist style. His works are on display in the Neue Nationalgalerie in Tiergarten and the Nationalgalerie on Museumsinsel.

Adolph von Menzel (1815–1905) A painter, graphic artist, draftsman, and illustrator, the self-taught Menzel is credited with anticipating impressionism in his paintings of the 1840s and 1850s.

He gained fame and popularity in many Berlin circles through his portraits, and was known to frequent the city's lively cafés. The Neue Nationalgalerie in Tiergarten has the world's largest collection of works by this Berliner artist.

Otto Nagel   (1894–1967) Nagel, also a Berliner, became one of the main representatives of proletarian art in Germany, with realistic portraits of Berlin's working class figuring importantly in his output. Dating mainly from the 1920s and 1930s, his works are on display at the Otto-Nagel-Haus in East Berlin.

Max Reinhardt   (1873–1943) Reinhardt, one of the legendary names in German theater, is credited with introducing German-language theater to the rest of the world. He served as director of the Deutsches Theater from 1905 to 1920 and again from 1924 to 1932. Reinhardt also founded the renowned Salzburg Festival.

Karl Friedrich Schinkel   (1781–1841) Schinkel was a gifted artist whose talents went beyond architecture—he worked as a landscape painter and stage designer in addition to pursuing a career as an architect, for which he received his training in Berlin. His works include the Neue Wache (New Guardhouse) on Unter den Linden, which today houses a memorial to victims of fascism and militarism, and the Alte Museum on Museumsinsel (Museum Island); the latter resembles a Greek temple. Particularly delightful is his summerhouse behind Schloss Charlottenburg, built in the style of an Italian villa and known today as the Schinkel Pavilion.

Andreas Schlüter   (1660–1714) Schlüter, Berlin's top baroque architect, is credited with giving the city a royal physical presence. Also a sculptor, he was greatly influenced by Michelangelo and Italian baroque sculpture during a trip to Italy in 1696; in fact Schlüter is best known for his 21 masks of dying warriors in the courtyard of the Arsenal on Unter den Linden (now the Museum of German History) and his equestrian statue of the Great Elector that now sits in the forecourt of Schloss Charlottenburg. As the court architect, he rebuilt the palace (no longer in existence), but fell out of favor when a tower he designed collapsed.

Heinrich Zille   (1858–1929) Zille is known for his sketches and caricatures of turn-of-the-century life in Berlin, including those depicting the poor and working class. Having come from a poor family himself, he had an eye for the absurd and the comic, and contributed regularly to satirical journals. Zille's works can be seen at the Berlin Museum in Kreuzberg.

6. RECOMMENDED BOOKS & FILMS

BOOKS

POLITICS & HISTORY

In *Before the Deluge: A Portrait of Berlin in the 1920s* (Harper & Row, 1986), Friedrich Otto captures the intellectual life of Berlin in the 1920s, when it was the third-largest city in the world and was home to such well-known people as Marlene Dietrich, Albert Einstein, Greta Garbo, Bertolt Brecht, Walter Gropius, Wassily Kandinsky, and Paul Klee.

Norman Geb's *The Berlin Wall: Kennedy, Khrushchev, and a Showdown in the Heart of Europe* (Times Books, 1988) explains Berlin's pivotal role in the Cold War.

Living with the Wall: West Berlin 1961–1985 (Duke Publishing Co., 1985) is Richard and Anna Merritt's description of Berlin as a divided city during the decades of the Wall.

For a history of Berlin from the reigns of the Great Elector and Frederick the Great through the rise of Bismarck to both world wars and the fall of the city in 1945, try Alexander Reissner's *Berlin 1675–1945: The Rise and Fall of a Metropolis* (Oswald Wolff, London, 1984).

Berlin Diary: The Journal of a Foreign Correspondent 1934–1941 (Little, Brown, 1988) is a personal narrative by well-known correspondent William L. Shirer, who went on to write one of the definitive books on Nazi Germany, *The Rise and Fall of the Third Reich* (Simon & Schuster, 1960).

Ann and John Tuna's *The Berlin Airlift* (Atheneum, 1988) re-creates the most massive airlift ever undertaken—11 months in 1948, when more than 200,000 flights brought 1.7 million tons of supplies to the people of Berlin.

FICTION

Having lived in Berlin from 1929 to 1933, Christopher Isherwood wrote about the people he met in the two novels contained in *The Berlin Stories* (New Directions, 1954). The more famous is *Goodbye to Berlin,* a fictionalized account of the last days of the Weimar Republic and the rise of the Nazis, which was the source for the stage play and movie *Cabaret.*

FILMS

Berlin Alexanderplatz (1980) Mammoth film by Rainer Werner Fassbinder that first played in movie houses and afterward on television. Story of a man's life in Berlin from 1927–1978.

Berlin Express (1948) Semi-documentary-style espionage thriller that uses actual footage of bombed-out Berlin, with Merle Oberon and Paul Lukas.

Berlin, Symphony of a Great City (1927) Documentary about life in Berlin. One of the first impressionistic documentaries.

Cabaret (1972) Bob Fosse's musical set in the Berlin of 1931, based on John van Druten's stage play that in turn was based on Christopher Isherwood's Berlin stories. It starred Liza Minnelli and Joel Grey.

Wings of Desire (1989) Wim Wenders' film is laid in contemporary Berlin, with Peter Falk and Bruno Ganz.

CHAPTER 2

PLANNING A TRIP TO BERLIN

Much of the anxiety associated with travel comes from not knowing what to expect. This chapter will help you prepare for your trip to Berlin, but don't stop here. Reading through the other chapters before leaving home will also provide useful information and will give you an idea of what Berlin is like and what you might like to see or do. Just learning that Berlin has many lakes great for swimming, for example, may prompt you to pack your swimsuit; on the other hand, learning that there are many nude beaches may prompt you to leave your suit at home.

1. INFORMATION, DOCUMENTS & MONEY

INFORMATION

The **German National Tourist Office (GNTO)** publishes a wealth of free, colorful items available to travelers, including a map of Germany, a general-information brochure about travel in Germany (including money and visa requirements), a brochure on Berlin itself, and one on the city's hotels.

If you'd like information and literature before leaving home, contact one of the GNTO offices:

United States: GNTO, 747 Third Ave., 33rd floor, New York, NY 10017 (tel. 212/308-3300)
GNTO, 444 South Flower St., Suite 2230, Los Angeles, CA 90017 (tel. 213/688-7332).
Canada: Office National Allemand du Tourisme, 2 Fundy, P.O. Box 417, Place Bonaventure, Montreal, P.Q. H5A 1B8 (tel. 514/878-9885).

England: GNTO, 61 Conduit St., London W1R OEN (tel. 01/734-2600).
Australia: GNTO, Lufthansa House, 12th floor, 143 Macquarie St., Sydney 2000 (tel. 02/221-1008).

DOCUMENTS

Citizens of the United States, Canada, Australia, and New Zealand need only a valid passport for entry into Germany and stays of up to three months. Visitors from the United Kingdom need only an identity card.

However, because of the changing situation in Germany, be sure to check before you go.

MONEY

The basic unit of currency in Germany is the **Deutsche Mark (DM).** One DM equals 100 pfennigs. Coins come in denominations of 1, 2, 5, 10, and 50 pfennigs, and 1, 2, and 5 DM. Bills are issued in denominations of 5, 10, 20, 50, 100, 500, and 1,000 DM. Note that new notes are being issued in 1991 which will be valid along with the older ones. These will include a new 200-DM note.

Currency unification between the two Germanys probably means that East German prices will rise to meet West German prices. Many establishments in East Berlin, including hotels and restaurants, at press time had simply changed their prices at a rate of one-to-one from the Reichsmark to the Deutsche Mark, other establishments are expected to change their prices radically. After all, under the former regime, even the price of beer was government-regulated.

Thus, travelers can expect fluctuation in prices during the next few years as East Berliners test the law of supply and demand and get used to a new currency. Although every effort has been made to report accurate prices for East Berlin, it's impossible to predict what the economic changes will be. Therefore, use those given here only as a guideline. Even in West Berlin, prices may change during the lifetime of this book—which means they will probably go up.

Although rates fluctuate continually, all conversions in this book are based on 1.65 DM to $1 U.S. (and then rounded off). To help you with money in Germany, there's a currency-conversion chart in the Appendix. However, keep in mind that the rates may have changed, so plan your budget accordingly.

As for credit cards, American Express, Diners Club, MasterCard, and VISA are the ones most readily accepted (and JCB, of course, in case you happen to have a Japanese credit card). All major hotels and many shops and restaurants accept plastic, particularly in West Berlin. In East Berlin, however, credit cards are usually accepted only in places frequented by international tourists, such as hotel restaurants. In addition, smaller establishments in both East and West are not equipped to deal with credit cards. You'll therefore want to carry a certain amount of cash with you, which you should keep secure in a money belt. Take only what you need for the day—keep the rest of your cash and traveler's checks in your hotel's safety-deposit box.

2. WHEN TO GO — CLIMATE, HOLIDAYS & EVENTS

Berlin is a tourist destination throughout the year. In fact, now that it's become one of the hottest destinations in Europe, it can be as lively and crowded in February as in August.

THE CLIMATE

Berlin is at about the same latitude as Vancouver and enjoys the changes of the four seasons. Its summers are generally mild and even pleasantly cool, which accounts for the fact that very few hotels and establishments bother with air conditioning. Spring and autumn can be glorious—my favorite time of year is October. Winters, on the other hand, can be quite severe, though not as bad as those in the northern regions of the United States. Though it rarely snows, the wind can be icy and it often rains. On the other hand, it sometimes warms up in February. In other words, be prepared for all kinds of weather, since temperatures and the amount of rainfall seem to vary from year to year. However, the following averages may help you plan your trip.

Berlin's Average Daytime Temperature and Rainfall

	Jan	Feb	Mar	Apr	May	June	July	Aug	Sept	Oct	Nov	Dec
Temp. (°F)	30	32	40	48	53	60	64	62	56	49	40	34
(°C)	−1	0	4	9	12	16	18	17	13	9	4	1
Rainfall Inches	2.2	1.6	1.2	1.6	2.3	2.9	3.2	2.7	2.2	1.6	2.4	1.9

HOLIDAYS

There are a few official and religious holidays to keep in mind. Some museums and restaurants are closed on certain holidays; most museums, for example, are closed on New Year's Day and Christmas. To avoid disappointment, be sure to telephone in advance if you wish to visit a certain establishment on a holiday.

Religious holidays in Berlin include Good Friday, Easter Sunday and Monday, Ascension Day, Whitsunday and Whitmonday, Day of

Prayer and Repentance (third Wednesday in November), and Christmas and the day after. Other holidays are New Year's Day, Labor Day (May 1), and German Unity Day (June 17).

THE YEAR IN BERLIN

If you're lucky, your trip may coincide with one of Berlin's cultural events. But if you do arrive during any of the major events described below, it's a good idea to reserve a hotel room in advance. For other events, including sporting events, art exhibits, or other one-time happenings, contact the German National Tourist Office nearest you. In Berlin, the organization in charge of arranging all major festivals is the **Berliner Festspiele GmbH,** Budapester Strasse 50 (tel. 030/25-48-90). The **Verkehrsamt Berlin** (tourist office), located in the Europa-Center on Budapester Strasse (tel. 030/262 6031), is another invaluable source of information.

BERLIN
CALENDAR OF EVENTS

FEBRUARY

✪ *INTERNATIONAL FILM FESTIVAL* *The calendar year starts off with a bang with this festival. which attracts stars, directors, movie critics, and film lovers from all over the world. Established back in 1951, it lasts almost two weeks and usually features films from 20 countries at the main showings. In addition, there are other movies shown round the clock under such headings as "International Forum of Young Filmmakers" and "New German Movies."*
    Where: *Various theaters* **When:** *Last part of February.* **How:** *Tickets, which run from about 10 DM to 15 DM ($6.05 to $9.10), can be purchased at the box offices.*

MAY

☐ **Theatertreffen** This festival, or "Theater Meeting," features German-language productions from throughout the German-speaking world, including Austria and Switzerland. You have to understand the language, therefore, to appreciate the various offerings. If you do and you love theater, you'll be in heaven.

JUNE/JULY

☐ Serenade concerts in Charlottenburg Palace. Call Verkehrsamt Berlin (tel. 25 48 90) for information.

SEPTEMBER

✪ *BERLINER FESTWOCHEN* *The Berlin Festival Weeks, one of the biggest events of the year, recognizes excellence in all fields of the arts. Included are symphonic, operatic, and theatrical performances.*

Where: *Various theaters* **When:** *September* **How:** *Ticket cost depends on the venue, and may be purchased at the box offices.*

OCTOBER/NOVEMBER

✪ *JAZZ-FEST BERLIN* A colorful mix of avant-garde and classical jazz musicians from around the world. There's everything from blues and swing to bebop, cool jazz, and free jazz.

Where: *Philharmonie.* **When:** *October and November* **How:** *Tickets costing from DM 10 ($6.05) to DM 30 ($18.20) may be purchased at the box office.*

DECEMBER

☐ **Weihnachtsmarkt,** from the Gedächtniskirche to Wittenberg-platz. This is the largest, most popular, and most convenient of the several traditional Christmas markets held around the city. Open daily from 11am to 9pm, it features more than 150 stalls selling cookies, candy, Christmas ornaments, and more. (Other Christmas markets include those in the Spandau Altstadt and on Alexanderplatz in East Berlin.) December 1 to Christmas Eve.

3. PREPARING FOR YOUR TRIP

HEALTH PREPARATIONS

No shots or inoculations are required for entry to Germany. If you need special medications, however, it's a good idea to bring them with you. Otherwise, German pharmacies are well equipped with their own brands of medicine, whether it's cough syrup or aspirin.

Medical and hospital services are not free in Germany, so ask your insurance company before leaving home if you are covered for medical emergencies or treatment abroad. If not, you may wish to take out a short-term traveler's medical policy before setting out. If an emergency arises during your stay in Berlin, consult Chapter 3, "Fast Facts" for emergency telephone numbers.

WHAT TO PACK

Since Germans are known throughout the world for the quality and quantity of their goods, and since they import just about everything else, you can probably find anything you might need in Berlin during your stay. Thus, pack as lightly as possible—if you shop, you'll probably end up leaving with a lot more than you came with.

Since Berlin has a moderate Continental climate (warm in summer and cold in winter), bring appropriate clothing. Also be prepared for unusual temperature changes, it can sometimes become quite cool on a summer's evening. Dress is generally fairly casual, but if you're going to the theater or opera, you'll want to pack one dressy outfit. Be sure to bring good walking shoes (ones already broken in), and at all times of year it's wise to have an umbrella. If you're staying in youth hostels, you'll want to bring your own towel.

4. TIPS FOR THE DISABLED

There are many organizations in Berlin for the disabled. For more information, including where to rent wheelchairs and which hotels are best equipped for the disabled, contact **Deutscher Paritätischer Wohlfahrtsverband,** Brandenburgische Strasse 80 (tel. 030/86-00-10); **Landesamt für Zentral Soziale Aufgaben,** Landesversorgungsamt, Sächsische Strasse 28-30 (tel. 030/86 71); or the Behindertenhilfe e. V. (tel. 030/302 10 45).

5. GETTING THERE

For most readers of this book, a trip to Berlin is likely to begin with a plane trip across the ocean to the European continent. Berlin itself is easily accessible by plane, train, or car. Below are some pointers to get you headed in the right direction.

BY AIR

Airlines that fly between North America and Germany include **Lufthansa,** the German national airline (tel. 718/895-1277 in New York City, 516/794-3930 in Nassau County, or toll free 800/645-3880 in other areas); **American** (tel. toll free 800/433-7300); **Delta** (tel. toll free 800/221-1212); **Pan Am** (tel. toll free 800/221-1111); and **TWA** (tel. toll free 800/892-4141). Contact your travel agent or specific carriers for current information.

To get a head start on your travel adventure, however, it seems only fitting to fly Germany's own Lufthansa, known throughout the world for its punctuality, dependability, and high quality of service. It operates the most frequent flights from the United States and Canada to Germany and also flies to the greatest number of cities in Germany.

Lufthansa offers daily direct flights to Berlin from Newark International Airport to Schönefeld Airport. Pan Am offers direct flights to Berlin's Tegel Airport from John F. Kennedy International Airport, Thursdays through Mondays. There are also many flights from Frankfurt to Berlin; **Euro/Berlin,** a Lufthansa affiliate, offers five flights daily.

TRANSATLANTIC PLANE FARES

Much more complicated are plane fares from North America to Germany, since the cheapest fares depend on the season and the day of the week you travel. In addition, airlines sometimes lower prices at the last minute to fill empty seats, or offer special promotional fares that are valid for certain times of the year and may include car-rental options. It pays, therefore, to shop around.

While first- and business-class fares are the same year-round, inexpensive tickets vary according to the season. The most expensive time to fly is during peak season, which is usually from June through September. The lowest fares are available during the winter months, usually November through March. Fares between the two extremes are usually available in April and May and again in October—the so-called shoulder seasons. To complicate matters, each season also has different rates for both weekday and weekend flights.

APEX (Advance Purchase Excursion)

You can cut the cost of your flight to Germany by purchasing your ticket in advance and complying with certain restrictions. Reservations, ticketing, and payment for APEX fares must be completed 30 days in advance and require a minimum stay of 7 days and a maximum stay of 21 days. The ticket is nonrefundable, and after it has been issued, no changes are permitted. Rates vary according to the season, with peak-season rates in effect June through September.

 **FROMMER'S SMART
TRAVELER—AIRFARES**

1. Shop all the airlines that fly to your destination.
2. Keep calling the airlines, since the availability of cheap seats changes daily. As the departure date nears, you might be able to obtain a seat at a great discount, since an airline would rather sell a seat than have it empty.
3. Read the advertisements of newspaper travel sections— they often offer special deals and packages.
4. You can also save money by buying your ticket as early as possible, since the cheapest fares such as APEX (Advance Purchase Excursion) usually require 30 days' advance purchase.
5. Ask whether there's a difference in price if you fly on a weekday—weekday flights are often $50 cheaper than weekend flights.
6. Travel off-season if you're trying to save money, since APEX and economy tickets often cost less if it's the off-season.

Weekday flights are approximately $50 cheaper than weekend flights. Lufthansa's special APEX fares, for example, range from as high as $770 for a round-trip flight from New York to Berlin on a weekend in summer to $528 for the same flight on a weekday in winter.

Economy Fares

In addition to its APEX fares, Lufthansa also offers some other options for budget travel. After APEX, its next most economical fare is its **Holiday Fare,** which permits no stopovers and carries a penalty for cancellation. Tickets must be purchased 21 days in advance and are valid for stays lasting from 7 days to 90 days, giving travelers greater flexibility. The peak-season round-trip fare from New York to Berlin is $969 on a weekday; the low-season fare for the same flight is $661.

If you're unable to purchase your ticket in advance or wish to stay longer than 90 days, you may want to purchase Lufthansa's **Excursion Fare,** which has no minimum stay and is valid for stays of up to one year. No advance purchase is necessary, and cancellations are allowed. The peak-season round-trip fare from New York to Berlin is $1,163 for a weekday, while the same flight during the off-season is $926.

In contrast, if you purchase Lufthansa's regular economy ticket, which carries no restrictions and allows one free stopover en route, the round-trip fare from New York to Berlin is $2,084 year-round. Similarly, Pan Am's normal economy round-trip ticket from New York to Berlin is $2,084.

First- and Business-Class Fares

If you wish to fly in style, you'll want to take advantage of luxuries provided to first- and business-class passengers. Lufthansa, for example, offers wider seats, travel kits, and more elaborate meals. Its fares are the same all year and allow an unlimited number of stopovers. The one-way business-class fare from New York to Berlin is $2,324, while first class is $4,220. Remember, however, that fares are subject to change without notice. Be sure to contact your travel agent or the airlines for current information.

Other Options

Certainly the best strategy for securing the lowest airfare is to shop around. Consult the travel sections of major newspapers, since they often carry advertisements for cheap fares. You may, for example, find bargains offered by so-called "bucket shops," which sell discounted tickets at reductions of about 20% to 30%. Tickets are usually restrictive, valid only for a particular date or flight, nontransferable, and nonrefundable.

Another option is a charter flight, which may offer a combination package that includes land transportation (such as rental car) and hotel accommodation. One reputable charter company is **Condor,** a Lufthansa subsidiary, which is located in Chicago (tel. 312/951-0005) and sells tickets to tour operators throughout the country. In New York, you can inquire about charter flights by calling the **Deutsches Reise Bureau** (tel. 212/818-0150).

FARES FROM FRANKFURT TO BERLIN

Although it's cheaper to purchase a ticket that will take you from North America all the way to Berlin, you may find yourself in Frankfurt. At press time the regular one-way economy fare from Frankfurt to Berlin was 240 DM ($145.45). The one-way business-class fare was 290 DM ($175), and first class was 317 DM ($192).

BY TRAIN

It's easy to get to Berlin by rail, since there are good connections to Frankfurt and Hamburg. The trip from Frankfurt to Berlin takes about 7 hours, and at press time it cost 112 DM ($67.85) for second class and 168 DM for first class ($101.80) one way. From Hamburg, with the trip taking about 3 hours, the one-way second- and first-class fares were 64 DM ($38.80) and 95 DM ($57.55), respectively.

BY CAR

Your main obstacle traveling by car is likely to be traffic. Until East Germans are used to going West and West Germans have already traveled East, the autobahns are bound to be clogged with day-trippers and vacationers out to explore new territories, especially on weekends. The East Germans are easy to spot—packed into tiny Trabants going at a snail's pace. West Germans, used to unlimited speeds on autobahns, are the ones looking impatient in their much bigger cars. Try to anticipate when traffic might be at its highest, such as on Saturdays or during exceptionally fine weather, or travel in the early morning or late at night.

In the recent past, the East German police were notorious for their speed traps and stiff fines, and they would nail you even if you were going only a couple of miles above the speed limit. It would be best to keep this in mind. In addition, keep alcoholic beverages in the trunk to be on the safe side.

CHAPTER 3

GETTING TO KNOW BERLIN

1. ORIENTATION
2. GETTING AROUND
3. NETWORKS & RESOURCES

This chapter will answer any questions you might have upon arrival in Berlin and during your stay, and furnish you with practical information, from how to get to your hotel from the airport to numbers to call during an emergency. Note that information about Berlin's airports, train stations and other transportation centers may change.

1. ORIENTATION

ARRIVING

BY AIR AT TEGEL AIRPORT

Located in West Berlin only 5 miles northwest of the city center, Tegel Airport (tel. 410 11) is the major airport for flights from Western Europe and North America. It's rather small as international airports go, consisting of one main hall and a circular-shaped passenger terminal. One of the first things you'll want to do upon arrival is stop at the Berlin information counter, located in the main terminal. Pick up a map of the city and available brochures. If you don't yet have a hotel reservation, the tourist office here will book one for you at a 3-DM ($1.80) fee. It's open daily from 8am to 11pm.

Other facilities at the airport include banks for money exchange, luggage storage, a post office from which you can make international calls, a first-aid station, a police station, car-rental firms, a restaurant, and shops selling film, newspapers, souvenirs, and travel necessities.

Getting to and from Tegel Airport

By Bus The best and least expensive way to get into town is on **city bus 9,** which departs about every 10 to 15 minutes just outside the arrival hall. The fare is 2.70 DM ($1.65) one way, and the trip to the city center takes approximately a half hour. The bus travels along the Kurfürstendamm, where most of Berlin's hotels are concentrated, all the way to Bahnhof Zoologischer Garten (Berlin's main train station) and Budapester Strasse. Ask someone at the airport tourist information counter which stop is most convenient to your hotel. Once inside the bus, you'll find each stop clearly displayed on a panel at the front.

By Taxi The easiest and quickest way to get into town, of course, is by taxi, which is not as prohibitively expensive as in many other major cities. It costs approximately 25 DM ($15.15) one way to the city center, and there are always plenty of taxis waiting to take you to your destination.

BY AIR AT SCHÖNEFELD AIRPORT

East Berlin's Schönefeld Airport, serves international flights as well as flights from Eastern Europe and the Soviet Union. Flights from Asia and Latin America also arrive there. There are several ways to get into town.

Getting to and from Schönefeld Airport

By Bus A special **airport bus** will take you directly to West Berlin's Zentraler Omnibusbahnhof (Central Bus Station) near the Radio Tower in Messedamm. The fare is 9 DM ($5.45). From there you can take a taxi, bus, or subway to your hotel.

By S-Bahn and Subway You can take the **S-Bahn** from Flughafen Schönefeld station to Ostkreuz station in East Berlin and transfer to another line from there. You can also travel by bus from the S-Bahn Schönefeld station to the U-Bahn Rudow station and there board the **subway** into the city center.

Note: This information may change, with the integration of Berlin's public transportation systems.

BY TRAIN

West Berlin — Bahnhof Zoologischer Garten

If you're arriving by train from Western Europe, you'll probably end up at Bahnhof Zoologischer Garten, Berlin's main train station and popularly called Bahnhof Zoo. It's located in the center of town, not far from the Kurfürstendamm with its hotels and nightlife. An underground and bus system connects the train station to the rest of the city. Bus 9, for example, travels along the Ku'damm and continues to Tegel Airport.

Your first stop at Bahnhof Zoo, however, should be at the tourist information counter, open daily from 8am to 11pm. In addition to picking up maps and brochures, you can also have your hotel reservation made here for a 3-DM ($1.80) fee. Both a post office and a money-exchange office are also located in the train station. For information on train schedules, call 194 19.

East Berlin

East Berlin's most important train stations for long-distance travel are the **Ostbahnhof** (used for international traffic) and **Bahnhof**

Berlin-Lichtenberg (used for travel inside East Germany). This setup may change in the future as the two countries merge their transportation systems, but in any case, both train stations are connected to the S-Bahn, the city's subway system.

BY CAR

If you've driven to Berlin, you may wish to seek out a hotel that offers parking space. Otherwise, there are many parking garages in the inner city open day and night. These include **Parkhaus am Zoo,** Budapester Strasse 38; **Parkhaus Europa-Center,** Nürnberger Strasse 5-7; **Parkhaus Los-Angeles-Platz,** Augsburger Strasse 30; and **Parkhaus Metropol,** Joachimstaler Strasse 14-19. All four are located within a few minutes' walk of the Ku'damm, the Gedächtniskirche, the Europa-Center, and Bahnhof Zoo.

BY BUS

Except in resort areas, bus travel is not a major option in Germany, so it is more likely that you'll use the good plane and rail connections between Berlin and most European cities. However, there are omnibus lines that serve smaller towns not accessible by train, including spa towns in the Harz and Franken regions of Germany. In any case, if you travel by bus, you'll arrive at the Zentraler Omnibusbahnhof (Central Bus Station), located near the Radio Tower at Messedamm. From there you can board a taxi or a city bus for your hotel; the nearest subway station is Kaiserdamm U-Bahn station. If you need omnibus information, dial 301 80 28.

TOURIST INFORMATION

There are several branches of **Verkehrsamt Berlin,** Berlin's tourist information office, ready to serve you. The main one, conveniently located in the Europa-Center, with its entrance on Budapester Strasse (tel. 030/262 60 31), is just a couple of minutes' walk from both Bahnhof Zoo and the Ku'damm. In addition to stocking maps and brochures about the city, the tourist office will also book a hotel room for you for a 3-DM ($1.80) fee. It's open daily from 7:30am to 10:30pm.

Other tourist offices are located at Tegel Airport (tel. 030/4101 31 34) and Bahnhof Zoo (tel. 030/313 90 63). Both are open daily from 8am to 11pm, and both will also book your hotel room.

If you need tourist information for East Berlin, stop by the **Information Center** at the TV tower on Alexanderplatz (tel. 0372/212 45 75). It's open Tuesday through Friday from 8am to 6pm, on Saturday and Sunday from 10am to 6pm, and on Monday from 1 to 6pm. Be sure to pick up a copy here of *Wohin,* published monthly in German. It tells what's being performed at East Berlin's famous Deutsche Staatsoper, the Berliner Ensemble (founded by Bertolt Brecht in 1949), and other superb theaters.

Unfortunately, there's nothing available in English that gives the

WHAT THINGS COST IN BERLIN U.S. $

Taxi from Tegel Airport to Bahnhof Zoo train station	15.15
Underground from Kurfürstendamm to Dahlem	1.65
Local telephone call	.18
Deluxe double room (at Bristol Hotel Kempinski)	181.00
Moderate double room (at Berliner Hof)	100.00
Budget double room (at Hotel Charlottenburg Hof)	33.00
Budget lunch for one (at Rogacki)	8.50
Deluxe dinner for one, without wine (at Carmer's)	40.00
Moderate dinner for one, without wine (at Hardtke)	17.00
Budget dinner for one, without wine (at Athener Grill)	5.00
Half liter of beer	2.40
Glass of wine	2.50
Coca-Cola in a restaurant	1.60
Cup of coffee	1.60
Roll of 100 ASA slide film, 36 exposures	5.40
Admission to Dahlem Gemäldegalerie	free
Movie ticket	5.90
Theater ticket to Schiller-Theater	4.85

latest information about what's going on culturally throughout Berlin (which is rather amazing considering the number of international visitors). Your best bet for current information on plays, operas, concerts, and other happenings is probably *Berlin Programm,* available at the tourist information office and at magazine kiosks for 2.50 DM ($1.50). Issued monthly, it also lists museums and their opening hours. Even if you can't read German, you should be able to figure out what's being performed where.

If you do read German, you'll probably want to pick up a copy of either *tip* or *zitty,* two German city magazines that alternate weekly with information on fringe theater, film, rock and folk music, and all that's happening on the alternative scene. *zitty* costs 3 DM ($1.80); *tip* costs 3.40 DM ($2.05).

CITY LAYOUT

Berlin is composed of 20 precincts. Of these, the most important for visitors are Charlottenburg in West Berlin and Berlin-Mitte in East

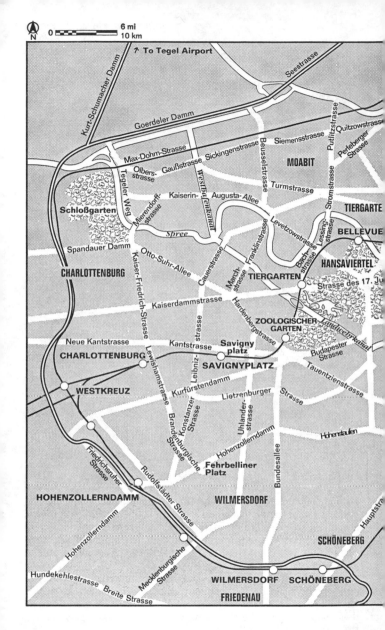

Berlin. Charlottenburg contains the famous Kurfürstendamm boulevard, most of the city's hotels, the main train station, the Europa-Center shopping and restaurant complex, many museums, and Schloss Charlottenburg (Charlottenburg Palace). Berlin-Mitte, so named because it was once the middle of Berlin, contains Museumsinsel (Museum Island), with a number of outstanding collections; a famous boulevard, Unter den Linden; a replica of old Berlin called the *Nikolaiviertel;* and Alexanderplatz, the heart of

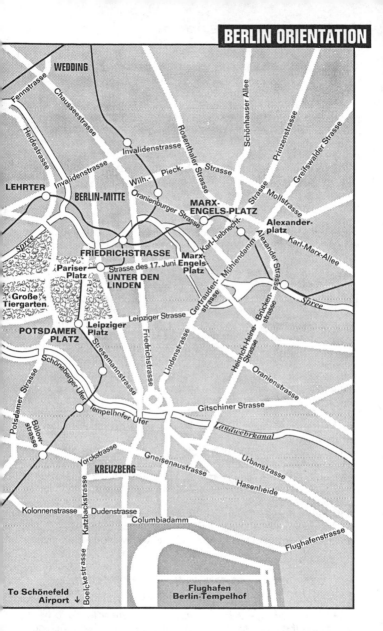

East Berlin. If you want, you can walk from Charlottenburg to Berlin-Mitte in less than two hours, a pretty stroll that takes you through the Tiergarten, the largest park in the city.

Running diagonally through the city is the Spree River. From the Grosser Müggelsee at the southeast end of Berlin, it runs through Köpenick, where it picks up the Dahme River; through East Berlin, where it's joined by the Panke River; past the Reichstag building and the Tiergarten; and on to Spandau, where it empties into the Havel

River. It was on the banks of the Spree River, halfway between Köpenick and Spandau, that two settlements called Berlin and Cölln sprang up centuries ago, growing and merging and eventually becoming the city we know today.

The layout of Berlin is markedly different from what it was just a year or two ago—there is no Wall slicing the city in half. Roads that had been severed are being reconnected, and grass and trees are covering the scars left from the Wall's removal. However, even though Berlin is whole again, it will take a while to heal, to overcome the tremendous challenges posed by uniting two cities that lived so long apart.

Thus, even though there is no longer any physical barrier between East and West, there is still a psychological one. The Wall may be gone, but for most Germans and Berliners, there is still an East and a West Berlin. I therefore use those terms throughout the book, but note that they refer now to geographical entities, not to political ones.

MAIN STREETS & SQUARES

The most famous street in West Berlin is the **Kurfürstendamm,** affectionately called the **Ku'damm.** About 2.5 miles long, it starts at the Kaiser-Wilhelm Gedächtniskirche (Kaiser Wilhelm Memorial Church), a ruined structure that has been left standing as a permanent reminder of the horrors of war. This is at the eastern end of the boulevard, and it's here that you'll find Bahnhof Zoo (Berlin's main train station), a large park called the Tiergarten, and the Europa-Center, a 22-story building with shops, an observation platform, and Verkehrsamt Berlin (the tourist information office). From the Europa-Center, **Tauentzienstrasse** leads straight to **Wittenbergplatz,** the location of KaDeWe, the largest department store on the European continent.

From the Gedächtniskirche, the Ku'damm stretches toward the west and is lined with many of the city's smartest boutiques, as well as many of its hotels. Just a five-minute walk north of the Ku'damm, off Knesebeckstrasse, is a square called **Savignyplatz,** noted for its bars and restaurants.

Wilmersdorfer Strasse, a pedestrian street located near a U-Bahn station of the same name, boasts several department stores, numerous shops, and restaurants. This is where most of the natives shop.

IMPRESSIONS

The two principles of Berlin architecture appear to me to be these. On the housetops, wherever there is a convenient place, put up the figure of a man; he is best placed standing on one leg. Wherever there is room on the ground, put either a circular group of busts on pedestals . . . or else the colossal figure of a man killing, about to kill, or having killed a beast . . . a dragon is the correct thing, but if that is beyond the artist, he may content himself with a lion or a pig.
—LEWIS CARROLL, 1867

Berlin's other famous boulevard—and historically much more significant—is **Unter den Linden** in East Berlin. This was the heart of pre-World War II Berlin, its most fashionable and its liveliest street. Its most readily recognized landmark is the Brandenburger Tor (Brandenburg Gate), and buildings along the tree-lined street have been painstakingly restored. Unter den Linden leads to Museumsinsel (Museum Island), which boasts the outstanding Pergamon Museum and a number of other great museums. Only a five-minute walk away is the modern center of East Berlin—**Alexanderplatz,** with its tall Fernsehturm (Television Tower). Nearby is the Nikolaiviertel (Nikolai Quarter), a reconstructed neighborhood of shops, bars, and restaurants built to resemble old Berlin.

FINDING AN ADDRESS

Although some of Berlin's streets are numbered with the evens on one side and the odds on the other, many are numbered consecutively up one side of the street and back down the other. The numbering system of the Ku'damm, for example, begins at the Gedächtniskirche and increases on the same side of the street all the way to end of the boulevard, then jumps to the other side of the street and continues all the way back. Thus, Ku'damm 11, site of the American Express office, is across the street from Ku'damm 231, the Wertheim department store. It's a bit complicated at first, but numbers for each block are posted on street signs.

For a bit of German, you might be interested in knowing that *Strasse* means "street" and *Platz* means "square." Generally speaking, streets south of the Ku'damm are named after important towns and regions—such as Augsburger Strasse, Nürnberger Strasse, and Pariser Strasse. Streets north of the Ku'damm are more likely to be named after famous Germans—such as Kantstrasse, Goethestrasse, and Schillerstrasse.

Keep in mind, too, that floors are numbered as they are in Britain, starting with the ground floor (called *Erdgeschoss* in German and thus marked *E* on elevators). The next floor up is therefore the first floor (which would be the American second floor), and so on.

In searching for an address, you should know that while the zip code for all of Berlin is 1000, the city is subdivided into postal codes. For example, Charlottenburg's postal codes include 12 and 15 near the area of the Gedächtniskirche; Spandau's code is 20; Kreuzberg has both 61 and 36. Most Berliners seem to know the various postal codes; so if in doubt, ask someone. In addresses, postal codes appear at the end, as in 1000 Berlin 15.

NEIGHBORHOODS IN BRIEF

Charlottenburg   This is West Berlin's most important precinct, named after Sophie Charlotte, wife of Prussia's Friedrich I. **Schloss Charlottenburg** (Charlottenburg Palace), which was built for

Sophie Charlotte, is here, as is a cluster of fine, nearby museums, including the **Ägyptisches Museum** (Egyptian Museum), with its famous bust of Nefertiti, and the **Bröhan Museum,** with its art nouveau collection. The majority of Berlin's hotels are in Charlottenburg, along with **Bahnhof Zoo** (the main train station), the **Ku'damm,** the **Europa-Center,** and such well-known theaters as the **Deutsche Oper, Schiller-Theater,** and **Theater des Westens.** Charlottenburg is huge, stretching from the Tiergarten all the way to the Havel River in the west.

Savignyplatz   Actually a part of Charlottenburg and just a 5-minute walk north of the Ku'damm, Savignyplatz is a pleasant square lined with restaurants and bars boasting outdoor seating. It's a great place to relax over a beer. Radiating out from Savignyplatz, or only a few minutes' walk away, are a number of other streets important for all you nightlife bloodhounds, including Kantstrasse, Schlüterstrasse, and Bleibtreustrasse.

Tiergarten   Tiergarten, which literally means "animal garden," refers to both the **Tiergarten park** and a precinct of the same name. Sandwiched in between Charlottenburg and Berlin-Mitte, it also encompasses a residential district called **Hansaviertel** (Hansa Quarter), the **Zoologischer Garten** (Berlin Zoo), the **Reichstag** (Parliament), the **Bauhaus-Archiv,** the **Philharmonie** (home of the famous Berlin Philharmonic Orchestra), and such museums as the **Neue Nationalgalerie** (New National Gallery), the **Kunstgewerbe Museum** (Museum of Applied Arts), and the **Musikinstrumenten Museum** (Museum of Musical Instruments). By the end of the century, several museums now in Dahlem will move to new homes in this museum district, making it the center for European art in West Berlin.

Hansaviertel   Stretching along the northern edge of Tiergarten park, the Hansaviertel is a residential district of housing projects, from one-family dwellings to apartment buildings. Each building was designed by a different architect as the result of an international gathering in 1957 of 50 leading architects, including Alvar Aalto, Walter Gropius, and Le Corbusier.

Dahlem   Once its own village and now a part of Zehlendorf precinct, Dahlem is home of West Berlin's Free University (formed after World War II, when the division of Berlin gave the city's only university to the Eastern Sector), the Max-Planck Institute, and, most important for visitors, a number of fine museums. These include the world-renowned **Gemäldegalerie** (Picture Gallery), with its European masterpieces from the 13th to 18th centuries, the **Skulpturengalerie** (Sculpture Gallery), the **Museum für Volkerkunde** (Ethnological Museum), the **Museum für Deutsche Volkskunde** (Museum of German Ethnology), the **Museum für Indische Kunst** (Museum of Indian Art), and the **Museum für Ostasiatische Kunst** (Museum of Far Eastern Art). After the Gemäldegalerie and the Skulpturengalerie move to new headquarters in the Tiergarten museum district by the end of the decade, Dahlem will serve as the city's showcase of non-European art.

Spandau   Located on the western edge of the city at the juncture of the Spree and Havel rivers, Spandau is older than Berlin itself, albeit by only five years. An independent city until swallowed up by Greater Berlin in 1920, Spandau still has its own flavor and character, including an **Altstadt** (old town) and an Italian-style **citadel** dating from the 16th century. Known also for its Christmas market in December, its shops (in the Altstadt), its woods and water recreation, it's a popular destination for both Berliners and visitors alike.

Kreuzberg   Once one of the poorest districts of Berlin, with a high concentration of immigrants, students, and others drawn by the low rents, Kreuzberg has become almost hip and is the scene of much of Berlin's counterculture. It is the most densely populated precinct of West Berlin, with as many as 30% of its inhabitants from Turkey, Greece, and Yugoslavia. About 65% of its apartments were built around the turn of the century. One of the most fun things to do in Kreuzberg is to visit the **Turkish Market,** held every Tuesday and Friday afternoon. Also in Kreuzberg is the **Berlin Museum,** depicting the fascinating history of the city; the **Martin-Gropius-Bar,** with its gallery of modern art; and the **Museum Haus am Checkpoint Charlie,** which documents the history of the Wall and of nonviolent revolutions around the world.

Berlin-Mitte   Once the cultural and political heart of Berlin, Berlin-Mitte fell on the Eastern side of the Wall after the city's division. It was here that Berlin originated back in the 13th century, when two settlements called Berlin and Cölln sprang up on opposite banks of the river. Included in the precinct, known as the First Precinct, is **Museumsinsel** (Museum Island), the restored **Nikolaiviertel** (Nikolai Quarter), and the boulevard **Unter den Linden.** Unfortunately, both the war and the postwar years took their toll on Berlin's historic district. What wasn't destroyed in the fighting was largely destroyed later under Communist rule, including Berlin's former royal palace, which had been the home of the Prussian monarchy for centuries; the ancient buildings on Fischerinsel, which were replaced by high-rises; and the old Acadamy of Architecture designed by Schinkel. Fortunately, those along Unter den Linden have been painstakingly restored.

IMPRESSIONS

The Wall is a kind of masterpiece of the squalid, the cruel, and the hideous, the most naked assertion one could find anywhere that life was not intended to be anything but nasty, brutish, and short.
—GORONWY REES, 1964

I love Germany so much I am glad there are two of them.
—FRANÇOIS MAURIAC, quoted by Roger Berthoud, 1978

Museumsinsel   Located in the middle of the Spree River, this is Berlin's oldest museum complex. Begun in the 1820s and falling under the jurisdiction of East Berlin after the war, this amazing collection of museums includes the outstanding **Pergamon Museum** with its architectural treasures.

Nikolaiviertel   Just southwest of Alexanderplatz in East Berlin and bounded on the other side by the Spree River, the Nikolaiviertel is a re-created neighborhood of old Berlin as it might have looked centuries ago. It's named after the **Nikolaikirche** (St. Nicholas's Church), Berlin's oldest church, which rises from the middle of the quarter. Grouped around the church are copies of buildings that used to exist and have been faithfully reconstructed down to the minutest historical details. In the Nikolaiviertel are approximately 30 town houses with 788 apartments (some with ceilings as high as 12 feet), as well as a number of restaurants, pubs, and shops.

Köpenick   Located in East Berlin at the southeast end of the city, Köpenick has a history stretching back to the 9th century and still has a much more provincial atmosphere than the inner city. An important industrial area, it is home primarily to the working class. It's a pleasant place for a stroll and boasts the 17th-century Köpenick Palace, now housing East Berlin's **Kunstgewerbe Museum** (Museum of Applied Arts).

MAPS

Unless the situation changes, the map issued by the Berlin tourist office is not adequate for an in-depth study of the city, primarily because it covers only the central part of West Berlin. Luckily, many hotels have free maps that help supplement the tourist-office map. As for East Berlin, maps are very scarce indeed, since the supply has not been able to keep up with the demand. It wouldn't hurt, however, to check the tourist office or the Europa Presse Center, a magazine and newspaper store in the Europa-Center, to see whether new and better maps of a united Berlin have been published.

2. GETTING AROUND

Berlin has an excellent public transportation network, including buses, the U-Bahn (underground), and the S-Bahn (overhead inner-city railway). All are run by Berlin's **BVG** (tel. 216 50 88), the largest public transportation department in Germany. If you have any questions regarding public transportation throughout Berlin, drop by the BVG information booth located in front of Bahnhof Zoo on Hardenbergerplatz. It's open daily from 10am to 6pm, and in addition to giving information, it also sells the various tickets outlined below, including the 24-hour ticket and the Sammelkarte.

BY PUBLIC TRANSPORTATION

One of the best things about Berlin's public transportation system is that the same ticket can be used for every branch of it—including the S-Bahn, the U-Bahn, and the buses. Furthermore, you can use the same ticket to transfer from one line to another, including public transportation in East Berlin. But even better is the fact that your ticket is good for up to two hours, allowing transfers, round trips, or even interruptions of your trip (you could, for example, go to Spandau for an hour or so and then return with the same ticket).

A single ticket costs 2.70 DM ($1.65). If you're traveling only a short distance (only six stops by bus or three stops by subway), you can purchase a **Kurzstreckenkarte** for 1.70 DM ($1.05). However, if you plan on traveling frequently by bus or subway, you're much better off buying a **Sammelkarte,** a card with five tickets at discounted rates. A normal Sammelkarte costs 11.50 DM ($6.95); a Sammelkarte with short-distance tickets costs 7 DM ($4.25). You can also buy a 24-hour ticket, which costs 9 DM ($5.45) for adults and 5 DM ($3.05) for children. And if you're going to be in Berlin for six days from Monday through Saturday, you might wish to purchase a six-day ticket for 26 DM ($15.75).

BY U-BAHN & S-BAHN

The fastest and easiest way to get around Berlin, especially during rush hour, is by underground (U-Bahn) or inner-city rail system (S-Bahn). Trains run from about 4am until midnight or 1am, except on Saturday night, when they run about an hour later. Some stations have ticket windows where you can purchase a single ticket or Sammelkarte; most, however, have only automatic vending machines for tickets. In any case, you must validate your ticket yourself at one of the little red boxes before boarding the train. This is on the honor system—and if you're caught without a ticket you'll be charged with a stiff fine.

To board the U-Bahn or S-Bahn line bound for your destination, you have to know that line's final stop. If, for example, you're in Bahnhof Zoologischer Garten and you wish to board the U-1 to Nollendorfplatz, you have to know that Nollendorfplatz is in the direction of Schlesisches Tor because you won't find Nollendorfplatz mentioned on any signs. If instead you board the U-1 going toward Ruhleben, you'll end up headed in the wrong direction. Refer to the subway map in this book or the map in all stations to determine the direction you need to go. It's not complicated, but Berlin has yet to figure out that everything would be a lot easier if directional signs included a list of stations along the way in addition to the final stop.

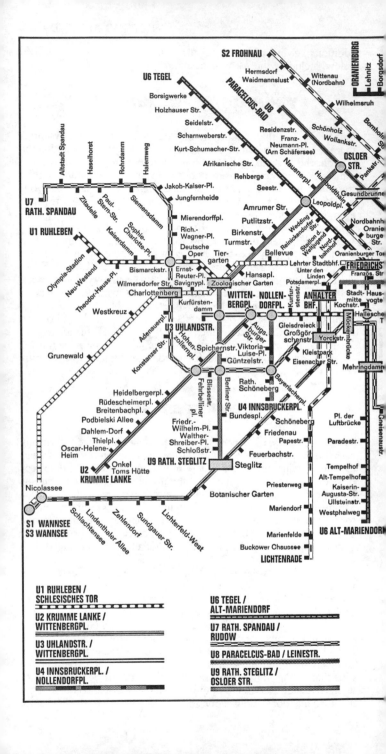

THE U-BAHN AND THE S-BAHN

U - OTTO-GROTEWOHL-STR./
PANKOW

U - ORANIENBURG/   U - ALEXANDERPL./
BERNAU   TIERPARK

S - FLUGHAFEN SCHÖNEFELD/
KÖNIGS WUSTERHAUSEN/
SPINDLERSFELD

S - WARTENBERG/   S - OSTKREUZ/
AHRENSFELDE/   FRIEDRICHSTRASSE
STRAUSBERG NORD   S - ERKNER / OSTKREUZ

S1 WANNSEE /
ANHALTER BHF.

S2 FROHNAU /
LICHTENRADE

S3 WANNSEE

You might be interested in knowing that since 1984, Berlin has been testing a new system, the magnetic-field aerotrain. Called the M-Bahn, this elevated train is now making a short run from Gleisdreieck U-Bahn station to the museum complex in Tiergarten, but is not yet extensive enough to be of much use to visitors.

BY BUS

Buses in Berlin carry more passengers than any other mode of transport. They are easy to use, and many are double-deckers, affording great views of the city. The problem at the present time, however, is that the entire city is integrating its bus system, and roads that had been severed by the Wall are being repaired. Thus, bus routes are changing and there's no way to predict how extensive the changes will be by the time you use this book. For the most part, however, you can expect bus lines running through West Berlin to be fairly consistent. If you have any questions, drop by the BVG booth at Bahnhof Zoo.

You can purchase a ticket from the bus driver, or use your Sammelkarte (described above). If you're transferring, simply show the bus driver your ticket. Apart from the normal day services, there are also special Nachtbusse (night buses) that run the entire night. You can pick up a brochure of their routes and schedules from the BVG booth at Bahnhof Zoo. In summer, there are special excursion buses marked with a triangle that make fast and convenient runs from Theodor-Heuss-Platz to recreation areas at Grünewald, from Wannsee station to Pfaueninsel, and from Nikolassee station to Wannsee Beach.

BY TAXI

If you need a taxi, you can find one at the many taxi stands in the city, or you can telephone one of several taxi companies: 6902, 26 10 26, 21 60 60, or 24 02 02. The meter starts at 3.40 DM ($2.05), plus 1.69 DM ($1) per kilometer. There's an extra 1-DM (60¢) surcharge on fares from midnight to 6am, Sundays and holidays. Luggage costs extra.

BY CAR

You don't need a car for trips within Berlin. Public transportation is excellent, and being burdened with a car means having to find a parking space. However, you may wish to rent a car for forays to the outskirts of town or such destinations as Potsdam. If you plan to stay overnight in East Germany, you should book your hotel room in advance.

You'll find driving in the outskirts of Berlin no more complicated than elsewhere in Germany. Driving is on the right side of the road, and standard international road signs are used. If you wish to rent a car, you'll need a valid driver's license (your U.S. license is fine) or an international driver's license. Third-party insurance is compulsory in Germany. Foreign visitors, with the exception of most European drivers, must either present their international insurance certificate (Green Card) or take out third-party insurance.

There are several well-known car-rental agencies in Berlin. **Avis** has a counter at Tegel Airport (tel. 030/410 13 148), as well as an office near Bahnhof Zoo at Budapester Strasse 43 (tel. 030/261 18 81). The latter office is open Monday through Friday from 7am to 6pm and on Saturday from 8am to 2pm. Prices here start at 195 DM ($118.20) for one day in an Opel Corsa or a Ford Fiesta, including 14% sales tax and unlimited mileage.

Hertz, another big name, also has a counter at Tegel Airport (tel. 030/410 13 315) and at Budapester Strasse 39 (tel. 030/261 10 53). The downtown office is open Monday through Friday from 7am to 6:30pm and on Saturday from 8am to 1pm. Its rates for an Opel Corsa or a Ford Fiesta start at 159 DM ($174.90) for one day, including 14% sales tax and unlimited mileage.

Keep in mind, however, that there are often special promotions with cheaper prices than those given above, including weekend rates. It pays to shop around.

BY BICYCLE

You'll probably want to forgo the experience of riding a bicycle in the center of Berlin's traffic-clogged streets, but it is a fast and pleasant way to see other parts of the city. It's important to know that you're allowed to take bicycles onto certain compartments of both the U-Bahn and S-Bahn. Thus, you may wish to rent a cycle, take the subway to the outskirts, and then begin your experience from there.

Fahrradbüro Berlin, Hauptstrasse 146 (tel. 784 55 62), rents bikes by the day for 12 DM ($7.25), plus a 15-DM ($9.10) deposit. It's located near the Kleistpark U-Bahn station and is open Monday, Wednesday, and Friday from 10am to 6pm and on Tuesday and Thursday from 2 to 6pm. On Saturday it's open from 10am to 2pm.

Another shop renting bicycles is **Räderwerk,** Körtestrasse 14 (tel. 691 85 90), located near the Südstern U-Bahn station. Charging 12 DM ($7.25) per day, plus a 100-DM ($60.60) deposit, it is open Monday through Friday from 10am to 1pm and 2 to 6pm, and on Saturday from 10am to 2pm. Be sure to bring your passport or some other piece of identification.

 BERLIN

This section is designed to make your stay in Berlin as problem-free as possible. However, keep in mind that the information below may have changed by the time you arrive. The concierge at your hotel may be able to help you if problems arise; another invaluable source is the Berlin tourist information office in the Europa-Center (tel. 262 60 31).

Airports   Berlin has two major airports. If you're arriving from North America or Western Europe, you'll arrive at **Tegel Airport** in West Berlin. If you're arriving from the Soviet Union or Eastern Europe, you'll arrive at East Berlin's **Schönefeld Airport.** For more information, refer to the beginning of this chapter under "Orientation."

American Express   The office is located in the center of town, across the plaza from the Gedächtniskirche at Kurfürstendamm 11 (tel. 882 75 75). It's up on the first floor (entrance is not directly on the Ku'damm but around the corner on Breitscheidplatz). It's open Monday through Friday from 9am to 5:30pm and on Saturday from 9am to noon.

Area Code   The telephone area code for West Berlin is 030; for East Berlin it's 0372. At last check, it still took a long-distance call to telephone between the two Berlins (though more lines were recently added and an expected result of reunification will be an integrated phone system). To call East Berlin from West Berlin, therefore, first dial area code 0372. From East Germany, dial 849 for West Berlin.

Auto Rentals   See the "Getting Around" section (above) for information on car-rental agencies and prices.

Babysitters   Some major hotels in Berlin provide babysitting services. Otherwise, call the **Babysitters Service,** Claudiusstrasse 6 (tel. 383 59 81).

Banks   They're open Monday through Friday from 9am to 1 or 3pm, with slightly longer hours one or two days of the week, depending on the bank.

Bookstores   Kiepert is a well-known bookstore within a 10-minute walk of Bahnhof Zoo, near the Technical University at the corner of Knesebeckstrasse and Hardenbergstrasse (tel. 311 00 940). It has maps and travel books, and is open Monday through Friday from 9am to 6:30pm and on Saturday from 9am to 2pm. The nearest U-Bahn station is Ernst-Reuter-Platz.

Buses   Berlin's double-decker buses are a fun way to see the city. Refer to the "Getting Around" section (above) for more information.

Business Hours   Downtown businesses and shops are open Monday through Friday from 9 or 10am to 6 or 6:30pm and on Saturday from 9am to 2pm. On the first Saturday of the month (called *langer Samstag*), shops remain open until 6pm. In addition, some shops remain open on Thursday until 8:30pm.

Banks are open Monday through Friday from 9am to 1 or 3pm, with slightly longer hours one or two days of the week depending on the bank.

Climate   Refer to Chapter 2, sections 2 and 3, for information on Berlin's climate and how to pack accordingly.

Currency   For a brief description of Germany's currency, the Deutsche Mark (DM), see Chapter 2, Section 1. In addition, a table in the Appendix gives exchange rates based on 1.65 DM to $1 U.S.

Currency Exchange   You can exchange money at any bank or at the American Express office (see listings above). There's an **exchange counter at Tegel Airport,** open daily from 8am to 10pm. You can also exchange money at the **Wertheim** and **KaDeWe department stores.**

If you need to exchange money outside banking hours, your best bet is the **Deutsche Verkehrs-Kredit-Bank** (tel. 881 71 17), an exchange office at Bahnhof Zoo. It's open Monday through Saturday from 8am to 9pm and on Sunday and holidays from 10am to 6pm.

Customs   If you are a citizen of a country outside Europe, you can bring duty-free into Germany 400 cigarettes or 100 cigars or 500 grams of tobacco, 1 liter of spirits, and 2 liters of wine. If you are an American or a Canadian residing in Europe, however, your allowance is only half that given above for tobacco products. If you come from a Common Market country, you may bring in 300 cigarettes or 75 cigars or 400 grams of tobacco, 1½ liters of spirits, and 5 liters of wine. You are also allowed a reasonable amount of perfume and coffee for your own personal use. You may bring gifts into Germany totaling 620 DM ($375.75), including a maximum of 115 DM ($69.70) in gifts from non–Common Market countries.

Dentists and Doctors   Some first-class hotels offer medical facilities or an in-house doctor. In addition, the Berlin tourist office in the Europa-Center has a list of English-speaking doctors and dentists in Berlin. If you need a doctor in the middle of the night or in an emergency, call 31 00 31.

Documents Required   The only document needed for travel to Berlin is a valid passport. No visas are necessary for travel to Germany. For more information, refer to Chapter 2, Section 1.

Driving Rules   See Chapter 2, Section 5, for information on driving to Berlin and the "Getting Around" section earlier in this chapter for information on driving in Berlin.

Drugstores   Called *Apotheken* in Germany, drugstores have normal business hours just like any other shops. However, there are always a few that stay open at night and during weekends and holidays, and all drugstores post a list of those that are open. Otherwise, to find out which pharmacies are open at night in West Berlin, call 11 41. In East Berlin, call 160. Note: Drugstores in Germany are pharmacies only. Stores selling cosmetics and sundries are called *Drogeries.*

Electricity   Berlin's electrical current is 220 volts AC, 50 cycles, which is much different from the American current of 110 volts, 60 cycles. In addition, plugs are different from those in the United States. You'll therefore need an adapter if you're bringing a hairdryer, electric razor, or other electrical appliance. The major hotels will probably have adapters you can use. Otherwise, you can purchase one at an electrical shop or a department store in Berlin.

Embassies and Consulates   The **U.S. Consulate** is in Dahlem at Clayallee 170 (tel. 832 40 87). For Americans who have lost their passports, it's open Monday through Friday from 8:30 to 11:30am; its visa section is open Monday through Friday from 8:30 to 9:30am.

The **Canadian Consulate,** on the 12th floor of the Europa-Center (tel. 261 11 61), is open Monday through Friday from 9am to noon.

The **British Consulate,** Uhlandstrasse 7-8 (tel. 309 52 93 or 309 52 92), is open Monday through Friday from 9am to noon and 2 to 4pm (visa section, only in the morning).

Emergencies   Throughout East and West Berlin, the emergency number for police is **110;** for fires and ambulances, it's **112.**

Eyeglasses   If you need a pair of eyeglasses, you'll find most shops in the area of the Ku'damm and Tauentzienstrasse. It's best to carry your prescription with you from home.

Hairdressers and Barbers   Many first-class hotels have beauty salons and barbershops, which may be your best bet for an English-speaking specialist.

Holidays   For Berlin's holidays, see Chapter 2, Section 2.

Hospitals   If you need emergency hospital treatment, the ambulance service will deliver you to the one best suited to your case. If you need a doctor in an emergency, telephone 31 00 31 in West Berlin and 12 59 in East Berlin. Otherwise, if you wish to check into a hospital and it's not urgent, contact your embassy for recommendations.

Information   Locations of the Verkehrsamt Berlin (tourist) office branches are given in the "Orientation" section at the beginning of this chapter.

Language   Useful phrases in German are listed in the Appendix. For food, see Chapter 1's "Food & Drink" section for a description of German cuisine that might appear on menus. If you wish to learn German in more depth, there are countless phrase books and language books on the market, including *German for Travellers* published by Berlitz.

Laundry and Dry Cleaning   All upper-bracket and most medium-priced hotels offer laundry and/or dry cleaning services. If not, ask the staff where the most conveniently located Laundromat is. Otherwise, there's a **Wasch Center** near the center of town at Leibnizstrasse 72 (on the corner of Kantstrasse) and another at Uhlandstrasse 53 (between Pariser Strasse and Düsseldorfer Strasse). Hours for both locations are 6am to 10:30pm. A wash cycle with detergent is 5 DM ($3.05), 1 DM (60¢) for a spin, and 1 DM for a dryer. For information, call 213 88 00 or 854 26 57.

Liquor Laws   Compared to U.S. liquor laws, Germany's seem rather liberal. As in many European countries, drinking beer or wine with a meal is so much a part of the culture that even teenagers receive a glass at home. However, laws against drunk driving in Germany have long been enforced and respected. In East Germany, drivers are not allowed even one drink.

Lost Property   **West Berlin's general-property office** is at Tempelhofer Damm 3 (tel. 69 91). For property lost on public transportation services, check the **BVG lost-and-found** at Potsdamer Strasse 184 (tel. 216 14 13).

At press time **East Berlin's general lost-property office** was at Wilhelm-Pieck-Strasse 164 (tel. 280 62 35 or 280 62 57). If you have lost something on public transportation in East Berlin, drop by the lost-property office at the S-Bahnhof at Marx-Engels-Platz (tel. 492 16 71). Be aware, however, that these addresses may change as both Berlins merge their transportation and governmental services.

Luggage Storage   There's luggage storage at both Tegel Airport and at the main train station, Bahnhof Zoologischer Garten (Bahnhof Zoo), where you'll also find lockers.

Mail   Mailboxes are yellow in Germany. Airmail letters to

North America cost 1.65 DM ($1) for the first 5 grams, while postcards cost 1.05 DM (64¢).

The **post office** in Bahnhof Zoo is open 24 hours a day for mail, telephone calls, and telegrams. You can have your mail sent here in care of Hauptpostlagernd, Postamt 120 Bahnhof Zoo, D-1000 Berlin 12 (tel. 313 97 99 for inquiries). You can also have your mail sent to you via the **American Express office,** Kurfürstendamm 11 (tel. 882 75 75), a service that is free if you have American Express traveler's checks or credit card. Otherwise, the service costs a steep 2 DM ($1.20) *per enquiry.*

If you want to mail a package, you'll have to go to one of the city's larger post offices. Two that are conveniently located are at Goethestrasse 2-3 and at Marburger Strasse 12-13, which is near the Europa-Center. Both are open Monday through Friday from 8am to 6pm and on Saturday from 8am to 1pm. Both sell cardboard boxes, complete with string and tape, which come in five sizes ranging in price from 1.10 DM (65¢) to 3.60 DM ($2.20).

In East Berlin, there's a post office open 24 hours at Strasse der Pariser Kommune 8-10. A post office in Palast der Republik on Marx-Engels-Platz is open daily from 10am to 10pm.

Maps   Refer to the "Orientation" section at the beginning of this chapter for information regarding maps.

Money   For a brief description of Germany's currency, the Deutsche Mark (DM), see Chapter 2, Section 1. In addition, a table in the Appendix gives exchange rates based on 1.65 DM to $1 U.S.

Newspapers and Magazines   At press time there were no newspapers and magazines published in English in Berlin. However, you can pick up English-language newspapers and magazines such as the *International Herald Tribune* and *Newsweek* at a newsstand called **Europa Presse Center,** located on the ground floor of the Europa-Center.

Photographic Needs   Film, batteries, and other photographic necessities are available at the **Wertheim** and **KaDeWe** **department stores,** described in Chapter 8.

Police   The emergency number for police throughout Berlin is **110.**

Radio and TV   For radio programs in English, tune in 90.2 FM (87.6 on cable) for the BBC, 87.9 AM (94 on cable) for the American Forces Network, and 98.8 FM (102.85 on cable) for the British Forces Broadcasting Services.

As for television, many medium- and upper-range hotels offer cable TV with CNN news broadcasts from the United States; a sports channel in English; Super Chanel, with programs from the United Kingdom; and MTV, a music channel.

Restrooms   If you ask for the "bathroom" in Germany, your host is going to think it mighty strange that you wish to take a bath in his home or restaurant. Rather, a restroom in Germany is called a *Toilette* and is often labeled *WC* in public places. Women's toilets are often marked with an *F* for *Frauen,* while men's are identified with an *H* for *Herren.*

In the center of Berlin there are public facilities at Wittenbergplatz and near the Europa-Center on Tauentzienstrasse. Other places to look for facilities include fast-food outlets, department stores, hotels, restaurants, and pubs. If there's an attendant, it's customary to tip 30 pfennigs (20¢).

Safety   Berlin is a safe city, particularly in places frequented by tourists such as the Ku'damm. However, as in any unfamiliar city, it's wise to stay alert and be aware of your immediate surroundings, because every society has its criminals. Wear a money belt, and don't sling your camera or purse over your shoulder, particularly at night or in crowded places; wear the strap diagonally across your body. This will minimize the possibility of becoming the victim of a crime. Keep your valuables in a safety-deposit box at your hotel.

Shoe Repairs   For quick service on shoe repairs, head for **Wertheim department store,** 231 Kurfürstendamm, or either **Karstadt** or **Hertie department store,** both on Wilmersdorfer Strasse, where you'll find a Mister Minit counter specializing in repairs. In East Berlin, there's an express shoe-repair shop called **Flinke Jette,** Alexanderplatz 1.

Taxes   Government tax is included in the price of restaurants, hotels, and goods in Germany. On many goods, however, tourists can obtain a refund of the Value-Added Tax—see Chapter 8 for information on how to obtain a refund. There is no airport departure tax.

Taxis   Refer to the "Getting Around" section of this chapter for information on taxis.

Telephone   Berlin's telephone system is not much different from that in the United States when it comes to a dial tone or a busy tone, but it does differ in the amount of telephone digits. Some telephone numbers have four digits, others may have seven or eight. Area codes in Germany are often enclosed in parentheses—such as (030) for West Berlin—and the rest of the digits are simply grouped into twos or threes. Thus, a seven-digit number in Berlin would be written (030) 881 47 68. If you come across a number with a dash, the number following the dash is the extension number, which you can reach directly simply by dialing the entire number.

Local telephone calls cost 30 pfennigs (20¢). If you want to make an international call, look for phone booths with the green "International" sign and make sure you have a handful of change. It's much easier to make long-distance calls from a post office, where you can also send telegrams. The main post office at Bahnhof Zoologischer Garten (West Berlin's main train station) is open 24 hours. It costs 12.30 DM ($7.45) to make a three-minute long-distance phone call to the United States. Try to avoid making telephone calls from your hotel room—a surcharge added to the bill may double or even triple the rate.

At press time it still took a long-distance call to telephone between the two Berlins. To call East Berlin from West Berlin, therefore, first dial area code 0372. From East Germany, dial 849 for West Berlin. Since this will change in the future, ask the tourist information office or the concierge in your hotel for the latest details.

Time   Berlin is 6 hours ahead of Eastern Standard Time in New York, 7 hours ahead of Chicago, and 9 hours ahead of Los Angeles. Berlin operates on Central European Time—except that it's officially 6 minutes and 22 seconds behind Central European Time. Don't ask me why. Germany goes on and off Daylight Saving Time at slightly different dates than the United States, with the result that Berlin is 7 hours ahead of New York for short periods in spring and fall. Since this can affect rail timetables, make sure you double-check if you're traveling during spring or fall.

Tipping   Since a service charge is usually included in hotel and restaurant bills, you are not obliged to tip. However, it is customary to round off restaurant bills to the nearest mark, which you give directly to the waiter or waitress rather than leave on the table. If your bill is 14 DM, therefore, say "15 DM" if you hand her a 20-DM note and you'll receive 5 DM in change. If a meal costs more than 20 DM ($12.10), most Germans will add a 10% tip. For taxi drivers, it's customary to round off to the nearest mark. Tip hairdressers or barbers 10%. Porters receive 2 DM ($1.20) per bag.

Water   Although the water is technically safe to drink in Berlin, take your cue from the Germans, who almost never drink their tap water. Instead, they ask for bottled water, either carbonated or noncarbonated.

4. NETWORKS & RESOURCES

If you need more information than what's given here, contact the tourist information office or telephone one of the organizations below for advice on where to turn.

FOR STUDENTS

Berlin's oldest university, now called Humboldt University, was founded in 1810 and suffered the fate of the divided city after World War II. Most departments and institutes of the university were located in the Soviet zone, and when some students were suspended for political reasons in 1948, teachers and students founded the Free University in West Berlin. Also in West Berlin is the University of Technology, located near Bahnhof Zoo.

Today, with a student population of well over 100,000, Berlin is Germany's largest "university city." As in most German cities, there are student cafeterias with budget-priced meals (see the dining chapter). Those museums that charge admission offer student discounts (most museums in Berlin, by the way, are free to everybody). In addition, some theaters (such as the renowned Schiller-Theater) offer unused tickets to students at a 50% reduction on the night of the performance.

For discounts, you'll need an International Student Card to prove you're a bona fide student. It's easiest to apply for the card at your own university, but if you've arrived in Berlin without one and can show proof of current student status, you can obtain one at **ARTU,** Hardenbergstrasse 9 (tel. 31 04 66). A travel agency, it's located in the district of the University of Technology, not far from Bahnhof Zoo. It also offers discounted plane fares around the world, as well as cheap train tickets to people under 26 years of age. It's open Monday through Friday from 10am to 6pm (on Wednesday from 11am to 6pm) and on Saturday from 10am to 1pm.

FOR GAY MEN & WOMEN

Berlin has a very active alternative scene, with many different organizations for gay men and women. For men who are interested in learning about the political and social scene in Berlin, there's the **Allgemeine Homosexuelle Arbeitsgemeinschaft,** Friedrichstrasse 12 (tel. 251 25 41). This organization will also offer advice on further groups to contact.

Kommunikations- und Beratungszentrum für Homosexuelle Männer und Frauen is a center of communication and counseling for both gay men and women and is located at Kulmer Strasse 20 (tel. 251 90 00).

For women, there's the **Lestra Frauenzentrum,** Stresemannstrasse 49 in Kreuzberg (tel. 251 88 12), a lesbian women's center actively involved in political and social issues of interest to gay women.

CHAPTER 4

BERLIN ACCOMMODATIONS

1. VERY EXPENSIVE
2. EXPENSIVE
3. MODERATE
4. INEXPENSIVE
5. BUDGET

As in most major cities of the world, your biggest daily expense in Berlin will be for accommodations. These range from deluxe hotels to modestly priced pensions, with a great many choices in between. What's more, unlike most big cities, Berlin boasts a wealth of accommodations smack in its center, clustered along or near its main boulevard, the Kurfürstendamm, called the Ku'damm for short. Another centrally located area of hotels is east of the Europa-Center and south of the Tiergarten, within a 15-minute walk of the Ku'damm. Even budget-range accommodations abound near the Ku'damm, but if you opt for a hotel removed from the hustle and bustle of the city center, you're never more than a short bus or subway ride from Bahnhof Zoologischer Garten (Bahnhof Zoo), Berlin's main train station.

As for East Berlin, it has not yet developed a tourist-oriented sector, though that is slowly changing. Presently there are only a few upper-range hotels. They are expensive, even by Western standards, but are not up to par with West Berlin's hotels in the same price category. Although personnel are friendly and try to be helpful, messages may disappear before being delivered, hotel restaurants are expensive, and it takes much longer to make international phone calls. What's more, most of Berlin's best restaurants and nightlife entertainments are in the West. However, business or your own interests may lead you to East Berlin, so I've included a few choices. Hopefully, there will be many more choices in the future, particularly in the medium- and budget-range hotels.

All rates given below include the 14% government tax and the service charge. In addition, note that most hotels, from budget to expensive, include a Continental or buffet-style breakfast in their rates. Many visitors report that they eat so much for breakfast that it tides them over until an early dinner, thus saving on lunch. If you thrive on breakfast, therefore, it would make sense to pay slightly more for a room that includes breakfast in its rates than to opt for one that doesn't.

Hot showers, even those in cheaper pensions (where the shower is down the hall), are also included in all room rates. The rates are much higher for rooms with private showers and toilets (a toilet is usually referred to as a WC, or water closet). If you're on a budget, therefore, you can save lots of money by taking a room without private facilities. If you do desire your own shower and WC, note that some hotels charge more for a bathtub than for a shower (bathtubs are somewhat of a rarity in Berlin's hotels and are considered a luxury). And incidentally, a "bathroom" in Germany refers to a room containing a bathtub (usually a room separate from the WC). If you're in a German home and ask for the bathroom, therefore, they may fear you're about to take a soak in their tub. Ask instead for the Toilette.

Another thing to keep in mind: Some hotels charge more for a twin-bedded room (a room with two beds), while others charge more for a double room (a room with one full- or king-size bed). Most hotels, however, charge the same for both a double room and a twin-bedded room (in which case I've referred to them simply as double, meaning the price for two persons). Finally, few hotels outside the expensive category have air conditioning—except for an occasional two weeks in August, it rarely gets hot enough to warrant it.

 FROMMER'S SMART TRAVELER—HOTELS

VALUE-CONSCIOUS TRAVELERS SHOULD TAKE ADVANTAGE OF THE FOLLOWING:

1. Lodging in the heart of town in all price categories, near the Ku'damm, the Europa-Center, shops, restaurants, and bars.
2. Rooms without private bathrooms or showers, which are much cheaper.
3. Rooms on upper floors of inexpensive pensions without elevators, which are often cheaper than rooms near the ground floor.
4. Winter discounts, offered primarily by expensive and moderately priced hotels but also by a few inexpensive hotels.
5. Accommodations that offer breakfast in the price.
6. Youth hotels and hostels, open throughout the year.

QUESTIONS TO ASK IF YOU'RE ON A BUDGET

1. Is breakfast included in the price? Is it buffet style, allowing you to eat as much as you want?
2. Are prices different for a double or a twin-bedded room? Some hotels charge more for a double, others for a twin, though most charge the same for both.
3. How much is the surcharge on local and long-distance telephone calls? You may pay almost twice as much for a call from your room than you would from a public telephone.
4. Is there parking space at the hotel, and if so, what is the charge per day? Some hotels outside the city center offer free parking.

The rates below are those charged through much of the year, including summer. However, many hotels in the upper-price category increase their rates during *Messen* (international conferences and conventions) and in the main tourist season in August, but offer discounts during the off-season winter months. Therefore, be sure to ask for the exact rate when making your reservations and whether you're being given a discount or paying more because of a Messe. Hotels that offer discounts or raise their rates in peak season or during a Messe are indicated. Most moderately priced and budget hotels keep the same rates year-round.

Keep in mind, too, that while every effort was made to be as accurate as possible, rates may change during the lifetime of this book—which means they may go up. Thus, to avoid misunderstanding or embarrassment when it comes time to pay the bill, be sure to ask the rate when making your reservations.

The hotels below are divided into five price categories. The very expensive hotels charge more than 300 DM ($182) for two persons but provide first-rate accommodations and a wide range of services, which may include free use of a health club and swimming pool, a concierge to help you with any problems that may arise, cocktail lounges or bars, and fine restaurants. Hotels in the next category, the expensive hotels, charge 230 DM to 300 DM ($139 to $182) for two persons and also offer comfortable rooms with all the usual amenities: private bathrooms, cable TVs offering programs in English or in-house videos, minibars, radios, and telephones. But don't expect the same roominess or facilities you'd find in a hotel of comparable price, say, in the Midwestern United States. However, prices often include breakfast, and some hotels in this category have swimming pools that guests can use for free. In addition, some hotels have outfitted all their rooms with a "trouser presser," a contraption that heats pants or skirts and gets rid of wrinkles. You may also encounter a free shoeshine machine, which has a rotating brush.

Moderately priced hotels, charging from 140 DM to 230 DM ($85 to $139) for a double, offer rooms with private showers and WCs and other amenities, which may include minibars. Inexpensive lodgings, ranging from 80 DM to 140 DM ($48.50 to $85) for a double room, offer accommodations with or without private showers and WCs. They are usually smaller hotels and pensions. Although a pension usually has fewer rooms and lower prices than a hotel, sometimes there is only a fine line between the two. Finally, budget accommodations include pensions that charge less than 80 DM ($48.50) for a double room, as well as rock-bottom youth hotels and hostels.

Note that in Germany floors are counted beginning with the ground floor (which would be the American first floor) and go up to the first floor (the American second floor) and beyond. Directions are given for each establishment listed below, including instructions from Tegel Airport or Bahnhof Zoologischer Garten (Bahnhof Zoo), as well as the nearest U-Bahn or S-Bahn station where relevant.

It's always a good idea to reserve a room in advance to avoid disappointment or time wasted searching for a room. In addition, rooms become scarce during the International Film Festival (end of February) and the Berlin Festival (running from the end of August to

October), as well as during frequent international conferences, fairs, and conventions (Messen) held in Berlin. And because of the exciting developments that have taken place in East Germany the past few years, Berlin has become a popular destination for visitors from around the world. Even winters, once slow periods for tourism in Berlin, are bustling with life.

Remember, if the recommendations below are full, the tourist office (tel. 262 60 31) will find a room for you for a 3-DM ($1.80) fee.

1. VERY EXPENSIVE

These top hotels are either on the Ku'damm or within a few minutes' walk, not far from the Europa-Center and Bahnhof Zoo. All rooms, of course, have private bathrooms.

ON OR NEAR THE KU'DAMM

BRISTOL HOTEL KEMPINSKI, Kurfürstendamm 27, D-1000 Berlin 15. Tel. 030/88 43 40, or U.S. toll free 800/426-3135. Fax 030/883 60 75. Telex 183553 kempi d. 315 rms, 44 suites. MINIBAR TEL TV **Bus:** 9 from Tegel Airport to Uhlandstrasse. **U-Bahn:** Kurfürstendamm.

$ Rates: 360–420 DM ($218–$255) single; 420–470 DM ($255–$ 285) double; 550 DM ($333) junior suite; from 900 DM ($545) suite. Extra bed 50 DM ($30.30). Children under 12 free in parents' rm. AE, DC, MC, V. Parking available.

A member of the Leading Hotels of the World, the Bristol Hotel Kempinski is considered by many to be the top hotel in Berlin. Certainly it's the best known. Although the present building dates from 1952 and has been renovated since then, its name stretches back before World War II, when the original Hotel Bristol was located on Unter den Linden and was regarded as one of Germany's foremost establishments. Today the hotel still exudes an old-world elegance, with antiques, chandeliers, and elaborate tapestries in the lobby. It occupies a prime spot on the Ku'damm; in fact, its restaurant Kempinski Eck is a favorite place for people-watching, with tables on the sidewalk in summer.

All rooms are luxuriously appointed, complete with cable stations and remote control for the TVs, hairdryers, magnifying makeup mirrors in the bathrooms, and vanity stools. Room styles vary, from those with modern furnishings to those with antiques or Chinese decor. No-smoking rooms are available.

Dining/Entertainment: Both the Kempinski and the Kempinski Eck offer dining in a relaxed atmosphere with a view of the Ku'damm. For a more elegant atmosphere, the Kempinski Grill excels in international cuisine and has long been considered a Berlin institution. After dinner, guests can retire to the Bristol Bar for a drink and dancing.

Services: Same-day laundry and dry cleaning service, limousine service.

Facilities: Indoor swimming pool, sauna, massage, solarium, fitness room, beauty parlor and barbershop, newsstand, flower shop, counter for theater tickets.

HOTEL STEIGENBERGER BERLIN, Los-Angeles-Platz 1, D-1000 Berlin 30. Tel. 030/210 80, or U.S. toll free 800/223-5652 or 800/SRS-5848. Fax 030/210 81 17. Telex 181444. 400 rms, 11 suites. AC MINIBAR TEL TV **Bus:** 9 from Tegel Airport to Tauentzienstrasse. **U-Bahn:** Kurfürstendamm, a 2-minute walk.

$ Rates: 245–285 DM ($148–$173) single, up to 400 DM ($242) single during Messen; 295–360 DM ($179–$218) double, up to 490 DM ($296) during Messen; from 700 DM ($424) suite. Extra bed 65 DM ($39.40). Children under 12 free in parents' rm. Breakfast buffet 26 DM ($15.75) extra. AE, DC, MC, V. Parking: 12 DM ($7.25).

This hotel, with a great location on a quiet square near the Gedächtniskirche and the Europa-Center, boasts excellent service and a well-trained, efficient staff. It's been a favorite haunt of visiting businesspeople and journalists ever since it opened in 1981, not only for its location but also for its facilities. If you want to be close to the hustle and bustle of the Ku'damm but without the accompanying noise, this is a good choice.

Rooms are virtually the same throughout and with the same amenities, including two sinks and magnifying makeup mirrors in the bathrooms, hairdryers, TVs with cable and pay videos, radios, soundproof windows that can also be opened, and air conditioners with control knobs. The more expensive rooms in each category are slightly larger in size.

Dining/Entertainment: The hotel's finest restaurant is the Park Restaurant, which offers classic international dishes, nouvelle cuisine that changes with the seasons, and more than 400 wines and spirits. The Berliner Stube is decorated in the tradition of old Berlin, with solid oak tables and period engravings of the city, and offers hearty German fare. The Café Charlotte has the atmosphere of a Viennese coffeehouse, with various coffees, cakes, and tarts, as well as international newspapers. The Cocktail Bar has a happy hour daily except Monday from 5 to 7pm, and there's piano music in the Piano Bar from 5pm.

Services: 24-hour room service, complimentary shoeshine, house doctor, babysitting.

Facilities: Indoor swimming pool, sauna, massage, solarium, shopping arcade, newsstand.

NEAR THE EUROPA-CENTER & THE TIERGARTEN

GRAND HOTEL ESPLANADE, Lützowufer 15, D-1000 Berlin 15. Tel. 030/26 10 11. Fax 030/262 91 21. Telex 185986 gespl d. 369 rms, 33 suites. A/C MINIBAR TEL TV **Bus:** 9 from Tegel Airport to Budapester Strasse, then a 5-minute walk.

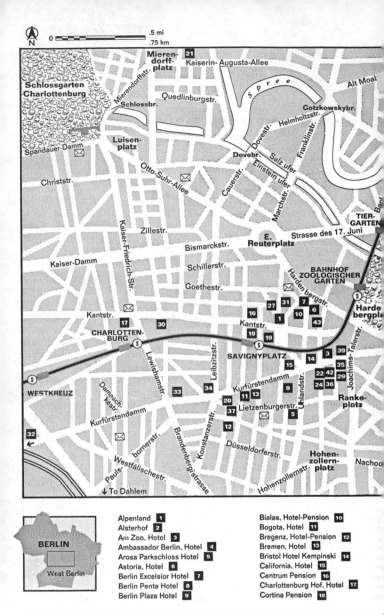

BERLIN

West Berlin

Alpenland **1**	Bialas, Hotel-Pension **10**
Alsterhof **2**	Bogota, Hotel **11**
Am Zoo, Hotel **3**	Bregenz, Hotel-Pension **12**
Ambassador Berlin, Hotel **4**	Bremen, Hotel **13**
Arosa Parkschloss Hotel **5**	Bristol Hotel Kempinski **14**
Astoria, Hotel **6**	California, Hotel **15**
Berlin Excelsior Hotel **7**	Centrum Pension **16**
Berlin Penta Hotel **8**	Charlottenburg Hof, Hotel **17**
Berlin Plaza Hotel **9**	Cortina Pension **18**

U-Bahn: Nollendorfplatz, a 5-minute walk.

$ Rates: 260–280 DM ($157–$170) single; 305–335 DM ($185–$203) double; 490 DM ($297) penthouse rm, double; from 800 DM ($485) suite. Extra bed 50 DM ($30.30). Children under 12 free in parents' rm. Breakfast buffet 20 DM ($12.10) extra. AE, DC, MC, V. Parking: 15 DM ($9.10).

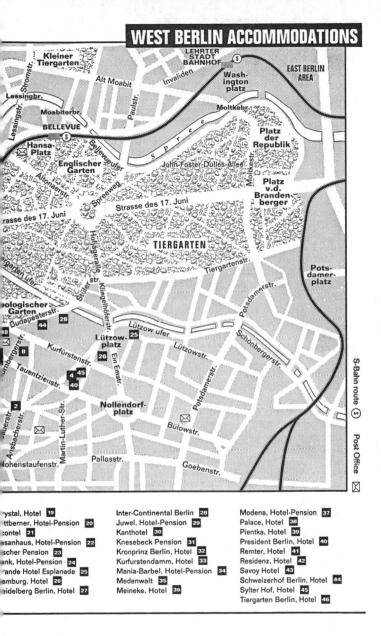

WEST BERLIN ACCOMMODATIONS

ystal, Hotel **19**
ttberner, Hotel-Pension **20**
:ontel **21**
asanhaus, Hotel-Pension **22**
scher Pension **23**
ink, Hotel-Pension **24**
rande Hotel Esplanade **25**
amburg, Hotel **26**
eidelberg Berlin, Hotel **27**

Inter-Continental Berlin **28**
Juwel, Hotel-Pension **29**
Kanthotel **30**
Knesebeck Pension **31**
Kronprinz Berlin, Hotel **32**
Kurfurstendamm, Hotel **33**
Mania-Barbel, Hotel-Pension **34**
Medenwalt **35**
Meineke, Hotel **36**

Modena, Hotel-Pension **37**
Palace, Hotel **38**
Pientka, Hotel **39**
President Berlin, Hotel **40**
Remter, Hotel **41**
Residenz, Hotel **42**
Savoy Hotel **43**
Schweizerhof Berlin, Hotel **44**
Sylter Hof, Hotel **45**
Tiergarten Berlin, Hotel **46**

S Privately owned by a Berliner, the Grand Hotel Esplanade opened in 1988 and quickly established itself as one of the best hotels in the city. Its lobby is modern and simple yet pleasant and refined, with gray-speckled marble floor and walls, black-leather chairs, and a rug the color of summer grass. As much as 1.8 million DM ($1.09 million) was spent on artwork alone. The hotel stands beside a canal, across from the Bauhaus-Archive (featuring the works of Walter Gropius and other famous designers).

Rooms are bright and cheerful, with white walls, beautifully crafted ash-wood furniture, and queen-size beds fitted with down quilts. Both the radios and cable TVs are operated by remote control, and the bathrooms have both makeup magnifying mirrors and hairdryers. Penthouse rooms are larger and have their own terraces. There are 30 no-smoking rooms.

Dining/Entertainment: Harry's New York Bar is one of the best and best-known bars in Berlin, good for a cocktail either before or after dinner in the Gourmet-Restaurant Harlekin. Buffet breakfast is served in the cheerful Orangerie, while Berlin specialties and beer are dished out in the Eck-Kneipe.

Services: Room service until midnight, shoeshine machines on each floor, in-house doctor and nurse, babysitting service.

Facilities: Indoor swimming pool, whirlpool, sauna, solaria, massage, hair salon, boutique.

INTER-CONTINENTAL BERLIN, Budapester Strasse 2, D-1000 Berlin 30. Tel. 030/260 20, or U.S. toll free 800/237-5469. Fax 030/260 280 760. Telex 184380. 530 rms, 70 suites. A/C MINIBAR TEL TV **Bus:** 9 from Tegel Airport to Budapester Strasse. **U-Bahn:** Bahnhof Zoologischer Garten, about a 7-minute walk.

$ Rates: 275–380 DM ($167–$230) single, 490 DM ($297) in peak season; 335–435 DM ($203–$264) double, 550 DM ($333) in peak season; from 575 DM ($348) suite. Extra bed 55 DM ($33.30). Breakfast buffet 24 DM ($14.55) extra. Winter discounts available. AE, DC, MC, V. Parking: 15 DM ($9.10).

Americans should feel at home at this branch of the international chain, Berlin's largest hotel. Its modern lobby is a bit sterile, but take a look at its glass-pyramid entryway, which predates those at the Louvre in Paris. The Inter-Continental has a good location near the zoo and the Tiergarten, and is not far from the Europa-Center. Rooms, many with views of the zoo or the Gedächtniskirche, are outfitted with the usual cable TVs, soundproof windows, and first-class amenities and services.

Dining/Entertainment: The rooftop Dachgarten Restaurant offers both superb views of the city and evening entertainment provided by a live band. Zum Hugenotten is the hotel's finest restaurant and serves traditional international cuisine; the Brasserie is its breakfast and snack restaurant; and the Kaminbar, with its open fireplace, is the place to go for a late-night drink with a view over Berlin.

Services: 24-hour room service, laundry and valet service.

Facilities: Indoor swimming pool, sauna, shopping arcade, beauty salon and barbershop, newsstand.

IN EAST BERLIN

GRAND HOTEL, Friedrichstrasse 158-164, DDR-1080 Berlin. Tel. 0372/209 23253, or U.S. toll free 800/223-6800. Fax 0372/229 4095. Telex 11-5198. 312 rms, 34 apartments and junior suites. A/C MINIBAR TEL TV **S-Bahn:** Friedrichstrasse.

$ Rates (including breakfast): 270–330 DM ($164–$200) single; 380 DM ($230) double; from 530 DM ($321) junior suite; from 770 DM ($467) apartment. AE, DC, MC, V. Parking: Free.

★ This would be a luxury hotel no matter where in the world it was. Opened in 1987, it is so cleverly designed that it looks as if it's been here forever. From its mock turn-of-the-century facade to its atrium lobby with a sweeping staircase (Scarlett O'Hara would have killed for this one), the hotel has a grand, elegant, yet cozy ambience. It has one of the best locations in the city, right off Unter den Linden, and even boasts its own lovely roof garden, where guests can sit and relax in the summer. There are plants throughout the hotel, as well as exotic orchids.

Even the rooms are what you'd expect in a first-class establishment, along with a few extras such as bathroom scales, telephones in the bathrooms, makeup magnifying mirrors, hairdryers, TVs with videos, and bathrobes. The apartments are decorated in various styles, including a Japanese apartment complete with futon, tatami, and beautifully papered walls. In short, this is one of Berlin's finest hotels, East or West.

Dining/Entertainment: Unsurprisingly, the Grand Hotel offers some of the best dining in the city. Le Grand Restaurant Silhouette, decorated in art nouveau style and with a different place setting of exquisite china for each table, offers superbly prepared courses served by an attentive staff. Zur Goldenen Gans looks like a house in the countryside and features roast goose and Thuringian potato dumplings, while Forellenquintett specializes in fish from the Spreewald. Stammhaus Kindl is the place to go for a foaming mug of beer; Pfauenauge is a classy cocktail bar.

Services: Limousine service, hotel doctor.

Facilities: Indoor swimming pool, whirlpool, massage, sauna, hairdresser, and beautician.

2. EXPENSIVE

ON OR NEAR THE KU'DAMM

AROSA PARKSCHLOSS HOTEL, Lietzenburger Strasse 79-81, D-1000 Berlin 15. Tel. 030/88 00 50. Fax 030/ 882 45 79. Telex 183397 or 182969. 91 rms. MINIBAR TEL TV **Bus:** 9 from Tegel Airport to Uhlandstrasse, then a 3-minute walk. **U-Bahn:** Uhlandstrasse, a 3-minute walk.

$ Rates (including buffet breakfast): 173–213 DM ($105–$129) single; 246–286 DM ($149–$173) double. Extra bed 50 DM ($30.30). AE, DC, MC, V. Parking: 10 DM ($6.05).

Just a few minutes' walk south of the Ku'damm, the Arosa Parkschloss has undergone extensive renovation in its lobby, including the addition of a fireplace. Its owners are a young couple with

IMPRESSIONS

An air of silence and dejection reigns in the streets, where at noonday scarcely any passengers are seen except soldiers.
—Sir N. W. Wraxall, 1779

It is distressing to see the multitude of soldiers here—to think of the nation's vitality going to feed 300,000 puppets in uniform. In the streets one's legs are in constant danger from officers' swords.
—George Eliot, 1854

---

plans to turn this small and personable hotel into one of the best in the city. With a staff that's efficient and courteous, it's one of the few hotels to boast both an outdoor pool and outdoor dining.

Rooms are fairly basic, but all come with radios and cable TVs. One of the best features of this hotel is its facilities for babies, from infant bathtubs to nursing tables and high chairs.

Dining/Entertainment: Of the hotel's two restaurants, one is a typical German pub with hearty German fare; the other, a more refined establishment offering nouvelle German cuisine, outdoor seating, and a bar.

Services: Room service, laundry service.

Facilities: Outdoor pool.

HOTEL BREMEN, Bleibtreustrasse 25, D-1000 Berlin 15. Tel. 030/881 40 76. Fax 030/882 46 85. Telex 184892 hobre d. 48 rms, 5 suites. MINIBAR TEL TV   **Bus:** 9 from Tegel Airport or Bahnhof Zoologischer Garten to Bleibtreustrasse, then a 1-minute walk.
$ Rates (including breakfast): 210 DM ($127) single; 250–270 DM ($151–$164) double. Children under 12 free in parents' rm. Discount offered Dec, Jan, and July. AE, DC, MC, V.

This quarter-century-old hotel was completely renovated in 1989, from its new marbled lobby to its pleasant breakfast room on the fifth floor. The latter, cheerfully decorated in peach and blue, has large windows overlooking turn-of-the-century facades across the street—a good way to start the day in Berlin. Rooms, decorated in soft pastels of mauve and sky-blue, have the modern conveniences of cable TVs with remote control, push-button phones, radios, and hairdryers. A good choice if you prefer a smaller hotel.

Dining/Entertainment: A bar in the hotel lobby is open round the clock.

Services: Room service, laundry and dry cleaning service, babysitting, shoeshine machine.

BERLIN EXCELSIOR HOTEL, Hardenbergstrasse 14, D-1000 Berlin 12. Tel. 030/31 991 or 31 993. Fax 030/319 92849. Telex 184781 exho d. 315 rms, 5 suites. A/C (in some rooms) MINIBAR TEL TV   **Bus:** 9 from Tegel Airport to Bahnhof Zoologischer Garten, then a 2-minute walk.
$ Rates (including buffet breakfast): 188 DM ($114) single; 238–268 DM ($144–$162) double; from 575 DM ($348) suite. Extra

bed 55 DM ($33.30). Children up to 2 free in parents' rm; children up to 12 an extra 18 DM ($10.90) in parents' rm. Crib available. AE, DC, MC, V. Parking: 12 DM ($7.25).

The Berlin Excelsior, near the train station and the university and about a 5-minute walk north of the Ku'damm, appeals to many of the city's international business guests because of its location, meeting rooms, simple and no-nonsense guest rooms, and dining facilities. Although the front of the hotel faces a busy street, rooms are soundproof. All come with hairdryers, cable TVs, safes, stocked minibars, and radios. Some rooms have small balconies, and doubles have large desks. The penthouse suites on the top floor are especially roomy, with huge windows overlooking the city.

Dining/Entertainment: The Rum Corner, just off the lobby, offers cocktails other than just those with rum. Diners have a choice between the casualness of the Store House Grill, built in the style of a Mississippi warehouse and offering steaks, fish, and a salad bar, and the more formal Restaurant Peacock, serving international cuisine.

Services: Babysitting, hotel doctor, shoeshine machines.

HECKER'S HOTEL, Grolmanstrasse 35, D-1000 Berlin 12. Tel. 030/88 900. Fax 030/889 02 60. Telex 184954 hhblnd. 52 rms. MINIBAR TEL TV **Bus:** 9 from Tegel Airport to Uhlandstrasse, then a 2-minute walk. **U-Bahn:** Uhlandstrasse, a 2-minute walk.

$ Rates: 200–260 DM ($121–$157) single; 250–320 DM ($151–$194) double. Extra bed 40 DM ($24.25). Children under 12 free in parents' rm. Breakfast buffet 15 DM ($9.10) extra. AE, DC, MC, V. Parking: Free.

Yet another older, more modest establishment that has undergone renovation, Hecker's Hotel calls itself Berlin's "small, private hotel." It has a good location between the Ku'damm and an interesting square called Savignyplatz. Rooms are decorated in a soothing pastel blue and feature walk-in closets, double doors to block out corridor noise, king-size beds, and radios. The more expensive rooms even have kitchenettes, good for longer stays.

Dining/Entertainment: The hotel's one restaurant, the Hecker's Deele, serves German cuisine from the Westphalia region.

Services: Room service.

Facilities: Drink vending machine on first floor.

SAVOY HOTEL, Fasanenstrasse 9-10, D-1000 Berlin 12. Tel. 030/31 10 30, or U.S. toll free 800/223-5652. Fax 030/311 33 33. Telex 184292. 116 rms, 14 suites. A/C (on 6th floor only) MINIBAR TEL TV **Bus:** 9 from Tegel Airport to Hardenbergstrasse. **U-Bahn:** Bahnhof Zoologischer Garten, a 3-minute walk; Kurfürstendamm, a 4-minute walk.

$ Rates: 195–240 DM ($118–$145) single; 280–420 DM ($170–$254) double; from 480 DM ($290) suite. Extra bed 60 DM ($36.35). Children under 12 free in parents' rm. Breakfast buffet 21 DM ($12.70) extra. AE, DC, MC, V.

S An old-timer by Berlin standards, this is one of my favorite hotels in the city, and judging by the people who have stayed here, I'm not alone. The late conductor Herbert von Karajan was a regular guest for 25 years; Benny Goodman and Maria Callas also stayed at the Savoy (it is close to the Theater des Westens, Schiller-Theater, and Deutsche Oper). When it first opened more than 60 years ago, it was an instant sensation because each room had its own private bathroom, a novel idea for the time. As one of the few buildings left standing after World War II, it served as British headquarters until 1955. Now, having recently been lovingly restored, this family-owned establishment is once again a great hotel. From its masculine Times Bar to the roof garden overlooking the city, the Savoy is a great choice in this category.

Its lobby is small and unassuming, with the emphasis on the rooms above. Each of these is slightly different, but all have trouser pressers, radios, cable TVs with remote control and free English video movies, and bathrooms with their own telephones, hairdryers, and bidets. Some doubles even have small kitchenettes, complete with hot plates, fridges, and utensils. The most expensive rooms are on the sixth floor, called the Belle Étage, where television sets also serve as computers, and fresh fruit and flowers are supplied daily.

Dining/Entertainment: The Times Bar, cozy and wood-paneled, is stocked with international newspapers. A sumptuous buffet breakfast, which includes everything from salmon to exotic fruits like kiwi, is served in the Belle Époque, where there's even outdoor seating in a small garden. It's also open for lunch and dinner, when the emphasis is on modern, health-conscious cuisine.

Services: Complimentary shoeshine.

Facilities: Fitness club, sauna, solarium.

NEAR THE EUROPA-CENTER & THE TIERGARTEN

HOTEL AMBASSADOR BERLIN, Bayreuther Strasse 42-43, D-1000 Berlin 30. Tel. 030/219 02, or U.S. toll free 800/223-6764. Fax 030/219 02380. Telex 184259 ambas d. **191 rms, 8 suites. MINIBAR TEL TV Bus:** 9 from Tegel Airport to Budapester Strasse, then a 4-minute walk. **U-Bahn:** Wittenbergplatz, a 2-minute walk.

$ Rates (including breakfast buffet): 228 DM ($138) single, 262 DM ($159) in peak season and during Messe; 295 DM ($179) double, 315 DM ($191) in peak season; from 435 DM ($264) suite. Extra bed 55 DM ($33.30). Winter discount available. AE, DC, MC, V. Parking: 8 DM ($4.85).

Located near Wittenbergplatz with its famous KaDeWe department store, this hotel has a simple lobby but a lot of extras, including good restaurants, comfortable rooms, and a heated pool with sunning area on the roof. Rooms all have soundproof windows, radios, and TVs, and one floor is exclusively for nonsmoking guests.

Dining/Entertainment: The Conti-Fischstuben is one of Berlin's better-known hotel restaurants, specializing in seafood. Schöneberger Krug dishes out international food and typical German meals. Drinks are served in the Bar Ambassador.

Services: Laundry and valet services.

Facilities: Indoor swimming pool, solarium, Finnish sauna, massage.

BERLIN PENTA HOTEL, Nürnberger Strasse 65, D-1000 Berlin 30. Tel. 030/21 00 70, or U.S. toll free 800/237-5469 or 800/225-3456. Fax 030/213 20 09. Telex 182877 bepen d. 415 rms, 10 suites. A/C MINIBAR TEL TV   **Bus:** 9 from Tegel Airport to Budapester Strasse, then a 2-minute walk.   **U-Bahn:** Wittenbergplatz or Kurfürstendamm, each a 3-minute walk.

$ Rates: 200 DM ($121) single; 240 DM ($145) double; from 430 DM ($261) suite. Extra bed 40 DM ($24.25). Breakfast buffet 20 DM ($12.10) extra. AE, DC, MC, V. Parking: 12 DM ($7.25).

Conveniently situated right across the street from the Europa-Center complex, this hotel is just a short walk from the Ku'damm, the Gedächtniskirche, the KaDeWe department store, and Bahnhof Zoo. A chain hotel, it has all the expected modern conveniences and facilities, from restaurants and bars to a swimming pool and comfortable rooms. There's a no-smoking floor, as well as special rooms for disabled persons. Each room is soundproof and comes equipped with combination bath/shower, radio, minibar, and cable TV with pay video, with bedside control panels for both the TV and radio.

Dining/Entertainment: The Globetrotter is the hotel's primary restaurant, serving breakfast and international meals. The Pinte Bierstube, with a rustic atmosphere typical of old Berlin bars, serves draft beer and German snacks. An especially good deal is the daily happy hour in the Follow Me Bar, when drinks are half price from 5 to 6:30pm and there's live piano music.

Services: House doctor and nurse, babysitting, complimentary coffee for early risers.

Facilities: Indoor swimming pool, sauna, solarium, massage, boutique, hair, beauty salon and barbershop.

HOTEL PALACE, Europa-Center, D-1000 Berlin 30. Tel. 030/25 49 70, or U.S. toll free 800/268-1234 or 800/237-5469. Fax 030/262 65 77. Telex 184825 eupal d. 258 rms, 4 suites. A/C MINIBAR TEL TV   **Bus:** 9 from Tegel Airport to Budapester Strasse, then a 1-minute walk.   **U-Bahn:** Bahnhof Zoologischer Garten or Kurfürstendamm, each a 2-minute walk.

$ Rates: 220–240 DM ($133–$145) single, from 285 DM ($173) during Messen and in peak season; 240–280 DM ($145–$170) double, from 330 DM ($200) during Messe and in peak season; from 490 DM ($297) suite. Extra bed 55 DM ($33.30). Buffet breakfast 24 DM ($14.55) extra. AE, DC, MC, V.

You can't get much closer to the Europa-Center than this—the Hotel Palace is right inside the huge complex with its casino and many shops and restaurants. A Best Western hotel, it enjoys an international clientele and has a comfortable, personable lobby filled with plants and fresh flowers. Hotel guests have free use of the Thermen, which is a large health spa with sauna and swimming pool in the Europa-Center.

Guests receive credit-card-size electronic "keys" to their rooms. The rooms are soundproof and offer individually controlled air conditioning, trouser pressers, radios, hairdryers, and cable TVs with remote control. The more expensive rooms, located in the newer Casino Wing, offer marble bathrooms with magnifying makeup mirrors and separate tubs and showers. No-smoking rooms are available.

Dining/Entertainment: La Reserve, specializing in French and international dishes, is located inside the hotel. In addition, the Palace operates two informal restaurants in the Europa-Center: Tiffany's, with its "outdoor" terrace dining; and Alt-Nürnberg, serving Bavarian and Berlin specialties. There's a bar just off the lobby.

Services: Laundry service, shoeshine service.

Facilities: Free use of Thermen swimming pool and sauna in Europa-Center.

HOTEL PRESIDENT BERLIN, An der Urania 16-18, D-1000 Berlin 30. Tel. 030/21 90 30. Fax 030/214 12 00. Telex 184018 presi d. 132 rms, 11 suites. A/C (in most rms) MINIBAR TEL TV **Bus:** 9, 19, 29, or 69 to An der Urania. **U-Bahn:** Wittenbergplatz, a 3-minute walk.

$ Rates (including buffet breakfast): 215 DM ($130) single, 255 DM ($154) in peak season; 255 DM ($154) double, 300 DM ($182) in peak season; from 490 DM ($297) suite. Extra bed 45 DM ($27.25). Children under 14 free in parents' rm. Off-season rates available. AE, DC, MC, V. Parking: 6 DM ($3.65).

Although it doesn't look like much from the outside and is easily overlooked, this small hotel is pleasant and personable on the inside and has recently renovated and upgraded its facilities. It stands about halfway between the Europa-Center and Nollendorfplatz, about a 5-minute walk from both. For the security-conscious, it has added such extras as peepholes in the doors and electronic credit-card-size room keys. All accommodations come with hairdryers, minibars, cable TVs with in-house videos, and radios.

Dining/Entertainment: As its name suggests, Die Saison offers seasonal dishes, as well as a salad buffet. There's one hotel bar, the President.

Services: Room service, shoeshine machines.

Facilities: Fitness room, sauna, steam bath, solarium.

HOTEL SCHWEIZERHOF BERLIN, Budapester Strasse 21-31, D-1000 Berlin 30. Tel. 030/269 60, or U.S. toll free 800/33-AGAIN or 800/237-5469. Fax 030/269 69 00. Telex 185501 swho d. 420 rms, 10 suites. A/C (in some rms) MINIBAR TEL TV **Bus:** 9 from Tegel Airport to Budapester Strasse, then a 2-minute walk. **U-Bahn:** Bahnhof Zoologischer Garten, a 7-minute walk.

$ Rates: 225–440 DM ($136–$267) single; 280–490 DM ($170–$297) double; from 750 DM ($454) suite. Extra bed 50 DM ($30.30). Children under 12 free in parents' rm. Breakfast buffet 22 DM ($13.30) extra. AE, DC, MC, V. Parking: 9 DM ($5.45).

S Established by a Swiss firm that prides itself on providing the best in Swiss hospitality, the Schweizerhof belongs to the Inter-Continental group and is practically across the street from the Inter-Continental Berlin. To live up to its Swiss name, the hotel displays lots of natural wood in its decor and offers native specialties in its Grill Restaurant. Its swimming pool is one of Berlin's largest. All around, it's one of the best hotels in its category.

Rooms are nice and pleasant, with radios and cable TVs (with video programs). The fifth floor is reserved for nonsmokers, and the deluxe rooms in the newer west wing even have balconies overlooking the zoo.

Dining/Entertainment: Breakfast buffet, offering everything from rye bread and Muesli to eggs and smoked ham, is served in the Alter Markt, a restaurant designed to look like a marketplace. The Grill Restaurant serves not only Swiss and German specialties but also international dishes and a changing four-course menu. There are also two bars.

Services: Complimentary shoeshine, laundry and dry cleaning, in-house nurse.

Facilities: Large indoor pool, sauna, solarium, massage.

HOTEL SYLTER HOF, Kurfürstenstrasse 116, D-1000 Berlin 30. Tel. 030/21 200. Fax 030/214 28 26. Telex 183317. 131 rms, 25 suites. MINIBAR TEL TV   **Bus:** 9 from Tegel Airport to Budapester Strasse, then a 5-minute walk.   **U-Bahn:** Wittenbergplatz, a 4-minute walk.
$ Rates (including buffet breakfast): 185 DM ($112) single; 275 DM ($167) double; from 230 DM ($139) junior suite. Extra bed 45 DM ($27.25). Discount in suites for longer stays. AE, DC, MC, V. Parking: 6 DM ($3.65).

Built in 1966 but renovated since then, the small and comfortable Sylter Hof has a cozy lobby that looks as if it could be someone's living room. Rooms are small but adequate, with radios and alarm clocks, cable TVs with pay videos, and minibars. The majority of rooms are singles; the 49 doubles have bidets. Beside the hotel is the cabaret Dollywood, with a variety show in English.

Dining/Entertainment: The Friesenstube serves German and international choices. There's a small bar for relaxation just off the reception area.

Services: Shoeshine machines.

Facilities: Beauty salon.

IN EAST BERLIN

METROPOL, Friedrichstrasse 150-153, DDR-1086 Berlin. Tel. 0372/22040. Fax 0372/2204209. Telex 114141. 307 rms, 33 apts and suites. A/C MINIBAR TEL TV **S-Bahn:** Friedrichstrasse.
$ Rates (including buffet breakfast): 220 DM ($133) single; 300 DM ($182) double; from 340 DM ($206) apt. AE, DC, MC, V.

Just a 2-minute walk from the Friedrichstrasse and across the street from the International Trade Center, the Metropol is a modern hotel filled mainly with business travelers. The courteous staff will help guests obtain theater tickets or restaurant reservations in East Berlin. Rooms are all the same size, each with wood furniture (including desk), minibar, direct-dial telephone, radio, alarm clock, and hairdryer.

Dining/Entertainment: Acquaint yourself with Cuban cuisine and drinks in La Habana. Friedrichstadt serves both a breakfast buffet and international dishes; the Specialty Restaurant's changing menu centers on different themes from different countries; and the Grill serves fast food. A nightclub with a disco and floor show opens at 9pm, while the Hall Bar serves drinks round the clock.

Services: Hotel doctor, babysitting, laundry, pressing and dry cleaning services, limousine service, 24-hour room service.

Facilities: Indoor swimming pool, massage, Finnish sauna, shopping arcade, hairdresser.

ON THE LIETZENSEE

HOTEL SEEHOF BERLIN, Lietzensee Ufer 11, D-1000 Berlin 19. Tel. 030/32 00 20. Fax 030/230 02 251. Telex 182943. 78 rms, 1 suite. MINIBAR TEL TV **Bus:** 94 or 50.

$ Rates (including buffet breakfast): 105 DM ($64) single with toilet only, 165–258 DM ($100–$156) single with bath; 275–300 DM ($167–$182) double with bath; from 440 DM ($267) suite. Extra bed 40 DM ($24.25). AE, DC, MC, V.

Idyllically situated on the bank of a picturesque lake with willow trees and a park, this hotel is as close as you can get to resortlike accommodations in the heart of the city. It's in a peaceful and quiet residential area of Charlottenburg, just a 10-minute walk from the Internationales Congress-Centrum (ICC) and the Funkturm (Radio Tower). There's a jogging path around the lake, and the hotel swimming pool is surrounded by glass walls that can be pushed open in the summer. Guests can dine outside on a terrace beside the lake, where there's also a bar.

As for the rooms, all doubles overlook the lake, but some singles face the street and are the same price as the lakeside singles, so be sure to ask for one with a view. Rooms on the second floor have small balconies. Amenities include hairdryers, magnifying makeup mirrors, cable TVs, radios, and minibars.

Dining/Entertainment: Au Lac, serving a different international menu every day, features evening piano music; guests can dine either outdoors on a terrace overlooking the lake or indoors in a romantic, candle-lit ambience. For drinks, there are both an outdoor terrace bar and an indoor bar with a rustic, open-beamed ceiling.

Services: Hotel doctor, babysitting.

Facilities: Swimming pool, sauna, solarium.

3. MODERATE

Unless otherwise indicated, all rooms in this category come with private shower/tub and WC.

HOTEL ASTORIA, Fasanenstrasse 2, D-1000 Berlin 12. Tel. 030/312 40 67. Fax 030/312 50 27. Telex 181745 asber d. 33 rms. MINIBAR TEL TV **Bus:** 9 from Tegel Airport to Bahnhof Zoologischer Garten, then a 3-minute walk.

$ Rates (including buffet breakfast): 155 DM ($94) single; 215 DM

FROMMER'S COOL FOR KIDS
Hotels

Arosa Parkschloss Hotel *(see p. 61)* This hotel offers a lot of services for babies, including infant bathtubs, nursing tables, and high chairs.

Econtel *(see p. 81)* In addition to having economically priced family rooms, the Econtel also boasts special facilities for the little ones, including cribs, bottle warmers, and surprise diversions and games.

($130) double. Extra bed 40 DM ($24.25). AE, DC, MC, V. Parking: 12 DM ($7.25).

Near the corner of Fasanenstrasse and Hardenbergstrasse between Bahnhof Zoo and the university, this small, modestly furnished family-owned hotel, about a 5-minute walk north of the Ku'damm, is almost 50 years old. Its hallways and rooms would be brighter if the carpet and furniture weren't such a dark brown, but otherwise the accommodations are perfectly adequate and have all the basic comforts: minibars, radios, hairdryers, safes, TVs, and tiled bathrooms.

Services: Babysitting.
Facilities: Bar.

BERLIN MARK HOTEL, Meinekestrasse 18, D-1000 Berlin 15. Tel. 030/88 00 20 or 880 02 802. Fax 030/880 02 804. Telex 186616 markh d. 217 rms. TEL **Bus:** 9 from Tegel Airport to Kurfürstendamm/Joachimstaler Strasse, then a 3-minute walk. **U-Bahn:** Kurfürstendamm or Uhlandstrasse, each a 3-minute walk.

$ Rates (including buffet breakfast): 109 DM ($66) economy single, 140 DM ($85) single in "comfort" rm; 170 DM ($103) economy double, 190 DM ($115) double in "comfort" rm; 215 DM ($130) economy triple, 250 DM ($151) triple in "comfort" rm; 240 DM ($145) economy quad. Children under 2 free in parents' rm; children 2 to 12 an extra 10 DM ($6.05) in parents' rm. AE, DC, MC, V.

This conveniently located hotel, on the corner of Lietzenburger Strasse and Meinekestrasse just a few minutes' walk south of the Ku'damm, caters strongly to youth groups and bus tours. Built in 1987, it offers two types of accommodations: economy rooms (all with two bunk beds), which can be rented to single travelers or as many as four persons, and which come only with bathrooms and telephones; and 66 "comfort" rooms, which come with such extra perks as color TVs, with remote control, minibars, and radios.

Dining/Entertainment: The Bistro restaurant, complete with a bar and an outdoor terrace, offers a buffet, snacks, desserts, and freshly baked breads.

BERLIN PLAZA HOTEL, Knesebeckstrasse 63, D-1000 Berlin 15. Tel. 030/88 41 30 or 884 13 444. Fax 030/884 13 754. Telex 184181 plaza d. 131 rms. MINIBAR TEL TV   **Bus:** 9 to Bleibtreustrasse, a 2-minute walk.   **U-Bahn:** Uhlandstrasse, a 3-minute walk.

$ Rates (including buffet breakfast): 155 DM ($94) single; 200 DM ($121) twin; 220 DM ($133) double. Extra bed 40 DM ($25.25). Crib available. Children under 2 free in parents' rm; children 2 to 12 an extra 18 DM ($10.90) in parents' rm. AE, DC, MC, V. Parking: 8 DM ($4.85).

With a good location just off the Ku'damm and friendly personnel, this older hotel recently underwent renovation. It features a pleasant hot-pink breakfast room with white curtains; its clean rooms are decorated in white and plum. No-smoking rooms are available.

Dining/Entertainment: The hotel's one restaurant, which has a summer terrace, serves specialties of Berlin, as well as beer and wine.

HOTEL AM ZOO, Kurfürstendamm 25, D-1000 Berlin 15. Tel. 030/88 43 70. Fax 030/884 37 714. Telex 183835 zooho d. 131 rms, 5 suites. MINIBAR TEL TV   **Bus:** 9 from Tegel Airport to Joachimstaler Strasse, then a 1-minute walk.   **U-Bahn:** Kurfürstendamm, a 1-minute walk.

$ Rates (including buffet breakfast): 180 DM ($109) single; 220–245 DM ($133–$150) double; from 285 DM ($173) suite. Extra bed 45 DM ($27.25). Children under 7, an extra 25 DM ($15.15) in parents' rm. AE, DC, MC, V. Parking: 8–15 DM ($4.85–$9.10).

Right on the Ku'damm, and only a 5-minute walk from Bahnhof Zoo train station, is another older hotel that has undergone such extensive renovation that it's modern in every sense of the word. Its lobby has a glass facade that looks out onto Berlin's famous boulevard, and rooms are soundproof so guests can get a good night's sleep. A fourth of the rooms face the Ku'damm; the rest face toward the back. First opened in 1911, the Hotel am Zoo has been family-run ever since.

Services: Room service (for drinks and snacks only), shoeshine machines, laundry and dry cleaning service.

Facilities: Bar.

KANTHOTEL, Kantstrasse 111, D-1000 Berlin 12. Tel. 030/32 30 26. Fax 030/324 09 52. Telex 183330 kanth d. 55 rms. MINIBAR TEL TV   **Bus:** 9 from Tegel Airport or Bahnhof Zoologischer Garten to Wilmersdorfer Strasse.   **U-Bahn:** Wilmersdorfer Strasse, a 1-minute walk.

$ Rates (including buffet breakfast): 144 DM ($87) single; 179 DM ($108) double. Extra bed 45 DM ($27.25). AE, DC, MC, V. Parking: 6 DM ($3.65).

About a 6-minute walk north of the Ku'damm, this simple, basic place is convenient to the Wilmersdorfer Strasse pedestrian shopping lane with its many department stores and boutiques. Built in 1981, the hotel offers clean rooms with soundproof windows, TVs (with pay videos), and radios. In summer, breakfast is served on an outdoor terrace.

HOTEL KRONPRINZ BERLIN, Kronprinzendamm 1, D-1000 Berlin 31. Tel. 030/89 60 30. Telex 181459 kropr d. 53 rms. MINIBAR TEL TV **Bus:** 9 from Tegel Airport to Adenauerplatz, then 19 or 29 to Henriettenplatz; from Bahnhof Zoologischer Garten, 19 or 29 to Henriettenplatz.

$ Rates (including buffet breakfast): 120–135 DM ($73–$82) single; 175–200 DM ($106–$121) double. Extra bed 45 DM ($27.25). Children under 12 free in parents' rm. AE, DC, MC, V.

The Kronprinz, with a lovely facade dating from 1894, stands in a quiet location on the far western edge of the Ku'damm, but is easily connected to the city center in less than 10 minutes by bus 19 or 29 (each of which travels up and down the Ku'damm). The hotel's interior is modern and renovated. Rooms vary in size but are outfitted with the same amenities. At day's end, guests tend to gather in the cozy bar for a bit of camaraderie and conversation.

Facilities: Bar.

HOTEL KURFÜRSTENDAMM, Kurfürstendamm 68, D-1000 Berlin 15. Tel. 030/88 28 41. Fax 030/882 55 28. Telex 184630 kuhot d. 30 rms, 4 suites (30 with private baths, 4 with WCs only). TEL TV **Bus:** 9 from Tegel Airport or Bahnhof Zoologischer Garten to Adenauerplatz, then a 1-minute walk. **U-Bahn:** Adenauerplatz.

$ Rates (including buffet breakfast): 85 DM ($51.50) single with WC, 118 DM ($72) single with bath; 170 DM ($103) double with bath; from 210 DM ($127) suite. Crib available. AE, DC, MC, V. Parking: Free.

True to its name, this modern hotel is on the Ku'damm, at its west end, about a 20 minute walk from the Gedächtniskirche and the Europa-Center. Recently renovated from top to bottom, it looks a bit out of place amid facades dating from earlier decades and its rooms are a bit unimaginative, but its prices are reasonable. Especially good are the four two-room suites, two of which even have their own terraces. Rooms face either the busy Ku'damm or the quieter back side of the hotel; specify which you prefer when making your reservation.

HOTEL LENZ, Xantener Strasse 8, D-1000 Berlin 15. Tel. 030/881 51 58 or 881 93 31. Telex 186883 lenz d. 28 rms. TEL TV **Bus:** 9 from Tegel Airport or Bahnhof Zoologischer Garten to Adenauerplatz, then a 3-minute walk. **U-Bahn:** Adenauerplatz.

$ Rates (including Continental breakfast): 115–160 DM ($70–97) single; 165–230 DM ($100–$139) double; 200 DM ($121) triple. AE, DC, MC, V.

A family-owned hotel, the Lenz is on a quiet residential street not far from Olivaer Platz. The building dates from 1916, reflected in the fact that each room and each floor is different. Some rooms are decorated with antique furniture; others have balconies. Some repeat guests get so attached to certain rooms that they request them over and over again. There's an elevator (activated by a key that each guest receives), and corridors are all nicely wallpapered. A pleasant place to stay.

Facilities: Bar.

**HOTEL MEINEKE, Meinekestrasse 10, D-1000 Berlin 15.
Tel. 030/88 28 11.** 60 rms. TEL TV **Bus:** 9 from Tegel
Airport to Uhlandstrasse, then a 4-minute walk. **U-Bahn:**
Uhlandstrasse, a 4-minute walk.

$ Rates (including Continental breakfast): 108–140 DM
($66–$85) single; 185–210 DM ($112–$127) double. Extra bed
40 DM ($24.25). AE, DC, MC, V.

About a 10-minute walk from Bahnhof Zoo south of the Ku'damm,
this hotel has its reception area up on the first floor, with rooms
spread over several floors serviced by an ancient elevator (indicative of
the Meineke's having been around since the beginning of the
century). Rooms are fairly large, and some that face the front have
small balconies (but also more traffic noise). The majority of rooms
face the back courtyard, where there's no view but it's much quieter.
Essentially, this is a place to lay your head with just the basics.

**HOTEL PIENTKA, Kurfürstendamm 12, D-1000 Berlin 15.
Tel. 030/88 42 50.** Fax 030/884 25 450. Telex 186695 hopie
d. 57 rms. MINIBAR TEL TV **Bus:** 9 from Tegel Airport to
Joachimstaler Strasse, then a 1-minute walk. **U-Bahn:**
Kurfürstendamm, a 1-minute walk.

$ Rates (including breakfast): 170–250 DM ($103–$151) single;
220–290 DM ($133–$176) double. Extra bed 40 DM ($24.25).
Crib available. AE, DC, MC, V.

⑤ Just a stone's throw from the Gedächtniskirche, the Pientka is
one of the best hotels in its category, especially if you like a
modern, crisp interior and plenty of sunshine. Reception is up
on the sixth floor, a sleek and spacious area with marble floors,
plants, and wide windows overlooking the rooftops on the other side
of the Ku'damm. Especially grand is the large outdoor terrace off the
lobby, where you can enjoy breakfast in the morning or simply relax
with a coffee or an evening drink, observing life on the busy
boulevard below. Rooms are modern, with safes, minibars, radios,
and TVs; those facing the Ku'damm are outfitted with soundproof
double-pane windows. All in all, a great place to stay.

Services: Room service.
Facilities: Bar.

**HOTEL RESIDENZ, Meinekestrasse 9, D-1000 Berlin 15.
Tel. 030/88 28 91 or 88 44 30.** Fax 030/882 47 26. Telex
183082 hore d. 67 rms, 4 apts, 9 suites. MINIBAR TEL TV **Bus:**
9 from Tegel Airport to Uhlandstrasse, then a 4-minute walk.
U-Bahn: Uhlandstrasse or Kurfürstenstrasse, each a 4-minute
walk.

$ Rates: 165 DM ($100) single; 210 DM ($127) double; 244 DM
($148) apartment; 569 DM ($345) suite. Extra bed 45 DM
($27.25). Breakfast 17 DM ($10.30) extra. AE, DC, MC, V.

About a 10-minute walk south of Bahnhof Zoo, the Hotel Residenz
was built around the turn of the century and boasts an elegant facade
and a very ornate art nouveau entryway. Because they were once part
of private apartments, rooms vary in size but are all the same price.
Most have high stucco ceilings, and some have balconies; those
facing the back of the building are quieter. Apartments consist of

large double rooms with kitchenettes, while suites have bedrooms, living rooms, and kitchens.

Dining/Entertainment: There is a good French restaurant called Grand Cru, plus a bar.

NEAR THE EUROPA-CENTER & THE TIERGARTEN

These hotels are all east or southeast of the Europa-Center and south of the Tiergarten, most within a 10-minute walk of the Gedächtniskirche and the Ku'damm.

ALSTERHOF, Augsburger Strasse 5, D-1000 Berlin 30. Tel. 030/21 99 60. Fax 030/24 38 49. Telex 243949. 144 rms. MINIBAR TEL TV **Bus:** 9 from Tegel Airport to Joachimstaler Strasse, then a 7-minute walk. **U-Bahn:** Augsburger Strasse, a 1-minute walk.

$ Rates (including buffet breakfast): 165–210 DM ($100–$127) single; 225–270 DM ($136–$164) double. Extra bed 44 DM ($26.65). Children under 14 free in parents' rm. Crib available. AE, DC, MC, V. Parking: 8–12 DM ($4.85–$7.25).

About a 4-minute walk south of the Europa-Center, this small place first opened about 25 years ago. Rooms tend to be undersize, but there are a number of facilities that make the Alsterhof worthwhile, including rental bicycles (8 DM [$4.85] for 5 hours) and an indoor pool. Rooms all have hairdryers, radios, trouser pressers, minibars, and TVs (cable and videos in the more expensive rooms). The most expensive doubles boast terraces.

Facilities: Indoor swimming pool, sauna, solarium, massage, German restaurant, bar.

HOTEL BERLIN, Lützowplatz 17, D-1000 Berlin 30. Tel. 030/260 50. Fax 030/260 52 716. Telex 184332. 487 rms, 21 suites. A/C (in new wing) TEL TV **Bus:** 9 from Tegel Airport or Bahnhof Zoologischer Garten to Schillstrasse, then a 2-minute walk. **U-Bahn:** Nollendorfplatz, about a 5-minute walk.

$ Rates (including buffet breakfast): 155–269 DM ($94–$163) single; 175–215 DM ($106–$130) double; 198–319 DM ($120–$193) twin; from 440 DM ($267) suite. Crib available. Family packages available. AE, DC, MC, V. Parking: 5 DM ($3.05).

One of Berlin's largest establishments, the Hotel Berlin consists of two parts—an older wing built three decades ago and offering economy rooms at reasonable prices, and a newer modern wing built in 1987 and offering luxury rooms at higher rates. Rooms in the old wing are small but come with hairdryers, radios, and cable TVs; those in the new wing are much nicer and have the extras of air conditioning, TVs with remote control, and makeup magnifying mirrors in roomy tiled bathrooms. There are several restaurants here, as well as a wide range of facilities usually available only in first-class hotels. You may wish to save money by staying in the cheaper older wing while still taking advantage of all that a large, upper-category hotel has to offer. Note, however, that it costs 20 DM ($12.10) to use the fitness center.

Dining/Entertainment: The Grill, a gourmet restaurant, serves seafood and international cuisine. There is a restaurant–piano bar called Globe for casual, quick meals, plus the Berlin Eck pub.

Services: Laundry service, shoeshine machines.

Facilities: Beauty salon and barbershop, fitness center with sauna, steam bath, and training machines.

HOTEL HAMBURG, Landgrafenstrasse 4, D-1000 Berlin 30. Tel. 030/26 91 61. Fax 030/262 93 94. Telex 184974. 240 rms. TEL TV **Bus:** 9 from Tegel Airport or Bahnhof Zoologischer Garten to Kurfürstenstrasse. **U-Bahn:** Wittenbergplatz, a 5-minute walk.

$ Rates (including buffet breakfast): 175–195 DM ($106–$118) single; 195–205 DM ($118–$124) twin; 230–255 DM ($139–$154) double. Extra bed 29 DM ($17.55); crib 16 DM ($9.70). AE, DC, MC, V. Parking: 8 DM ($4.85).

Just off the busy Kurfürstenstrasse (not to be confused with the Kurfürstendamm) on a quiet side street, this simple hotel is more than 25 years old. Rooms look as if they've changed little since the 1960s (including a carpetlike wallpaper that may once have been considered mod), but they have the basic comforts of cable TVs and radios.

Services: Room service.

Facilities: Restaurant and bar.

HOTEL REMTER, Marburger Strasse 17, D-1000 Berlin 30. Tel. 030/24 60 61. Fax 030/213 86 12. Telex 183497 horem d. 34 rms. TEL TV **Bus:** 9 from Tegel Airport to Budapester Strasse, then a 2-minute walk. **U-Bahn:** Kurfürstendamm, about a 3-minute walk.

$ Rates (including buffet breakfast): 120–135 DM ($73–$82) single; 175–200 DM ($106–$121) double. AE, DC, MC, V.

Though the tiny Remter has a good location almost in front of the Europa-Center, it is off on a side street with much less traffic. Catering mostly to businesspeople, it has a small reception area up on the first floor and offers rooms with radios, safes, and TVs.

IN GRÜNEWALD

SCHLOSSHOTEL GEHRHUS, Brahmsstrasse 4-10, D-1000 Berlin 33. Tel. 030/826 20 81. 31 rms (25 with baths), 2 suites. TEL TV (in some rms) **Bus:** 9 to Kurfürstendamm, then 19 to Hagenplatz or 29 to Roseneck, followed by a 5-minute walk.

$ Rates (including breakfast): 80–125 DM ($48–$76) single without bath, 130–170 DM ($79–$103) single with bath; 170 DM ($103) double without bath, 190–245 DM ($115–$148) double with bath; from 245 DM ($148) suite. AE, DC, MC, V. Parking: Free.

This palace hotel looks as though it should be in a movie—as indeed it has been (Romy Schneider made her last film here). Built in 1912–14 as the private residence of Kaiser Wilhelm II's personal attorney, it is one of the few palaces to have survived World War II and sits amid some of the most expensive homes in Berlin, in a wealthy neighborhood called Grünewald. Ornate inside and out, it features an Italian Renaissance–style lobby with velvet wallpaper, chandeliers, and a gilded carved ceiling, and rooms from another era that vary in size. Ask to see the private-function rooms—they haven't changed since 1912–14. In fact, the hotel has made few concessions to the modern age (even the rooms have old furniture and few modern comforts) and borders on the edge of neglect, which somehow adds to the prevailing aura (come to think of it, the place would serve as a perfect setting for an Agatha Christie novel). Schlosshotel Gehrhus is surrounded by the palace grounds, and in summer guests can dine outdoors on the terrace. The only disadvantage of staying here is the location, away from the heart of Berlin (about a 15-minute taxi ride). However, if you're a nostalgic romantic who grows weak in the knees over grand old hotels from another age, you won't be able to resist this place. Highly recommended.

Facilities: French restaurant.

NEAR GÜNTZELSTRASSE STATION

QUEENS HOTEL, Güntzelstrasse 14, D-1000 Berlin 31. Tel. 030/87 02 41. Telex 182948. 110 rms. MINIBAR TEL TV **U-Bahn:** U-9 from Bahnhof Zoologischer Garten to Güntzelstrasse, then a 2-minute walk.

$ Rates: 160 DM ($97) single; 190–200 DM ($115–$121) double. Extra bed 45 DM ($27.25). AE, DC, MC, V. Parking: Free.

The Queens is located south of the city center near Güntzelstrasse station, with direct U-9 subway service to the Kurfürstendamm (two stops) and Bahnhof Zoo (three stops). If you like walking, you can stroll to the Ku'damm in about 20 minutes. Member of a German chain of hotels, the Queens is a modern place with rooms similar to those you'd find anywhere in the world, all with TVs (with pay videos), radios, alarm clocks, trouser pressers, and minibars.

Facilities: Bar.

4. INEXPENSIVE

Many of the hotels in this category give the option of rooms with or without private showers and WCs. Those without, of course, are cheaper, with free showers down the hall. Be sure to reconfirm the rates when making your reservation, since rates may go up. However, they probably won't differ more than a couple of marks from the prices given below.

ON OR NEAR THE KU'DAMM

ALPENLAND, Carmerstrasse 8, D-1000 Berlin 12. Tel. 030/312 39 70 or 312 48 98. Fax 030/313 84 44. 43 rms (6 with showers only, 6 with showers and WCs). TEL (in some rms) **Bus:** 9 from Tegel Airport to Uhlandstrasse, then a 6-minute walk. **S-Bahn:** Savignyplatz, a 3-minute walk.

$ Rates (including Continental breakfast): 65–70 DM ($39.40–

$42.40) single without shower or WC, 75–80 DM ($45.45–$48.50) single with shower, 90–100 DM ($54.55–$60.60) single with shower and WC; 95–100 DM ($54.55–$60.60) double without shower or WC, 105–110 DM ($63.65–$66.65) double with shower, 130–140 DM ($78.80–$85) double with shower and WC. Extra bed 35 DM ($21.20). No credit cards accepted.

North of the Ku'damm near Savignyplatz, which has a number of trendy bars and restaurants, the Alpenland is decorated in Tyrolean fashion, with lots of wood, some antiques, and dried-flower arrangements in the lobby and breakfast room. Catering mostly to group travelers, it offers accommodations spread on four floors; there is no elevator. With high ceilings and outfitted with safes, rooms face either the front or the back of the hotel—those facing the back are quieter but the view is not as interesting. Although the building is a bit old and run down, the pension itself is clean. It's less than a 10-minute walk from Bahnhof Zoo.

ARTEMISIA, Brandenburgische Strasse 18, D-1000 Berlin. Tel. 030/87 89 05. 8 rms (all with showers and WCs). TEL **Bus:** 9 from Tegel Airport or Bahnhof Zoologischer Garten to Adenauerplatz, then a 5-minute walk. **U-Bahn:** Konstanzer, a 1-minute walk.

$ Rates (including buffet breakfast): 100–110 DM ($60.60–$66.65) single; 130–160 DM ($78.80–$96.95) double; 45 DM ($27.25) per person in 4-bed dormitory rm. Children under 6 free in parents' rm; children 6 to 12 half price. AE, MC, V.

⭐ This is a wonderful pension—*for women only*. Opened in 1989, it is a modern, spotless, cheerful, and thoughtfully planned establishment that gives much attention to the needs of female travelers. Reception is up on the fourth floor (there's an elevator), and there's a sunny breakfast room, as well as a rooftop terrace and winter garden (perfect for writing those postcards). Also on the premises are a small library and a hotel bar with a fireplace. The walls of the corridor serve as a changing art gallery. Rooms are beautifully done, with a mixture of antiques and sleek modern furniture. Each accommodation is dedicated to a famous "forgotten" woman (such as the composer Fanny Mendelssohn-Hensel, who lived in her brother's shadow) and contains a few items in memory of her, as well as a hairdryer, full-length mirror, and desk. The dormitory room is actually two separate rooms, with two beds in each and a shared bathroom. Boys up to 14 years of age can stay here with their mothers. The only disadvantage to this place is its limited number of rooms—I wish it were much larger. Highly recommended.

HOTEL BOGOTA, Schlüterstrasse 45, D-1000 Berlin 15. Tel. 030/881 50 01. Fax 030/88 35 88. Telex 0184946. 130 rms (12 with showers, 65 with showers and WCs). TEL **Bus:** 9 from Tegel Airport or Bahnhof Zoologischer Garten to Bleibtreustrasse stop, then a 1-minute walk. **U-Bahn:** Adenauerplatz, a 6-minute walk.

$ Rates (including Continental breakfast): 55 DM ($33.35) single without shower or WC, 70 DM ($42.40) single with shower, 89 DM ($53.95) single with shower and WC; 90 DM ($54.55) double without shower or WC, 115 DM ($69.70) double with shower, 150 DM ($90.90) double with shower and WC; 122 DM ($73.95) triple without shower or WC, 155 DM ($93.95) triple with shower, 197 DM ($119.40) triple with shower and WC. AE, DC, MC, V.

S If you like older hotels, you'll like the Bogota, an old-fashioned establishment with character. The building itself is a century old and features high ceilings; a stairway that wraps itself around an ancient elevator, which nevertheless is one of the more "modern" additions to the hotel; and lobbies on each floor reminiscent of another era. No two rooms are alike, and there's a cozy TV room where you can spend a relaxing evening. The hotel is just off the Ku'damm, not far from Olivaer Platz.

HOTEL-PENSION BREGENZ, Bregenzer Strasse 5, D-1000 Berlin 15. Tel. 030/881 43 07. 23 rms (5 with showers, 10 with showers and WCs). TEL **Bus:** 9 from Tegel Airport or Bahnhof Zoologischer Garten to Leibnizstrasse, then a 3-minute walk. **U-Bahn:** Adenauerplatz, a 5-minute walk.
$ Rates (including Continental breakfast): 50–53 DM ($30.30–$32.10) single without shower or WC, 60–63 DM ($36.35–$38.20) single with shower, 72–75 DM ($43.65–$45.45) single with shower and WC; 85–88 DM ($51.50–$53.35) double without shower or WC, 98–105 DM ($59.40–$63.65) double with shower, 120–125 DM ($72.70–$75.75) double with shower and WC; 140–145 DM ($84.85–$87.90) quad with shower, 160–168 DM ($96.95–$101.80) quad with shower and WC. Crib available. MC.

This family-run pension, on a quiet residential street just a few minutes' walk south of Olivaer Platz and the Ku'damm, is located on the fourth floor (yes, there is an elevator). Each room is different, but all are clean and roomy and have double doors separating them from the corridor, which helps cut down on noise. The staff will make bookings for the theater and for sightseeing tours.

HOTEL CALIFORNIA, Kurfürstendamm 35, D-1000 Berlin 15. Tel. 030/882 64 22. Fax 030/882 64 50. 40 rms (all with baths). TEL TV **Bus:** 9 from Tegel Airport to Uhlandstrasse, then a 1-minute walk. **U-Bahn:** Uhlandstrasse, a 1-minute walk.
$ Rates (including Continental breakfast): 95–120 DM ($57.55–$72.70) single; 135–160 DM ($81.80–$96.95) double. Extra bed 35–45 DM ($21.20–$27.25). AE, MC, V.

Right on the Ku'Damm, with a reception area on the third floor (reached by elevator), the California is a modern, simple, and pleasant place to stay. It was recently renovated from top to bottom, and rooms all have tall ceilings, safes, and TVs. Only one room faces the Ku'damm and has its own balcony; the rest of the rooms all face toward the back of the building, which is a lot quieter. There are vending machines selling drinks, but there's also a bar, and a solarium that costs 5 DM ($3.05) for 10 minutes.

HOTEL CYSTAL, Kantstrasse 144, D-1000 Berlin 12. Tel. 030/312 90 47 or 312 90 48. Telex 184022. 32 rms (18 with showers, 10 with showers and WCs). TEL TV (available) **Bus:** 9 from Tegel Airport to Bleibtreustrasse; 49 from Bahnhof

Zoologischer Garten to Savignyplatz (3 stops). **S-Bahn:** Savignyplatz, a 2-minute walk.

$ Rates (including Continental breakfast): 65 DM ($39.40) single without shower, 70 DM ($42.40) single with shower, 80 DM ($48.50) single with shower and WC; 90 DM ($54.55) double without shower or WC, 100 DM ($60.60) double with shower, 120 DM ($72.70) double with shower and WC; 150 DM ($90.90) triple with shower and WC. Crib available. AE, MC, V. Parking: Free.

This is a typical older hotel, the kind that was once plentiful throughout Germany but is slowly dying out in the era of rampant renovation. There's nothing special about the place—indeed, the building has none of the flair you'd expect from a building 90 years old. Corridors are narrow, rooms are simple, and showers have been added as afterthoughts, many of them as freestanding closets against the wall. Yet, there's something German about the place, and rooms are spotlessly clean. The older couple running the place, John and Dorothee Schwarzrock (John is an American), are entertaining, friendly, and outgoing, and are happy to see Americans. There's a small bar for hotel guests.

HOTEL-PENSION DITTBERNER, Wielandstrasse 26, D-1000 Berlin 15. Tel. 030/881 64 85 or 882 39 63. 22 rms (15 with showers only, 7 with baths). TEL TV (on request) **Bus:** 9 from Tegel Airport or Bahnhof Zoologischer Garten to Leibnizstrasse, then a 1-minute walk. **U-bahn:** Adenauerplatz, a 6-minute walk.

$ Rates (including Continental breakfast): 70 DM ($42.40) single with shower, 90 DM ($54.55) single with bath; 102 DM ($61.80) double with shower, 135 DM ($81.80) double with bath. No credit cards accepted.

The 30-year-old Dittberner is beautifully decorated, with a Japanese screen, antiques, and artwork in the lobby; woodblock prints and posters in the corridors; and thickly upholstered chairs, white tablecloths, and fresh flowers in the breakfast room. The pension is situated on the third floor of an older building (guests receive a special key for the elevator) above an exclusive gallery. In fact, the best room is the one that overlooks a small courtyard containing the gallery's sculpture garden. Little wonder that guests return again and again, including a number of artists. The Dittberner is found just off the Ku'damm, near Olivaer Platz.

HOTEL-PENSION FASANENHAUS, Fasanenstrasse 73, D-1000 Berlin 15. Tel. 030/881 67 13. 25 rms (15 with showers only, 10 with baths). **Bus:** 9 from Tegel Airport to Uhlandstrasse, then a 2-minute walk. **U-Bahn:** Uhlandstrasse, a 1-minute walk.

$ Rates (including Continental breakfast): 65 DM ($39.40) single with shower, 85 DM ($51.50) single with bath; 95 DM ($57.55) double with shower, 130 DM ($78.80) double with bath; 125 DM ($75.75) triple with shower, 160 DM ($96.95) triple with bath. Crib available. No credit cards accepted.

This delightful pension has a great location not far from the very expensive Bristol Hotel Kempinski and the Käthe-Kollwitz Museum, about a 7-minute walk from Bahnhof Zoo. On a fashionable street lined with many older buildings, the Fasanenhaus is reached via an incredibly ornate entry stairway. It has a very pleasant breakfast room with exposed ceiling beams, adjoining a living room with a TV and large French doors that open onto a balcony with potted plants. Rooms are large, with high ceilings typical of Berlin's older buildings.

HOTEL-PENSION FUNK, Fasanenstrasse 69, D-1000 Berlin 15. Tel. 030/882 71 93. 15 rms (11 with showers only, 1 with shower and WC). TEL   **Bus:** 9 to Uhlandstrasse, then a 2-minute walk.   **U-Bahn:** Uhlandstrasse, a 1-minute walk.

$ Rates (including Continental breakfast): 60 DM ($36.35) single without shower, 70 DM ($42.50) single with shower; 105 DM ($63.65) double with shower only or with bath; 135 DM ($81.80) triple with shower only or with bath. No credit cards accepted.

Walk up the sweeping white-marbled staircase to reach this first-floor pension. Clean, orderly, and nicely decorated with French provincial reproduction furniture and flowered wallpaper in its high-ceilinged rooms, it is located down the street from the pension listed above and is convenient to the Europa-Center, Gedächtniskirche, and Bahnhof Zoo. Herr Groth, the proprietor, speaks English.

HOTEL HEIDELBERG BERLIN, Knesebeckstrasse 15, D-1000 Berlin 12. Tel. 030/31 01 03 or 31 08 53. 40 rms (34 with baths). TEL   **Bus:** 9 from Tegel Airport to Bahnhof Zoologischer Garten, then a 10-minute walk.

$ Rates (including Continental breakfast): 55–75 DM ($33.35–$45.45) single without bath, 85–130 DM ($51.50–$78.80) single with bath; 95–130 DM ($57.55–$78.80) double without bath, 110–160 DM ($66.65–$100) double with bath. Crib available. DC, MC, V. Parking: Free.

Standing north of Savignyplatz about a 10-minute walk from the Ku'damm or Bahnhof Zoo, this casual establishment caters primarily to youth groups but also takes in individual travelers. Its reception desk is located in its ground-floor café, which dispenses coffee, drinks, and snacks in addition to room keys. An elevator delivers guests to the rooms above, all of which have safes and are clean and bright (white walls). In addition, all but those on the first floor have small balconies, and some even have kitchenettes.

HOTEL-PENSION JUWEL, Meinekestrasse 26, D-1000 Berlin 15. Tel. 030/882 71 41. 22 rms (15 with showers only, 3 with showers and WCs). TEL   **Bus:** 9 from Tegel Airport to Uhlandstrasse, then a 2-minute walk.   **U-Bahn:** Uhlandstrasse or Kurfürstendamm, each a 2-minute walk.

$ Rates (including Continental breakfast): 69 DM ($41.80) single with shower, 105 DM ($63.65) single with shower and WC; 105 DM ($63.65) double with shower, 140 DM ($84.85) double with shower and WC. Crib available. No credit cards accepted.

Near Café Kranzler (one of Berlin's most famous coffeehouses) and just off the Ku'damm, this unpretentious small pension has high ceilings and stark white walls, adorned with pictures of local Berlin artists. The breakfast room is decorated with proprietor Roswitha Schreiterer's patchwork quilts; she has more than 80 in her private collection (including a few Amish quilts), only a few of which are on display at any one time. Since all but two rooms face a back street, the location is very quiet. Some of the singles, however, are quite small.

HOTEL-PENSION MANIA-BÄRBEL, Kurfürstendamm 62, D-1000 Berlin 15. 030/883 54 98 or 883 61 61. 10 rms (7 with showers only). TEL **Bus:** 9 from Tegel Airport or Bahnhof Zoologischer Garten to Olivaer Platz, then a 1-minute walk. **U-Bahn:** Adenauerplatz, a 2-minute walk.

$ Rates (including Continental breakfast): 55 DM ($33.35) single without shower, 75 DM ($45.45) single with shower; 105 DM ($63.65) double without shower, 125 DM ($75.75) double with shower; 135 DM ($81.80) triple with shower. No credit cards accepted.

Ⓢ A small and delightful pension at the west end of the Ku'damm (about a 20-minute walk from the Gedächtniskirche and the Europa-Center), it's owned by Peter and Marion Hölzer, a friendly couple who strive to give guests the personal touch they feel is missing in the larger hotels. Rooms are airy and comfortable, decorated in old-world style, and the triple even has a balcony overlooking the Ku'damm. All those watercolors you see lining the corridors were done by Marion herself. You'll like this place. Enter through the building's imposing marble-and-wood entryway on the ground floor, and then take the elevator to the pension on the second floor.

MEDENWALDT, Kurfürstendamm 225, D-1000 Berlin 15. Tel. 030/881 70 34 or 881 70 35. 29 rms (18 with showers only, 4 with showers and WCs). TEL TV (in some rms) **Bus:** 9 from Tegel Airport to Joachimstaler Strasse, then a 1-minute walk. **U-Bahn:** Kurfürstendamm, a 1-minute walk.

$ Rates (including buffet breakfast): 65 DM ($39.40) single without shower or WC, 75 DM ($45.45) single with shower, 90 DM ($54.55) single with shower and WC; 90 DM ($54.55) double without shower or WC, 100–110 DM ($60.60–$66.65) double with shower, 130–150 DM ($78.80–$90.90) double with shower and WC. Extra bed 30 DM ($18.20). V.

It would be impossible to find a better location than this: on the Ku'damm right across the street from the famous Café Kranzler and not far from the Gedächtniskirche. This upstairs pension, complete with an elevator, offers high-ceilinged rooms, most of which face toward the quieter back side of the building. Those that face the Ku'damm have double-paned windows—still not enough to keep out the traffic noise. But the view, of course, is infinitely more interesting.

HOTEL-PENSION MODENA, Wielandstrasse 26, D-1000 Berlin 15. Tel. 030/881 52 94 or 883 54 04. 21 rms (9 with showers only, 5 with showers and WCs). **Bus:** 9 from Tegel Airport or Bahnhof Zoologischer Garten to Leibnizstrasse, then a 1-minute walk. **U-Bahn:** Adenauerplatz, a 6-minute walk.

$ Rates (including Continental breakfast): 58 DM ($35.15) single without shower or WC, 68 DM ($41.20) single with shower, 78–80 DM ($47.25–$48.50) single with shower and WC; 88 DM

($53.35) double without shower or WC, 98 DM ($59.40) double with shower, 125 DM ($75.75) double with shower and WC; 125 DM ($75.75) triple with shower, 145 DM ($87.85) triple with shower and WC. No credit cards accepted.

On the second floor of a lovely building dating from the turn of the century, the Modena is located off the west end of the Ku'damm near Olivaer Platz. A good choice in terms of price and location, it's managed by Frau Kreutz, who keeps the rooms spotlessly clean. She'll give you a key to operate the old-fashioned elevator, an ancient-looking box still common in old buildings all over Berlin.

IN EAST BERLIN

HOTEL ADRIA, Friedrichstrasse 134, DDR-1040 Berlin. Tel. 0372/280 51 05. Telex 114942. 68 rms (5 with baths). TEL TV **S-Bahn:** Friedrichstrasse, a 4-minute walk.
$ Rates: 75 DM ($45.45) single without bath; 130 DM ($78.80) double without bath; 230 DM ($139.40) apt with bath. No credit cards accepted.

Although the Adria is too expensive for what it offers, it's one of the few medium-range hotels in East Berlin and is conveniently situated not far from Unter den Linden. Rooms haven't been renovated in years (if ever) and the carpet is worn, but they're large and clean. The two-room apartments are huge, with fridges and gigantic bathrooms. The staff members are friendly, and one of them operates the elevator—ring once from the ground floor, five times if you need to board from the fifth floor. A hotel restaurant is open from 6am to midnight, and there's a first-floor bar that offers dancing. You may enjoy staying here, just for the novel experience.

NEAR GÜNTZELSTRASSE STATION

HOTEL-PENSION STEPHAN, Güntzelstrasse 54, D-1000 Berlin 31. Tel. 030/87 41 21. 8 rms (3 with showers only). **U-Bahn:** U-9 from Bahnhof Zoologischer Garten to Güntzelstrasse, then a 2-minute walk.
$ Rates (including Continental breakfast): 45 DM ($27.25) single; 85 DM ($51.50) double. No credit cards accepted.

This pension is located south of the city center near Güntzelstrasse station, which is served by the U-9 subway line. If you like walking, you can stroll to the Ku'damm in about 20 minutes. Located in an older house with superhigh ceilings, the pension serves breakfast in a cozy living room with lots of plants and flowers and a color TV. A few of the rooms are wonderfully decorated with old-fashioned furniture; the singles are fairly small.

NEAR SCHLOSS CHARLOTTENBURG

ECONTEL, Sömmeringstrasse 24, D-1000 Berlin 10. Tel. 030/34 40 01. Fax 030/344 70 34. Telex 17308048. 205 rms (all with baths). TEL TV (in some rms) **Bus:** 9 from Tegel Airport to Jakob-Kaiser-Platz, then U-Bahn 7 to Mierendorffplatz, followed by a few minutes' walk.
$ Rates: 85–115 DM ($51.50–$69.70) single; 105–130 DM

($63.65–$78.80) twin; 125–135 DM ($75.75–$81.80) double; 120–130 DM ($72.70–$78.80) triple; 130–145 DM ($78.80–$87.85) quad. Children under 12 free in parents' rm. Breakfast 13 DM ($7.85) extra for adults; 6.50 DM ($3.95) for children aged 6 to 12, free for children under 6. MC. Parking: 6 DM ($3.65).

With accommodations especially designed for families, young travelers, and even female travelers and businesspeople, this economy hotel tries to appeal to everyone. The family rooms, outfitted with bunk beds to sleep three or four persons, offer special facilities for babies and children, including cribs, bottle warmers, and surprise diversions for little ones. The "Lady Class" rooms feature sofas, magnifying makeup mirrors, hairdryers, typewriters on request, and a few other amenities, while the business rooms offer desks, sofas, minibars, trouser pressers, and typewriters upon request. All accommodations have radios and safes; 40 have TVs; and 4 have small balconies. There are also no-smoking rooms. The Econtel's modern lobby is pleasant, with a high ceiling, plants, and a wall of glass.

NORTH OF THE TIERGARTEN

HOTEL LES NATIONS, Zinzendorfstrasse 6, D-1000 Berlin 21. Tel. 030/392 20 26. Telex 186861. 42 rms (5 with showers only, 14 with showers and WCs). TEL TV (in some rms) **Bus:** 90 from Bahnhof Zoologischer Garten to Alt Moabit, then a 2-minute walk. **U-Bahn:** U-9 from Bahnhof Zoologischer Garten to Turmstrasse station (2 stops), then a 5-minute walk.

$ Rates (including Continental breakfast): 55–63 DM ($33.35–$38.20) single without shower or WC, 75–80 DM ($45.45–$48.50) single with shower; 100 DM ($60.60) double without shower or WC, 115–125 DM ($69.70–$75.75) double with shower, 150 DM ($90.90) double with shower and WC. Extra bed 20 DM ($12.10). Crib available. AE, DC, MC, V. Parking: Free.

Easily and quickly connected to Bahnhof Zoo and the Ku'damm via a direct subway line, this small, comfortable hotel offers clean, pleasant rooms that have recently been renovated with new furniture, carpeting, and wallpaper. Those rooms facing the front that have private bathrooms also have small balconies. Proprietor Frau Hilde Meier speaks English, as does her front-desk staff, and there's a small hotel bar.

HOTEL TIERGARTEN BERLIN, Alt-Moabit 89, D-1000 Berlin 21. Tel. 030/391 30 04 or 391 41 79. Fax 030/393 86 92. Telex 186812 tgt d. 35 rms (5 with showers only, 30 with showers and WCs). TEL TV **U-Bahn:** U-9 to Turmstrasse, then a 3-minute walk.

$ Rates (including buffet breakfast): 75–85 DM ($45.45–$51.50) single with shower, 105–140 DM ($63.65–$84.85) single with shower and WC; 110–135 DM ($66.65–$81.80) double with shower, 155–200 DM ($93.94–$121.20) double with shower and WC. AE, DC, MC, V.

Ⓢ The reception area of this small hotel is up on the first floor, in a beautiful building with a facade dating from 1890. Each room is different in size, furnishings, and atmosphere—one room, for example, is wood-paneled, another has a detailed stucco ceiling. All rooms are large, high, and airy, and outfitted with cable TVs (with videos), radios, and alarm clocks. The breakfast room still retains its turn-of-the-century charm and elegance. In short, this is a fine little hotel, the kind you'd come back to again and again.

5. BUDGET

Many of the establishments listed below haven't changed much over the decades—large, airy rooms with high ceilings and a shared bathroom down the hall. (If you saw *Cabaret,* then you'll know that the entertainer played by Liza Minnelli lived in such a rented room, as did many Berliners of the time.) These rooms provide basic comforts—i.e., beds and sinks—and some also have showers and/or WCs. Be aware that in the lifetime of this book, prices may go up a couple of marks, especially in 1992. Ask the rate when making your reservations.

ON OR NEAR THE KU'DAMM

All these selections are located in the heart of town, most within a 7-minute walk of West Berlin's most famous boulevard.

HOTEL-PENSION BIALAS, Carmerstrasse 16, D-1000 Berlin 12. Tel. 030/312 50 25 or 312 50 26. Telex 186506. 40 rms (10 with showers and WCs, 2 with WC only). TEL (in some rms) **Directions:** A 6-minute walk from Bahnhof Zoologischer Garten.
$ Rates (including Continental breakfast): 50–60 DM ($30.30–$36.40) single without shower or WC, 70 DM ($42.40) single with WC, 80 DM ($48.50) single with shower and WC; 65–85 DM ($39.40–$51.50) double without shower or WC, 120 DM ($72.70) double with shower and WC. Extra bed 30–35 DM ($18.20–$21.20) in rm without shower or WC, 45 DM ($27.25) in rm with shower and WC. No credit cards accepted.

The Bialas, a cross between a hotel and a pension, is located on a quiet street off Savignyplatz, less than a 10-minute walk from the Ku'damm. Its reception area is up on the first floor of an older building, with rooms spread over several floors. The cheapest rooms are those on the fifth floor—quite a hike, since there is no elevator.

PENSION CENTRUM, Kantstrasse 31, D-1000 Berlin 12. Tel. 030/31 61 53. 7 rms (none with bath). TEL (in most rms) **Bus:** 9 from Tegel Airport to Bleibtreustrasse, then a 7-minute walk. **S-Bahn:** Savignyplatz, a 2-minute walk.
$ Rates: 35–40 DM ($21.20–$24.25) single; 65–75 DM ($39.40–$45.45) double. Breakfast 7 DM ($4.25) extra. No credit cards accepted.

This small family-run pension is now in its second generation of owners, an English-speaking native Berliner and her Dutch husband. A 10-minute walk west of Bahnhof Zoo past Savignyplatz, the Centrum in an older building dating from 1880, with stucco ceilings and double-paned windows.

HOTEL CHARLOTTENBURG HOF, Stuttgarter Platz 14, D-1000 Berlin 12. Tel. 030/324 48 19. 45 rms (28 with showers and WCs). TEL (in rms with showers and WCs) TV (available) **Bus:** 9 from Tegel Airport or Bahnhof Zoologischer Garten to Bahnhof Charlottenburg, then a 1-minute walk. **S-Bahn:** Charlottenburg, a 1-minute walk.

$ Rates: 40–70 DM ($24.25–$42.40) single without shower or WC, 55–80 DM ($33.35–$48.50) single with shower and WC; 55–80 DM ($33.35–$48.50) double without shower or WC, 70–110 DM ($42.40–$66.65) double with shower and WC. Extra bed from 30 DM ($18.20). Discounts in winter or for longer stays. No credit cards accepted.

⑤ A great choice in terms of price, facilities, and location, this is one of Berlin's finest budget hotels. Rooms are bright and cheerful, with white walls, colorful pictures adorning them, and modern furniture. The staff is young and friendly. You can rent a TV for 5 DM ($3.05), with cable offering English programs, but there's also a communal TV lounge where you can watch cable programs free of charge. And although breakfast is not included in the price, you'll probably want to go to the adjoining Café Voltaire with its large windows, plants, and artwork, where Continental breakfast costs a low 5 DM ($3.05).

PENSION CORTINA, 140 Kantstrasse, D-1000 Berlin 12. Tel. 030/313 90 59. 21 rms (5 with showers). TEL (in some rms) **Bus:** 9 from Tegel Airport to Schlüterstrasse, then a 6-minute walk. **S-Bahn:** Savignyplatz, a 2-minute walk.

$ Rates: 45 DM ($27.25) single without shower; 70 DM ($42.49) double without shower, 80 DM ($48.50) double with shower; 90 DM ($54.55) triple without shower, 110 DM ($66.65) triple with shower. Breakfast 8 DM ($4.85) extra. No credit cards accepted.

Owned by a native Berliner and her Italian husband, the Cortina is in a century-old building. The breakfast room has been pleasantly remodeled in bright, cheerful colors and most of the rooms are large, each one slightly different in size and shape. One family-size room can sleep up to six people. Reception is up on the first floor.

JUGENDGÄSTEHAUS AM ZOO, Hardenbergstrasse 9a, D-1000 Berlin 12. Tel. 030/312 94 10. 17 rms (none with bath). **Directions:** A 10-minute walk from Bahnhof Zoologischer Garten.

$ Rates: 35 DM ($21.20) single; 60 DM ($36.35) double; 25 DM ($15.15) per bed in dormitory rm. No credit cards accepted.

It's easy to miss this no-frills budget establishment appealing to young backpackers and school groups—no sign outside advertises its existence and the building itself looks a bit run-down and neglected. But take the elevator up to the fourth floor (that is, if the elevator is working) and you'll find a youth hotel with all the normal facilities.

Rooms have just the basics: beds and sinks. There's an age limit of 27, but any age is welcome if there's room. Note, however, that no reservations are accepted for single or double rooms, so call when you get to town and inquire whether they're available. Otherwise, there are also larger dormitory-style accommodations with four to eight beds per room. Facilities include a bar, which is open from 9:30pm to an astonishing 6am. Near the university and the Mensa student cafeteria.

PENSION KNESEBECK, 86 Knesebeckstrasse, D-1000 Berlin 12. Tel. 030/31 72 55. TEL (in 2 rms) TV (available) **Bus:** 9 from Tegel Airport to Bahnhof Zoologischer Garten, then a 7-minute walk.   **S-Bahn:** Savignyplatz, a 3-minute walk.

$ Rates (including Continental breakfast): 40–50 DM ($24.25–$30.30) single; 70–80 DM ($42.40–$48.50) double; 30 DM ($18.20) per person in family rm. AE.

Owned by English-speaking and friendly Jutta Jorende, this older pension has some modern twists, including artistic light fixtures in the breakfast room and plants that make the place more livable and pleasant. Ten rooms face an inner courtyard, making them very quiet, and there's a large family room with four beds. The place is less than a 10-minute walk north of the Ku'damm, past Savignyplatz.

NEAR THE EUROPA-CENTER

Both these pensions are located in the same building (there's no elevator), a block from the Europa-Center and an 8-minute walk south of Bahnhof Zoo.

PENSION FISCHER, Nürnberger Strasse 24a, D-1000 Berlin 30. Tel. 030/24 68 08. 10 rms (none with bath). **Bus:** 9 from Tegel Airport to Joachimstaler Strasse, then a 5-minute walk.   **U-Bahn:** Augsburger Strasse, a 1-minute walk.

$ Rates: 40 DM ($24.25) single; 60 DM ($36.35) double; 85 DM ($51.50) triple; 110 DM ($66.65) quad. Breakfast 6 DM ($3.65) extra. No credit cards accepted.

With a great location within easy walking distance of the Ku'damm, Gedächtniskirche, Europa-Center, and KaDeWe department store, this second-floor pension is a pleasant place to stay. Accommodations are clean, high-ceilinged, and airy—with large windows letting in plenty of sunshine—and they have old-fashioned tiled heaters of the sort that once heated all German homes. Some rooms face a quiet inner courtyard. The breakfast room is especially nice, cozy with plants, flowers, and a TV. An automatic machine dispenses cups of coffee or hot chocolate, and there's a refrigerator for guests' use.

NÜRNBERG ECK, Nürnberger Strasse 24a, D-1000 Berlin 30. Tel. 030/24 53 71. 8 rms (none with bath).   **Bus:** 9 from Tegel Airport to Joachimstaler Strasse, then a 5-minute walk. **U-Bahn:** Augsburger Strasse, a 1-minute walk.

$ Rates: 45 DM ($27.25) single; 80 DM ($48.50) double; 105 DM ($63.65) triple. Breakfast 7 DM ($4.25) extra. No credit cards accepted.

This old-fashioned pension (first floor) looks as if it could have been used as a set for *Cabaret*—a look that the owners have consciously cultivated. Rooms are very nice, with comfortable old-style furniture, stucco ceilings, and massive doors. Fresh flowers decorate the hallway.

NEAR GÜNTZELSTRASSE STATION

PENSION MÜNCHEN, Güntzelstrasse 62, D-1000 Berlin 31. Tel. 030/854 22 26. 9 rms (2 with showers and WC). **U-Bahn:** U-9 from Bahnhof Zoologischer Garten to Güntzelstrasse (3 stops), then a 3-minute walk.

$ Rates: 41 DM ($24.85) single without shower and WC; 70 DM ($42.40) double without shower and WC, 105 DM ($63.65) double with shower and WC. Breakfast 8 DM ($4.85) extra. No credit cards accepted.

The third-floor Pension München, reached by elevator, is only two subway stops from the Ku'damm, or less than a 30-minute walk. You can tell immediately upon entering that this place belongs to an artist—the artwork on the walls, the vases of flowers, the artistic way everything is arranged. Frau Renate Prasse, the charming proprietress, is in fact a sculptress, and she rents rooms that are bright, white, and spotless. You'll like this place.

IN KREUZBERG

JUGENDHOTEL INTERNATIONAL, Bernburgerstrasse 27-28, D-1000 Berlin 61. Tel. 030/262 30 81 or 262 30 82. Telex 186575. 70 rms (12 with bathrooms). TEL & TV (in rms with baths). **Bus:** 29 from Bahnhof Zoologischer Garten to Anhalter Bahnhof, then a 3-minute walk.

$ Rates (including Continental breakfast): 40 DM ($24.25) single without bath, 65 DM ($39.40) single with bath; 76 DM ($46.05) double without bath, 120 DM ($72.70) double with bath; 165 DM ($100) triple with bath; 35 DM ($21.20) per bed in multibed dormitory rm. No credit cards accepted.

Located near Potsdamer Platz, this hotel translates as "International Youth Hotel," but in reality it attracts not only youth groups but also individuals and families, many of them from Eastern Europe. Rooms are nicely furnished in natural woods. Those with private bathrooms face a quiet inner courtyard and have telephones, color TVs, large wardrobe spaces, and tables and chairs. All rooms—singles, doubles, and multibed dormitory rooms—have sinks. Facilities include a restaurant serving inexpensive meals.

PENSION KREUZBERG, Grossbeerenstrasse 64, D-1000 Berlin 61. Tel. 030/251 13 62. 13 rms (none with bath). **Bus:** 19 from Kurfürstendamm to Grossbeerenstrasse; 9 from Tegel Airport to Adenauerplatz, then 19 to Grossbeerenstrasse. **U-Bahn:** Möckernbrücke, about a 6-minute walk.

$ Rates: 36 DM ($21.80) single; 60 DM ($36.35) double; 80 DM ($48.50) triple; 100 DM ($60.60) quad. Breakfast 7 DM ($4.25). No credit cards accepted.

A pension for more than 50 years, the Kreuzberg was recently taken over by two energetic young men who are renovating the place themselves. Catering largely to backpacking youth and offering perfectly acceptable rooms, it ranks as one of Berlin's best values. Breakfast is buffet-style.

HOTEL TRANSIT, Hagelberger Strasse 53-54, D-1000 Berlin 61. Tel. 030/785 50 51. 39 rms (all with showers only). **Bus:** 19 from Ku'damm to Mehringdamm; 9 from Tegel Airport to Adenauerplatz, then 19 to Mehringdamm. **U-Bahn:** U-1 from Bahnhof Zoologischer Garten to Möckernbrücke, then U-7 to Mehringdamm.

$ Rates (including buffet breakfast): 45 DM ($27.25) single; 70 DM ($42.40) double; 25 DM ($15.15) per person in 6-bed rm. AE, MC, V.

Attracting a large international clientele of young travelers, Hotel Transit opened in 1987 in a converted former tobacco factory. Its entryway is in an inner courtyard of the old brick building; reception, up on the third floor, is reached via elevator. Rooms throughout are painted a stark white, with high ceilings and new fixtures. The buffet in the airy breakfast room offers unlimited coffee or tea. Guests often use breakfast as an opportunity to exchange travel advice and tips. This hotel is great for the price.

NEAR RATHAUS SCHÖNEBERG

STUDENTEN-HOTEL BERLIN, Meininger Strasse 10, D-1000 Berlin 62. Tel. 030/784 67 20 or 784 67 30. Telex 0181287. 50 rms (none with bath). **Bus:** 73 from Bahnhof Zoologischer Garten to Schöneberg Platz, then a 4-minute walk. **U-Bahn:** Schöneberg.

$ Rates (including Continental breakfast): 62 DM ($37.55) double; 29 DM ($17.55) for bed in multibed dormitory rm. No credit cards accepted.

This simple establishment is located near John F. Kennedy Platz and Rathaus Schöneberg. Despite its designation as a student hotel, it also welcomes nonstudents and guests of any age. In a building that resembles a student dormitory, it offers 20 double rooms and rooms with four or five beds. There's a game room with a pool table, soccer game, and pinball machine.

YOUTH HOSTELS

Technically, a youth-hostel card is required for stays at Berlin's youth hostels, but nonmembers can circumvent this by paying an extra 5 DM ($3.05) per night for a "guest" card. After 6 nights, this guest card automatically qualifies as a youth-hostel card. An alternative is to purchase a youth-hostel card right away for 30 DM ($18.20). Both cards are available at the hostels themselves, and there's no age limit. However, "seniors," those 27 years and older, pay a slightly higher rate. Keep in mind that curfew at these youth hostels is at midnight.

JUGENDGÄSTEHAUS AM WANNSEE, Badeweg 1, D-1000 Berlin 38. Tel. 030/803 20 34. Telex 186606. 264 beds. **S-Bahn:** S-3 to Nikolassee, then a 7-minute walk.

$ **Rates** per person (including breakfast and sheets): 22 DM ($13.35) for juniors 26 and younger; 25 DM ($15.15) for seniors 27 and older. Lunch 6 DM ($3.65) extra, dinner 7.50 DM ($4.55). No credit cards accepted.

This is Berlin's newest and most modern youth hostel, a handsome brick building with red trim. It's located close to Wannsee, a lake popular for swimming and boating in summer, with bathing facilities nearby. Rooms have four beds each, with showers per every two rooms. A good place to stay in summer if you're in need of a relaxing environment.

JUGENDGÄSTEHAUS BERLIN, Kluckstrasse 3, D-1000 Berlin 30. Tel. 030/261 10 97. 364 beds. **Bus:** 29 from Bahnhof Zoologischer Garten to Kluckstrasse, then a 1-minute walk. **U-Bahn:** Kurfürstenstrasse, a 12-minute walk.

$ **Rates** per person (including breakfast and sheets): 22 DM ($13.35) for juniors 26 and younger; 25 DM ($15.15) for seniors 27 and older. Lunch or dinner 6 DM ($3.65) extra. No credit cards accepted.

This modern building houses the most popular youth hostel in the city, primarily because it is the most conveniently located. In fact, it's so popular that you should write at least a month in advance to reserve a room. All rooms are dormitory style, with four to six beds per room, and everyone gets a locker with a key.

JUGENDHERBERGE ERNST REUTER, Hermsdorfer Damm 48-50, D-1000 Berlin 28. Tel. 030/404 16 10. 110 beds. **Directions:** From Tegel Airport, bus 8 to Kurt Schumacher Platz, then U-Bahn 6 to Tegel stop, then bus 15 to Jugendherberge stop; from Bahnhof Zoologischer Garten, U-9 to Leopoldplatz, then U-6 to Tegel station, then bus 15 to Jugendherberge stop.

$ **Rates** per person (including breakfast and sheets): 16.90 DM ($10.25) for juniors 26 and younger; 19.90 DM ($12.20) for seniors 27 and older. Dinner 7.50 DM ($4.55) extra. No credit cards accepted.

The disadvantage to staying here is that it's on the far outskirts of Berlin, at least 35 minutes from the city center (longer if connections are bad and you have to wait for the bus). However, it's surrounded by woods in a peaceful part of town and offers table tennis and a TV lounge. All rooms have eight beds.

BERLIN DINING

I t's tough being in a city where there is so much choice. Pork knuckles with Sauerkraut? Vegetable curry? Sushi? Pizza? Nouvelle cuisine? Altogether there are an estimated 5,000 pubs and restaurants in West Berlin alone, and the number seems to increase almost daily. I wouldn't be surprised to hear that Berlin boasts more international restaurants than any other city in Germany; certainly it offers more ethnic diversity in dining than many cities with twice its population.

One reason, of course, is Berlin's large foreign population and its many international visitors. But even young Germans are more likely to go out for Greek or Italian food than they are for their own heavier cuisine. In the four years I lived in Germany, my German friends and I rarely went out to German restaurants, primarily because that's what we ate at home. According to a recent survey, only half the Germans surveyed said they preferred their own cuisine. And in Berlin, ethnic restaurants are among the city's cheapest.

That's not to say that there aren't excellent German restaurants in Berlin in all price categories. The Germans are known around the world for their hearty portions, with typical meals consisting of meat accompanied by potatoes, dumplings, or noodles. German entrées are almost always complete meals in themselves—a platter with a main dish and various side dishes. As for the restaurants themselves, many in the medium-priced and budget range are worth visiting both for the food and the experience, for they are often boisterous, lively establishments, good places to mix with the locals and to strike up a conversation. Germans are not known for their reticence, especially in their neighborhood pub/restaurant, and especially after they've downed a few beers.

1. DINING HINTS

The vast majority of Berlin's restaurants are found on and around the Ku'damm, including Savignyplatz, Wilmersdorfer Strasse, and the

Europa-Center. This is where you'll find the greatest concentration of German Gaststätten (neighborhood restaurant/pubs), as well as ethnic restaurants serving international cuisine. In addition to the many take-out establishments here, there are also a number of Imbisse, stand-up food stalls serving everything from sausages to french fries.

Because the area around the Ku'damm encompasses such a large and long area (the Ku'damm stretches 2½ miles), I've divided it into several geographic regions to make your dining selections easier. After all, if you're shopping on Wilmersdorfer Strasse, you're probably more interested in knowing what's available in the immediate area rather than in the area near the Gedächtniskirche or the Europa-Center. Thus, all restaurants below are presented according to their location, including those on or within a 5-minute walk of the Ku'damm, those on or near Wilmersdorfer Strasse, those near the Europa-Center and Wittenbergplatz, those in East Berlin, and those in Dahlem. If you're more interested in dining according to cuisine (such as Greek or Indian), check the "Restaurants by Cuisine" list at the end of this chapter.

As a gauge for what a meal will cost, including appetizer, main course, a glass of wine or beer, and dessert, expect to spend at least 60 DM to 100 DM ($36.36 to $60.60) per person in the very expensive restaurants, 40 DM to 60 DM ($24.25 to $36.36) in the expensive ones, 20 DM to 40 DM ($12.10 to $24.25) in those that are moderately priced, 10 DM to 20 DM ($6.05 to $12.10) in inexpensive establishments, and less than 10 DM ($6.05) in the budget restaurants. As you can see, dining is very reasonable in Berlin, in all price categories. If you opt for the less expensive items on the menu and cut out appetizers and desserts, you can even dine at the expensive restaurants for much less than the prices given above. Thus, even if you're on a budget, don't automatically assume that the more pricey places are beyond your means. Be sure to check out the expensive category for restaurants that also have moderately priced entrées. It's possible, for example, to eat at a restaurant in the expensive category for 25 DM ($15.15) if you watch what you eat and cut out all alcohol.

Keep in mind that most Germans take their big meal of the day at lunch, which in most restaurants is served from about 11:30am to 2pm. Some restaurants offer lunch specials or a lunch menu during this time, at prices cheaper than those charged for their dinners. The most popular dinner hours are from 7 or 8 to 10pm. Some of the more expensive places close during the afternoon hours, while others are open only at night. The vast majority of restaurants, however, are open throughout the day. Thus, to avoid waiting for a table, try to eat in the off hours.

Reservations are a necessity for most of the expensive restaurants, especially for dinner. In addition, some of the more reasonably priced establishments are so popular that you'll never get a table unless you reserve one beforehand. As for East Berlin, restaurants are so few and far between that reservations are absolutely essential for all but the cheapest ones. Some are booked solid months in advance. In the budget-priced eateries of East Berlin, be prepared for long queues, especially if it's a weekend, when it's especially prudent to eat in mid-afternoon. I've indicated restaurants that require or recommend reservations.

As for dining etiquette, except for the more expensive restaurants, where you'll be seated by the management, it's considered perfectly fine to seat yourself wherever there's an empty place, even if the rest of the table is occupied. But simply sitting down would be rude, so ask first whether the seat is free and whether your fellow diners object. In East Berlin it's customary, and usually compulsory, to give your coat or jacket to the coat clerk at the *Garderobe,* for which the clerk expects a small tip of a mark or so (60¢).

For waiters and waitresses, you should also leave a small tip, even though tax and service charge are included in all restaurant bills. For meals costing less than 20 DM ($12.10), simply round off to the nearest mark. For meals costing more than 20 DM, most Germans will add a 10% tip. Unlike United States, where tips are left on the table, in Germany tips are indicated to the server before change is given back. If your bill is 14 DM and you want to give your waiter a 1-DM tip, say "15 DM" when you hand her your 20-DM bill. If she doesn't understand English (or your high school German), simply hand back the 1 DM.

And by the way, in East Berlin take at least 30 pfennigs with you on a trip to the restaurant's WC, to pay the woman in charge of the toilets. Some of the larger, tourist-oriented establishments in West Berlin also charge for use of their public facilities, though this is increasingly rare.

In addition to the restaurants listed in this chapter, check the nightlife chapter for pubs and other places that serve food in addition to wine and beer.

2. ON OR NEAR THE KU'DAMM

All these restaurants are either on, or within a 5-minute walk of, the Ku'damm, including those around Savignyplatz.

VERY EXPENSIVE

ANSELMO, Damaschkestrasse 17. Tel. 323 30 94.
  Cuisine: ITALIAN   **Reservations:** Recommended for dinner.
  U-Bahn: Adenauerplatz, a 3-minute walk.
$ Prices: Pastas 9–23 DM ($5.45–$13.95), entrées 34–55 DM ($20.60–$33.35). AE.
  Open: Tues–Sun noon–midnight.
Anselmo was one of the first restaurants in Berlin to raise Italian cuisine to a stylish and expensive dining experience. Although other great Italian restaurants have come onto the scene, this small and exclusive establishment still pulls in a faithful clientele, as well as curious newcomers—drawn, perhaps, to the flamboyance that has

become Anselmo's trademark. The dining area has an aura of ultramodern chic, with white-leather and chrome furniture, white tables with fresh flowers (orchids during my last visit), palm and ficus trees, tanks of bubbling water, and sophisticated lighting. Or you may prefer a table on the outdoor terrace. In any case, Anselmo is located near the far western end of the Ku'damm, off Lehniner Platz. If you're coming from the area near the Gedächtniskirche, you'll probably want to take a taxi; otherwise, it's about a 20-minute walk.

For starters, you might try the day's ravioli, lasagne, or spicy noodles, or perhaps some homemade rigatoni with gorgonzola. Main courses on the Italian-German-English menu include scampi in lobster sauce, salmon in mustard sauce, breast of duck with marsala, and lamb cutlet with garlic and rosemary. There's a bar where you can wait for your table or have an after-dinner drink. You'll want to dress up in your best for this place, if only to keep the waiter from looking you up and down; if you wear designer clothes, all the better.

CARMER'S, Carmerstrasse 2. Tel. 312 31 15.
Cuisine: CONTINENTAL **Reservations:** A must. **S-Bahn:** Savignyplatz or Bahnhof Zoologischer Garten, each about a 4-minute walk.
$ Prices: Appetizers 15–25 DM ($9.09–$15.15), entrées 25–40 DM ($15.15–$24.25). AE, MC, V.
Open: Lunch Mon–Fri noon–3pm; dinner daily 6–11pm.

You'll eat lunch with Berlin's powerhouse elite if you come here during the week, as this is a favorite place for a business lunch. (It's north of the Ku'damm, just off Hardenbergstrasse.) When it reopens for dinner, Carmer's manages to be both intimate and romantic—but it still draws in Berlin's high society. Maybe that's because it offer's the city's only curbside valet service, where a young man helps you out of your car and drives it off to the nearest parking garage. Walls of this small, upscale restaurant are decorated with artwork by up-and-coming artists. Service, swift and excellent, is under the watchful eye of the charming proprietress, who graciously greets her guests.

The handwritten menu changes weekly, but past dishes have included fish medallions with truffle butter and noodles, filet of plaice with leeks and wild rice, Sauerbraten with grilled apple and noodles, rib-eye steak with salad and potatoes, and roast beef with rémoulade and fried potatoes. It would be hard to resist starting your meal with an appetizer such as carpaccio of salmon with fresh cream and salmon roe, or a mousse of asparagus with shrimp, but leave room for one of the luscious desserts.

RISTORANTE DA ANTONIO, Rankestrasse 26. Tel. 24 72 50.
Cuisine: ITALIAN **Reservations:** Recommended, especially for dinner. **U-Bahn:** Kurfürstendamm, less than a 2-minute walk.

FROMMER'S SMART TRAVELER—RESTAURANTS

VALUE-CONSCIOUS TRAVELERS SHOULD TAKE ADVANTAGE OF THE FOLLOWING:

1. Daily specials offered by many restaurants. These specials are not on the regular menu and usually include a main course and side dishes.
2. Fixed-price lunches, generally available from about 11am to 2pm, which include an appetizer or soup, main course, and dessert—at prices much cheaper than those found on the dinner menu.
3. Inexpensive entrées, such as Würste or stews, offered by some of the more expensive restaurants, where even budget travelers can dine in style.
4. Berlin's wide variety of ethnic cuisine at very reasonable prices. There are many restaurants serving Chinese, Turkish, Greek, Indian, and Italian food.
5. Restaurants and food counters in department stores, an especially good value in Berlin.
6. Berlin's stand-up food stalls (called *Imbisse*), selling Würste, french fries, and other fast foods.
7. Coffee shop chains such as Tschibo, with coffee costing 1.20 DM (70¢) a cup.

QUESTIONS TO ASK IF YOU'RE ON A BUDGET

1. Is there an extra charge for each piece of bread consumed? Many restaurants charge extra every time you reach for the basket in the middle of your table.
2. Does the entrée come with side dishes? If so, it may be all you want to order, unless you have a voracious appetite.
3. Is there a special of the day or a fixed-price lunch not listed on the regular menu? It's especially important to ask about specials if you're reading from an English menu, since specials of the day are often printed only in German.

$ Prices: Appetizers, soups, and pastas 8–20 DM ($4.85–$12.10), entrées 29–38 DM ($17.55–$23.05); fixed-price meals 70–95 DM ($42.40–$57.55). AE, MC, V.

Open: Mon–Sat noon–3pm and 6:30pm–midnight.

Located down the street from the Hotel Steigenberger Berlin and not far from the Ku'damm, this is one of Berlin's best Italian restaurants. Cozy and avant-garde, with flowers everywhere and very graphic artwork adorning the walls, it is very popular with the well-to-do staying in the area's many first-class hotels. In fact, it's one of the establishments most recommended

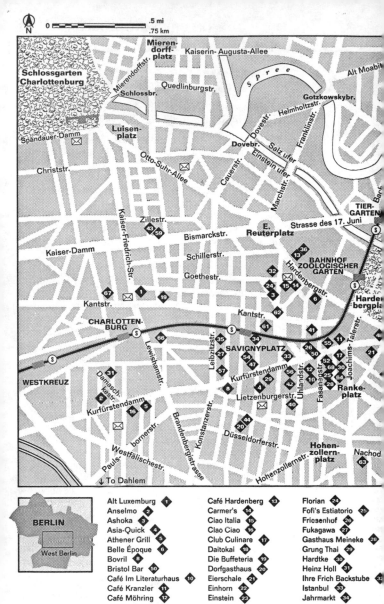

Alt Luxemburg	1	Café Hardenberg	13	Florian	24
Anselmo	2	Carmer's	14	Fofi's Estiatorio	25
Ashoka	3	Ciao Italia	15	Friesenhof	26
Asia-Quick	4	Ciao Ciao	16	Fukagawa	27
Athener Grill	5	Club Culinare	17	Gasthaus Meineke	28
Belle Époque	6	Daitokai	18	Grung Thai	29
Bovril	8	Die Buffeteria	19	Hardtke	30
Bristol Bar	50	Dorfgasthaus	20	Heinz Holl	31
Café Im Literaturhaus	10	Eierschale	21	Ihre Frich Backstube	32
Café Kranzler	11	Einhorn	22	Istanbul	33
Café Möhring	12	Einstein	23	Jahrmarkt	34

by hotel concierges near the Ku'damm. Customers aren't disappointed.

The handwritten menu is small and changes seasonally, but most people simply ask for the recommendation of the chef, who creates dishes according to what's fresh and available—from a pasta dish with black noodles to salmon with avocado. Two or three set menus are offered daily, ranging from a four-course meal to a larger "surprise menu," a potpourri of many courses in small portions.

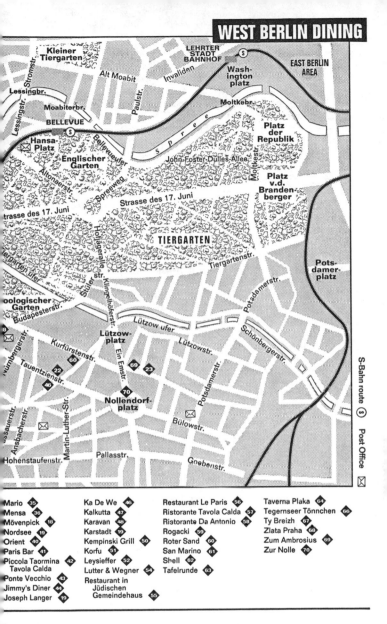

WEST BERLIN DINING

Mario 35	Ka De We 46	Restaurant Le Paris 56	Taverna Plaka 64
Mensa 36	Kalkutta 47	Ristorante Tavola Calda 57	Tegernseer Tönnchen 66
Mövenpick 18	Karavan 48	Ristorante Da Antonio 58	Ty Breizh 67
Nordsee 19	Karstadt 19	Rogacki 59	Zlata Praha 68
Orient 40	Kempinski Grill 50	Roter Sand 60	Zum Ambrosius 69
Paris Bar 41	Korfu 51	San Marino 61	Zur Nolle 70
Piccola Taormina Tavola Calda 42	Leysieffer 52	Shell 62	
Ponte Vecchio 43	Lutter & Wegner 54	Tafelrunde 63	
Jimmy's Diner 44	Restaurant in Jüdischen Gemeindehaus 55		
Joseph Langer 19			

EXPENSIVE

FLORIAN, Grolmanstrasse 52. Tel. 313 91 84.
   Cuisine: CONTINENTAL   **Reservations:** A must.   **S-Bahn:** Savignyplatz, a 3-minute walk.
$ Prices: Appetizers 13.50–18 DM ($8.20–$10.90), entrées 23–31 DM ($13.95–$18.80). Cash only.
   Open: Daily 6pm–3am.

Serving a changing menu of French, German, and other European-inspired dishes, Florian (just north of Savignyplatz) cultivates a devil-may-care atmosphere. No effort has been wasted in decorating the dining room—simply white-clothed tables on a wooden floor with nary a piece of artwork on the painfully bare walls. Florian is so devoid of worldly pretense that it's "in"; in fact, it seems as if everyone is trying to get into the place.

The changing daily menu, handwritten in a hurry, offers such appetizers as salmon with horseradish on iceberg lettuce, an Italian minced-meat casserole with tomato sauce and parmesan, and goose-liver pâté. Main courses might include roast beef in a béarnaise sauce with roast potatoes; chicken fricassee with mushrooms, buttered rice, and salad; and roast lamb with herbs and a potato casserole. I'd tell you more, but I have trouble deciphering that handwritten menu (which, by the way, is in German). Check it out for yourself.

FOFI'S ESTIATORIO, Fasanenstrasse 70. Tel. 881 87 85.

Cuisine: GREEK **Reservations:** Imperative. **U-Bahn:** Uhlandstrasse, a 1-minute walk.

$ Prices: Appetizers and salads 8–20 DM ($4.85–$12.10), entrées 22–39 DM ($13.35–$23.65). Cash only.

Open: Daily 7:15pm–3am.

This very popular restaurant has all the right ingredients for success—good location (a stone's throw from the Ku'damm), great food, interesting interior, sidewalk tables, and a mothering Greek owner named Fofi who greets strangers as warmly as she does her many regulars. The walls are covered with abstract and modern art, and the background music is likely to be easygoing jazz. In summer, try for an outdoor table.

The menu lists the usual national Greek dishes, including such appetizers as bean salad, dolmades (meat and rice rolled in grape leaves), keftedes (fried meatballs), and a Greek salad. Entrées range from grilled scampi and moussaka (eggplant and minced-meat casserole) to souvlaki, kebab, and lamb. There's also a changing menu with international dishes, as well as an abundant supply of Greek wines and spirits. If you're a devoted fan of Greek cuisine, you owe it to yourself to eat here. The sign on the facade says Estiatorio, but everyone calls it Fofi's.

FUKAGAWA, Leibnizstrasse 43. Tel. 324 35 16.

Cuisine: JAPANESE **Reservations:** Recommended.

S-Bahn: Savignyplatz, a 3-minute walk.

$ Prices: Sushi à la carte 6.50–9 DM ($3.95–$5.45) a piece; mixed sushi plates 31–38 DM ($18.80–$23.05). Cash only.

Open: Fri–Wed 6–11pm.

There are millions of places like this all over Japan—a minuscule room with only three tables and a sushi bar, where a knife-wielding chef deftly prepares slices of tender raw fish—but sushi is still relatively new to Germany. Enter through the door and you'll be greeted by shouts of "*Irashaimase!*" ("Welcome!"), followed by a steaming hot towel (cold in summer) and tea brought to you by the Japanese waitress.

If you've never had sushi before, I recommend that you start with my favorite, maguro (tuna). It tastes like very rare beef, not fishy at all. You might also like to try ika (squid) or whatever catches your fancy behind the refrigerated display case. Saké, of course, nicely complements sushi, but Sapporo or Kirin Japanese beer is equally good.

HEINZ HOLL, Damaschkestrasse 26. Tel. 323 14 04.
  Cuisine: GERMAN/CONTINENTAL **Reservations:** Imperative. **U-Bahn:** Adenauerplatz, a 4-minute walk.
$ Prices: Appetizers and soups 7–23 DM ($4.25–$13.95), entrées 20–35 DM ($12.10–$21.20). AE, MC.
  Open: Mon–Sat 7pm–1am. **Closed:** Sun and holidays.

Another Berlin institution, this place is so small, cozy, and personable that being here is like being part of an intimate social gathering. Named after its owner, located here for almost a quarter of a century, the restaurant continues to draw a devoted clientele, among them personalities from Berlin's social circles.

Although its ambience speaks strongly in the restaurant's favor, its food is even more of a recommendation. This is a good place to try Sülze (jellied meat, served with potatoes and rémoulade), Kohlroulade (stuffed cabbage rolls), Wiener Schnitzel, Tafelspitz (boiled beef with vegetables), beef Stroganoff, or Argentinian steak. Don't neglect the daily specials, however, which may include fresh fish and other items in season. There's a bar where you can sip a pre-dinner cocktail or an after-dinner drink.

RESTAURANT LE PARIS, Kurfürstendamm 211. Tel. 881 52 42.
  Cuisine: FRENCH **Reservations:** Recommended.
  U-Bahn: Uhlandstrasse, a 1-minute walk.
$ Prices: Appetizers, soups, and salads 7–23 DM ($4.25–$13.95), entrées 23–35 DM ($13.95–$21.20). Cash only.
  Open: Daily noon–midnight.

Right next to the Maison de France building on the Ku'damm, this dependably good bistro is cheerful with checkered tablecloths and artwork by French artists. Windows are pushed open wide to the boulevard in summer, when there are also 60 tables placed outside. A beacon to all those in the area who crave traditional French food, the place boasts a steady and faithful clientele.

The handwritten menu changes daily, offering the best of what's fresh. February, for example, is oyster season. Other items that might appear on the bill of fare include the ubiquitous goose foie gras as an appetizer, salmon on a bed of spinach, entrecôte de charolais, beef filet, and lamb cutlets. There are 250 different kinds of wine.

LUTTER & WEGNER, Schlüterstrasse 55. Tel. 881 34 40.
  Cuisine: GERMAN/CONTINENTAL **Reservations:** Imperative. **S-Bahn:** Savignyplatz, a 1-minute walk.
$ Prices: Entrées 16–37 DM ($9.70–$22.40). AE, DC, MC, V.
  Open: Daily 6:30pm–3am (last order midnight).

⭐ A combination wine bar and restaurant, Lutter & Wegner has been here since 1811 and still has that incomparable old-world style. It's simple and unpretentious, yet refined and civilized, with a dark-paneled wainscot, white tablecloths, candles, and pleasant background music. Catering to a professional and artistic crowd, it also has a small bar where you can come simply for a drink.

The often-changing menu always offers daily specials, which may include Tafelspitz, fish, or noodle casserole with cheese, mushrooms, and leeks. The salads, among the cheapest items available, are so huge that they're meals in themselves. Since this is a wine bar, indulge in one of its selections from Franken, the Rhine area, Baden, the Mosel Valley, or France. A glass starts at about 7 DM ($4.25).

MARIO, Leibnizstrasse 43. Tel. 324 35 16.
    Cuisine: ITALIAN **Reservations:** Recommended.
    S-Bahn: Savignyplatz, a 3-minute walk.
$ Prices: Appetizers and pastas 16–24 DM ($9.70–$14.55), entrées 39–49 DM ($23.65–$29.70). Cash only.
    Open: Sun–Fri noon–3pm and 6:30–11pm.

Located right next to the Fukagawa sushi bar (described above) and under the same management, this is a modern, uncluttered Italian *ristorante,* its white walls decorated with abstract art. The emphasis here is clearly on the food, as shown by the faithful clientele and the fact that many consider this the best Italian restaurant in town.

Most customers eschew the standard menu, which is small and insufficient, and instead go for one of the chef's many daily specials. Every day brings an array of at least 10 daily appetizers, five homemade pasta dishes, and almost two dozen selections of fish and other main courses. Whatever you order, you won't be disappointed.

PARIS BAR, Kantstrasse 152. Tel. 313 80 52.
    Cuisine: FRENCH **Reservations:** Recommended.
    S-Bahn and U-Bahn: Uhlandstrasse or Bahnhof Zoologischer Garten, each about a 3-minute walk.
$ Prices: Entrées 32–90 DM ($19.40–$54.55). Cash only.
    Open: Mon–Sat noon–2am.

It looks and feels like a typical bistro—crowded and noisy, with contemporary posters on the walls. (Despite its name, it's primarily a restaurant.) Even a casual glance around this seemingly informal eatery, however, reveals that most of its customers are smartly dressed, looking like the business types, journalists, film people, and upscale artists that they are. This is clearly one of Berlin's top places to see and be seen, a place for the successfully established and those who wish they were. With a French staff, it's been at this location for more than 30 years—between the Gedächtniskirche and Savignyplatz, near the Theater des Westens.

The menu offers traditional French cuisine, including steak and fish. There are also daily specials, as well as a good selection of desserts. And of course, the choice of French wines is what you'd expect in a restaurant like this.

RISTORANTE TAVOLA CALDA, Leibnizstrasse 45. Tel. 324 10 48.
    Cuisine: ITALIAN **Reservations:** Imperative for lunch or dinner. **S-Bahn:** Savignyplatz, a 3-minute walk.
$ Prices: Pastas and pizzas 10–13 DM ($6.05–$7.85), entrées 27–38 DM ($16.35–$23.05). Cash only.
    Open: Daily noon–11pm.

S A tiny one-room restaurant with a marble floor, clinically white walls, abstract art, and peach-colored tablecloths, Ristorante Tavola Calda is another favorite of lovers of Italian cuisine—giving Mario down the street stiff competition. Evenings are romantic, despite the fact that tables are close together. The place is trendy without being clichéd.

Its pastas and pizzas are especially good, and at such moderate prices that you can dine here quite reasonably. If you opt for one of its higher-priced lamb, beef, or seafood dishes, however, you're in for a special treat, since all are wonderfully prepared and presented.

ZLATA PRAHA, Meinekestrasse 4. Tel. 881 97 50.
   Cuisine: CZECHOSLOVAKIAN/HUNGARIAN **Reservations:** Recommended for dinner. **U-Bahn:** Uhlandstrasse or Kurfürstendamm, each about a 2-minute walk.
$ Prices: Appetizers 9.50–15 DM ($5.75–$9.10), entrées 19–38 DM ($11.50–$23.05). AE, DC, MC, V.
   Open: Mon–Sat noon–midnight.

Zlata Praha specializes primarily in food from Prague but offers dishes from Hungary and Austria as well. It is decorated in a hushed drawing-room style, with red-velvet chairs, dark furnishings, white tablecloths, and candles and fresh flowers on each table; portraits of noblemen and ladies adorning the walls conjure up the time when the Austro-Hungarian Empire still ruled much of eastern Europe. The atmosphere is subdued, and would be almost solemn if it weren't for the many customers who seem to know one another and become livelier with each round of Czech beer or spirits.

Most dishes are prepared with a liberal dose of paprika (red pepper), from paprika chicken with homemade noodles to paprika Schnitzel. Also available: stuffed peppers; Bohemian-style pork chops with onions and red cabbage; Stroganoff; steak; and goose liver with ham and mushrooms. I'm fond of the Hungarian filet casserole, with a very spicy paprika-tomato sauce and layers of homemade noodles.

MODERATE

BOVRIL, Kurfürstendamm 184. Tel. 881 84 61.
   Cuisine: CONTINENTAL **U-Bahn:** Adenauerplatz, about a 4-minute walk.
$ Prices: Fixed-price lunches 13–25 DM ($7.85–$15.15), fixed-price dinners 21–35 DM ($12.70–$21.20). AE, DC, MC, V.
   Open: Mon–Sat 11:30am–2am, Sun 5pm–2am.

A pleasant restaurant, on the Ku'damm just north of Olivaer Platz, Bovril provides a healthy mix of old and new in its decor. The facade gives a hint of art nouveau, while the interior features lamps, ceiling fans, red-plastic sofas that look very 1950s, and contemporary murals. In summer, tables are spread outside along the boulevard. The handwritten menu changes twice daily, with lunch served to 4pm and dinner available from 6pm. There are two- and three-course meals, as well as à la carte selections that may range from fettuccine to beefsteak. Make a reservation if you want to come during dinner hours.

CHUNG, Kurfürstendamm 190. Tel. 882 15 55.

Cuisine: CHINESE   **U-Bahn:** Uhlandstrasse or Adenauerplatz, each about a 6-minute walk.

$ Prices: Appetizers 4.50–15.50 DM ($2.75–$9.40), entrées 13–30 DM ($7.85–$18.20); fixed-price lunches 10.50–11 DM ($6.35–$6.65). AE, MC, V.

Open: Daily 11:30am–midnight.

Occupying a prime spot on the Ku'damm, with a glass-enclosed dining room that extends right over the sidewalk, this ornately decorated restaurant features Chinese lanterns hanging from the ceiling and an obliging staff. The best deals are the special fixed-price lunches, available only Monday through Friday until 3pm (excluding holidays), which consist of a choice of soup or spring roll, along with almost two dozen entrée choices. An English menu offers a seemingly endless list of main dishes, including beef with seasonal vegetables, fish filet Cantonese style with pork and mushrooms, pork with bamboo shoots and mushrooms, chicken Shanghai style, beef with mixed vegetables and bird's nest flavoring, and roast duck.

CIAO CIAO, Kurfürstendamm 156. Tel. 892 36 12.

Cuisine: ITALIAN   **U-Bahn:** Adenauerplatz, a 1-minute walk.

$ Prices: Appetizers and soups 7–30 DM ($4.25–$18.20), pizzas and pastas 11–24 DM ($6.65–$14.55), entrées 20–37 DM ($12.10–$22.40). MC, V.

Open: Sun–Thurs noon–2am, Fri and Sat noon–3am.

An informal Italian restaurant standing on the far west end of the Ku'damm past Adenauerplatz, Ciao Ciao makes a lively place to dine, with an animated Italian staff and plenty to watch if you can get a seat outside in summer. While the food is not always up to par, given the prices, the atmosphere is so good that few people seem to mind. In fact, it can get so crowded on a summer's evening that you should make a reservation for dinner. To be on the safe side, order the carpaccio and one of the dozen choices of pizza or pasta, the latter including cannelloni, tagliatelle, tortellini, and rigatoni. Scampi is served half a dozen different ways.

DORFGASTHAUS, Sächsische Strasse 7. Tel. 882 60 60 or 881 92 39.

Cuisine: GERMAN   **Directions:** A 5-minute walk south of the Ku'damm, south of Bleibtreustrasse.

$ Prices: Soups and salads 5.50–14.50 DM ($3.35–$8.80), entrées 11.50–32.50 DM ($6.95–$19.70). AE, MC, V.

Open: Daily 11:30am–1am.

Decorated in old-Berlin style with a wood-plank floor, antique light fixtures, and an abnormally long bar dominating one wall, Dorfgasthaus nevertheless has an aura of trendiness. Whereas many Gaststätten seem to survive primarily on a clientele of older customers, this one also draws in the younger generation, who come for a hearty dose of Leberknödelsuppe, Schnitzel, steak, and Sauerbraten. The Filet-teller Baden-Baden is a platter of pork medallions with a mushroom sauce and green peppers, along with side dishes of broccoli with cheese, béarnaise sauce, and homemade Spätzle (noodles). You'll need to go on a diet after you've eaten this meal.

FRIESENHOF, Uhlandstrasse 185-186. Tel. 883 60 79.
   Cuisine: GERMAN   **U-Bahn:** Uhlandstrasse, about a 2-minute walk.
$ Prices: Appetizers 5–16 DM ($3.05–$9.70), entrées 13.50–31 DM ($8.20–$18.80). MC, V.
   Open: Daily 11:30am–midnight.
This rustic family-style restaurant near the elevated tracks of the S-Bahn specializes in German food from Friesland (northern Germany near the Baltic Sea). The dining halls resemble the interior of a half-timbered farmer's house, with brick walls and exposed beams, wooden ceilings, and dried flowers on the tables. Winter brings such Friesland specialties as Grünkohl mit Pinkel (a cabbage dish). Other items on the menu include homemade Sülze with rémoulade, potatoes, and onions, farmer's platter with various cuts of meat and side dishes, Schnitzel, steak, and fish typical of the Baltic. The Friesische Reispfanne consists of meat strips with curry, vegetables, and rice.

GRUNG THAI, Ku'damm Passage, Kurfürstendamm 202. Tel. 881 53 50.
   Cuisine: THAI   **U-Bahn:** Uhlandstrasse, less than a 4-minute walk.
$ Prices: Appetizers and soups 5–11.50 DM ($3.05–$6.95), entrées 13.50–30 DM ($8.20–18.20). AE, DC, MC, V.
   Open: Daily noon–3am.
Located in a small mall at the corner of the Ku'damm and Knesebeckstrasse, Grung Thai strives to provide the right atmosphere with elephant statues and other Thai artifacts, a pedicab, and live music-and-dance entertainment every Friday and Saturday evening starting at 9pm. There are more than 100 items on the menu, including my favorites: chicken soup with coconut milk and lemon grass, Thai noodles with seafood, and a spicy beef salad. There are also curries, salads, and fish, pork, and beef dishes. Wash it all down with Singha beer, Thai's national drink. After midnight you must enter the restaurant through the passage on Knesebeckstrasse.

HARDTKE, Meinekestrasse 27 A & B. Tel. 881 98 27.
   Cuisine: GERMAN   **U-Bahn:** Uhlandstrasse, less than a 2-minute walk.
$ Prices: Appetizers 5.50–15 DM ($3.35–$9.10), entrées 10–29 DM ($6.05–$17.55). Cash only.
   Open: Daily 10am–1am.
Just a minute's walk from the Ku'damm, this popular restaurant has been dishing out hearty Teutonic fare for almost 40 years. Many visiting natives make a point of eating here at least once, and on any given evening the place is usually packed with middle-aged and retired German men and women. Because this restaurant has its own butcher shop, its meat has the reputation of being especially fresh, and its homemade sausages are excellent. The dining area is divided into two separate halls (hence the A and B addresses). Both have the rustic appearance of a typical Gaststätte and both offer the same menu, including Berliner Eisbein with vegetables, Sauerkraut, and potatoes; B*rathering* with potatoes; Sauerbraten or Schweinebraten with red cabbage and potato dumplings; and Schnitzel. You could easily spend 30 DM ($18.20) on a

great meal, or dine on sausages for 10 DM ($6.05). Try the fresh blood and liver sausage, the gigantic Bockwurst with potato salad, the Bratwurst with potatoes and Sauerkraut, or the Wurst platter. All around, this is one of the best places in town for a typical German meal.

RESTAURANT IN JÜDISCHEN GEMEINDEHAUS, Fasanenstrasse 79. Tel. 884 20 339.

Cuisine: KOSHER **U-Bahn:** Uhlandstrasse, a 2-minute walk.

$ Prices: Appetizers 8–10 DM ($4.85–$6.05); fixed-price meals 17–27 DM ($10.30–$16.35). Cash only.

Open: Mon, Fri, and Sun 12:30–3pm; Tues–Thurs 12:30–9pm. **Closed:** Sat.

This simple dining hall in the Jewish Community House, the only place in town for kosher foods, offers a daily menu of Jewish and Israeli specialties. Appetizers may range from tuna salad or falafel with pita to moussaka or stuffed cabbage roll. There are about five different daily fixed-price meals that include soup and dessert. Main courses may consist of Gulasch, roast veal, or lamb chops.

ISTANBUL, Knesebeckstrasse 77. Tel. 883 27 77 or 312 92 55.

Cuisine: TURKISH **S-Bahn:** Savignyplatz, less than a 2-minute walk.

$ Prices: Soups and salads 7–9.50 DM ($4.25–$5.75), appetizers 9.50–12 DM ($5.75–$7.25), entrées 12–29 DM ($7.25–$17.55). AE, DC, MC.

Open: Daily noon–midnight.

One of Berlin's oldest Turkish restaurants, this family-run establishment remains firmly entrenched as one of the best—quite a feat considering Berlin's large Turkish population and abundance of Turkish dining spots. Try to get a seat in the back room, which is decorated in mosque style. On Fridays and Saturdays, a belly dancer entertains after 9:30pm. You might wish to start your meal with a Turkish apéritif called Raki, which is sun-ripened raisins flavored with anise. For an appetizer, try the yaprak dolmast (vine leaves stuffed with rice, pine nuts, currants, and herbs) or the hummus (chick peas with garlic). Main courses range from so-called Turkish pizza (flat bread with chopped meat) to dönerkebab (veal grilled on a rotating spit and served with rice), shish kebab (skewered meat and vegetables), and a wide variety of lamb dishes. If you've never had the pleasure of sampling Turkish cuisine, this is a good place to do so.

SAN MARINO, Savignyplatz 12. Tel. 313 60 86.

Cuisine: ITALIAN **S-Bahn:** Savignyplatz, a 1-minute walk.

$ Prices: Pizzas and pastas 7–10 DM ($4.25–$6.05), entrées 15–30 DM ($9.10–$18.20). AE, MC, V.

Open: Daily 11am–1am.

Similar to the many other trattorias in Berlin, San Marino has the advantage of an ideal location right on Savignyplatz, just a few minutes' walk north of the Ku'damm. In summer you can dine outside on the square, with a pleasant view of grass and trees, and afterward go for a drink in one of the many bars in the neighborhood. In winter you dine indoors surrounded by plants. Although there are steaks and seafood on the menu, all you need order is one of the personal-size pizzas or pasta dishes, all priced at less than 10 DM ($6.05). It would be hard, however, to resist a couple of glasses of Lambrusco or Chianti as well.

SHELL, Knesebeckstrasse 22. Tel. 312 83 10.
   Cuisine: INTERNATIONAL/VEGETARIAN   **S-Bahn:** Savigny-platz, less than a 2-minute walk.
$ Prices: Soups and salads 6.50–18 DM ($3.95–$10.90), entrées 16.50–30 DM ($10–$18.20). MC, V.
   Open: Mon–Sat 9am–midnight, Sun 10am–midnight.
Shell occupies what was once a corner gas station (hence its cheeky name) and now dispenses beer instead of petrol. A simple and pleasant restaurant on Savignyplatz, it has a curved facade with huge windows that benefit the several indoor palm trees and cacti. Popular with the many young residents of the area, Shell features international dishes, many of them light or vegetarian. The main menu, available throughout the day and evening, lists such diverse selections as risotto with black rice, cashews, crab, and vegetables; tofu with sweet chili, vegetables, sprouts, and noodles; a vegetable plate with hollandaise, potatoes, and salad; Tafelspitz; and pork chops. In addition, there's also a lunch menu, available until 6pm, with prices of daily specials running less than 20 DM ($12.10). An evening menu offers daily specials for less than 30 DM ($18.20). My only complaint is that service tends to be slow—come here only if you have time, or, if you prefer, for a cup of coffee or a beer.

TAVERNA PLAKA, Joachimstaler Strasse 14. Tel. 883 15 57.
   Cuisine: GREEK   **U-Bahn:** Kurfürstendamm, less than a 2-minute walk.
$ Prices: Appetizers and salads 10–12 DM ($6.05–$7.25), entrées 15–28 DM ($9.10–$16.95). Cash only.
   Open: Mon–Fri 4pm–1am; Sat, Sun, and holidays noon–2am.
This first-floor Greek restaurant, just off the Ku'damm, is decorated in cheerful Mykonos white and blue, with flowers and candles on each table. The Greek waiters are friendly and accommodating, the recorded music is mainly Greek instrumental, and the food is good no matter what you order or how much you spend. There are the usual moussaka, fish, souvlaki, and gyros on the menu, but if you're on a budget, order the Mesedes Plaka for 10 DM ($6.05). Although it's an appetizer plate, it's plentiful—dolmades (stuffed grape leaves), eggplant salad, feta cheese, and a sampling of other Greek delicacies—and the waiter didn't blink twice when that's all I ordered. An alternative is the huge Greek salad (called choriatiki). A fun place to dine.

INEXPENSIVE

Be sure to read over the selections above in the moderate category, as many restaurants listed there have inexpensive main courses in addition to higher-priced ones. Both Ciao Ciao and Shell, for example, offer pizza and pasta dishes at very reasonable prices; Hardtke offers homemade sausages; and Shell and Istanbul offer inexpensive entrées as well. If you skip the appetizer and alcohol, you can dine in these restaurants for less than 20 DM ($12.10).

CLUB CULINARE, basement of Wertheim department store, Kurfürstendamm 231. Tel. 88 20 61.
  Cuisine: GERMAN/SNACKS **U-Bahn:** Kurfürstendamm, a 1-minute walk.
$ Prices: 6–25 DM ($3.65–$15.15). Cash only.
  Open: Mon–Fri 9am–6pm, Sat 9am–2pm (to 6pm first Sat of the month).

Most German department stores have grocery departments in their basements, and Wertheim is no exception. Unusual, however, are its several sit-down counters, where various types of snacks and meals are sold. Simply walk around until you find a counter offering the food that's most tempting to you. Among the choices: salads (several dozen kinds), stews, pastas, potato pancakes, grilled chicken, desserts, and wines.

GASTHAUS MEINEKE, Meinekestrasse 10. Tel. 882 31 58.
  Cuisine: GERMAN **U-Bahn:** Uhlandstrasse or Kurfürstendamm, each a few minutes' walk.
$ Prices: Appetizers 5–15 DM ($3.05–$9.10), entrées 9.50–25 DM ($5.75–$15.15). Cash only.
  Open: Daily noon–1am.

Although less than a decade old, this Gaststätte was cleverly designed to look like an old Berliner pub, with a wooden floor, a dark-paneled wainscot, and wooden benches built into private niches in the front-room wall. The place serves as both a bar and a restaurant, dishing out hearty helpings of homemade Leberwurst, Kasseler Rippenspeer with bread and butter, Brathering, Berliner Boulette, Bauernsalat (farmer's salad), Leberkäs, Sülze, Eisbein, Schnitzel, Forelle (trout), and Rumpsteak. Like everyone else around you, order a beer to wash it all down. Gasthaus Meineke is located just a few minutes' walk south of the Ku'damm, near Lietzenburger Strasse.

JAHRMARKT, Bleibtreustrasse 49. Tel. 312 14 33.
  Cuisine: GERMAN **Reservations:** Imperative. **S-Bahn:** Savignyplatz, a 1-minute walk.
$ Prices: Soups and salads 4.50–12 DM ($2.70–$7.25), entrées 15.50–24 DM ($9.40–$14.55). Cash only.
  Open: Mon–Fri noon–midnight, Sat and Sun 5:30pm–midnight.

The wonderful Jahrmarkt, one of the best deals in town, looks as if it might be expensive, because the patrons who flock here tend to be well dressed. More than 20 years old, it took over an earlier restaurant that served people waiting for their trains, and it seems to have altered little over the decades. Simply decorated, with wooden floor and tables, it offers a changing daily menu of huge platters at very reasonable prices, most of them for less than 18 DM ($10.90). Examples: Schnitzel with potatoes and Sauerkraut; cabbage with smoked sausage and potatoes; beef Gulasch with kidney beans, paprika, and onions, plus side orders of potatoes and mixed salad;

pork chops with vegetables, french fries, and salad; and Viennese-style grilled beef with onions, served with fried potatoes and mixed salad. The first Sunday of each month features a warm and cold buffet table, and in summer there's outdoor seating.

KALKUTTA, Bleibtreustrasse 17. Tel. 883 62 93.

Cuisine: INDIAN   **S-Bahn:** Savignyplatz, about a 2-minute walk.

$ Prices: Entrées 11–20 DM ($6.65–$12.10); fixed-price lunches 9.50–13 DM ($5.75–$7.85). AE, MC, V.

Open: Daily noon–midnight.

Just off the Ku'damm, amid the many bars of Bleibtreustrasse, this tiny and unpretentious restaurant offers great Indian curries, a generous use of spices giving them an extra pizzazz. With painted murals on the wall and the obligatory Indian background music, the place attracts a young clientele, most of them well traveled and many of whom have been to India. Dinner offers a wide assortment of tandoori, vegetable curries, and fish, as well as pork, chicken, beef, and veal dishes. Lunch is more economical, with special fixed-price lunches of vegetable curry, chicken korma, or mutton offered until 4pm.

KORFU, Savignyplatz Bogen 604. Tel. 312 64 23.

Cuisine: GREEK   **S-Bahn:** Savignyplatz, less than a 1-minute walk.

$ Prices: 5–18 DM ($3.05–$10.90). Cash only.

Open: Daily noon–2am.

Savignyplatz Bogen is a string of establishments located under the S-Bahn tracks between Savignyplatz and Bleibtreustrasse. Korfu, just off Bleibtreustrasse, is a modestly decorated Greek eatery, with just a few wooden tables and chairs. A good place for a midnight snack, a cheap meal, or take-out, it sells gyros, bean salad, Greek salad (Bauernsalat), souvlaki, lamb cutlets, and moussaka. If you aren't familiar with Greek food or like variety, and there are two of you, order the Korfu Grillteller, which comes with an assortment of dishes and costs 33 DM ($20) for two persons.

ORIENT, Lietzenburgerstrasse 77. Tel. 881 24 60.

Cuisine: MIDDLE EASTERN   **U-Bahn:** Uhlandstrasse, about a 3-minute walk.

$ Prices: 6.50–18 DM ($3.95–$10.90). Cash only.

Open: Daily noon–3am.

Specializing in Middle Eastern and Mediterranean dishes, the Orient stands on the corner of Lietzenburgerstrasse and Uhlandstrasse. It offers take-out food, but you may want to sit in its simple one-room dining area—outfitted with plastic tablecloths and a Middle Eastern motif on the walls—where you'll be serenaded by recorded music. There are a dozen items on the simple menu, many priced under 10 DM ($6.05), including falafel, kebab, maali (a vegetarian dish of cauliflower, potatoes, and eggplant), gyros, and muhamara (puréed red paprika with walnuts). There are also daily specials, all displayed behind the take-out counter.

BUDGET

Check the listings for Club Culinare, Korfu, and the Orient above under "Inexpensive," as these offer some entrées for less than 10 DM ($6.05).

ASHOKA, Grolmanstrasse 51. Tel. 313 20 66.
  Cuisine: INDIAN **S-Bahn:** Savignyplatz, less than a 4-minute walk.
$ Prices: 4.50–10 DM ($2.70–$6.05). Cash only.
  Open: Daily 10am–2am.
Just north of Savignyplatz, this tiny hole-in-the-wall has an open kitchen that takes up half the restaurant. Popular with students living in the area, it offers more than a dozen vegetarian dishes alone, along with half a dozen meat choices and a daily fixed menu. For an appetizer, try the pakoras, a kind of biscuit with cauliflower and other vegetables, with a dash of chutney.

ASIA-QUICK, Lietzenburger Strasse 96. Tel. 882 15 33.
  Cuisine: CHINESE **U-Bahn:** Uhlandstrasse, about a 6-minute walk.
$ Prices: 7–14 DM ($4.25–$8.50). Cash only.
  Open: Mon–Fri noon–midnight.
About a 2-minute walk south of the Ku'damm near Bleibtreustrasse, Asia-Quick is a simple and pleasant place for Chinese fast food. Decorated in bright red and white, it offers soups and appetizers for less than 5 DM ($3.05), while most of the main dishes are less than 12 DM ($7.25). Its meat dishes come in three styles: chop suey (with soy sauce), sweet-and-sour, and Szechuan (spicy). Meats to choose from include fish, pork, beef, and chicken; there are also rice, noodle, and vegetarian dishes. As in many restaurants throughout Asia, there is even a TV in the corner. You can either eat here or order take-out.

ATHENER GRILL, Kurfürstendamm 156. Tel. 892 10 39.
  Cuisine: GREEK/ITALIAN **U-Bahn:** Adenauerplatz, a 1-minute walk.
$ Prices: 3.50–11 DM ($2.10–$6.65). Cash only.
  Open: Sun–Thurs 11am–4am, Fri and Sat 11am–5am.
⑤ A good choice if you can't decide whether you want Greek or Italian—or if you want both. An imaginatively done cafeteria, it's located at the far western end of the Ku'damm, past Adenauerplatz (look for a modern brick building). Its menu is written on the wall. After deciding what you want, pay the cashier and then hand your ticket to the cook at the appropriate counter. Counters are divided into various specialties, with Greek food at one counter, pizzas at another, wines at yet another. You'll find fish, spaghetti, moussaka, souvlaki, gyros, ice cream, and salads, to mention a few of the dishes available. The Greek and Italian wines start at a low 1.50 DM (90¢) per glass, certainly one of the cheapest prices in town.

JIMMY'S DINER, Pariser Strasse 41. Tel. 882 31 41.
  Cuisine: AMERICAN/MEXICAN **Directions:** A 5-minute walk south of the Ku'damm, on the corner of Sächsische Strasse and Pariser Strasse.
$ Prices: 7–14 DM ($4.25–$8.50). Cash only.

Open: Sun–Thurs 4pm–4am, Fri and Sat 4pm–6am.

Just like back home—that is, if your town still has a '50s-style diner. This remake has booths with bright-red plastic furniture, lots of chrome, and old advertisements on the walls. Drive-in speakers dangle above the window. Popular with young Berliners who were probably born in the '70s, it has an eclectic menu, from corn on the cob or "Aunt Mary's chicken" to "quarter pownders," sandwiches, spareribs, spaghetti, tacos, enchiladas, and chili con carne. It even sells Mexican beers. The menu is good for a few laughs, interspersed with funny sayings like "If you think you have a reservation, you're in the wrong place." The music ranges from Mexican to country, along with hits from the '50s and '60s. A bit of unreality in the heart of Berlin—and for the homesick, much cheaper and quicker than a ticket home. Also, good for a hamburger fix, if that's what you need.

KARAVAN, Kurfürstendamm 11. Tel. 881 50 05.

Cuisine: TURKISH **U-Bahn:** Kurfürstendamm or Bahnhof Zoologischer Garten, each less than a 2-minute walk.

$ Prices: 3–8 DM ($1.80–$4.85). Cash only.

Open: Daily 8am–11pm.

Because of its large Turkish population, Berlin boasts a number of Turkish restaurants and stand-up food stalls. This simple place, beside the American Express office and just across the plaza from the Gedächtniskirche, is a cross between the two—tiny and very informal, with a few stools along a counter. Better yet, order your food take-out and eat it on one of the public benches around the Gedächtniskirche, a prime spot for people-watching. I especially recommend the Turkish pizza, which has a thick, soft crust and a thin spread of minced meat and spices. There's also a changing daily special for 7.50 DM ($4.55), as well as Turkish sandwiches and salads. Since all the food is visible behind the glass counter, simply point at what looks best. A good and convenient place to sample this ethnic food at very inexpensive prices.

There's another branch nearby called Meister Snack, located under the eaves of the Bilka department store on the corner of Joachimstaler Strasse and Kantstrasse. It offers the same Turkish food.

PICCOLA TAORMINA TAVOLA CALDA, 29 Uhlandstrasse. Tel. 881 47 10.

Cuisine: ITALIAN **U-Bahn:** Uhlandstrasse, less than a 3-minute walk.

$ Prices: 4.50–13.50 DM ($2.70–$8.20). Cash only.

Open: Daily 10am–2am.

Just a glance inside should convince you that this is one of the most popular self-service Italian restaurants in town. Its cheap prices attract hungry customers throughout the day and night, especially its pizza by the slice for 1.50 DM (90¢). But the menu on the wall lists other choices as well, including more than 25 different kinds of personal-size pizzas, omelets, risotto dishes, beefsteak, and such pastas as spaghetti, ravioli, lasagne, and cannelloni. Wine and beer are also available. Order at the counter and the cooks—all Italian—will have your order ready in a flash. There's plenty of dining space in the rear rooms, or you can order take-out.

3. NEAR THE EUROPA-CENTER & WITTENBERGPLATZ

VERY EXPENSIVE

DAITOKAI, Europa-Center. Tel. 261 80 90.
   Cuisine: JAPANESE   **Reservations:** Not necessary.
   Bahn: Kurfürstendamm or Wittenbergplatz, each about a 3-minute walk.
$ Prices: Entrées 40–55 DM ($24.25–$33.35); fixed-price lunches 10.50–38 DM ($6.35–$23.20); fixed-price dinners 69–105 DM ($42.80–$63.65). AE, DC, MC, V.
   Open: Tues–Sun noon–2:30pm and 6–10:30pm.

On the second floor of the Europa-Center, this Japanese teppanyaki restaurant specializes in grilled steaks, seafood, and vegetables. Traditionally decorated with slatted-wood screens, a pond with vermilion-colored carp, and lanterns, the large dining area contains several long tables, each outfitted with a grill where the chef prepares your meal before your eyes. A waitress in kimono takes your order for drinks—ask for Japanese beer (brands include Sapporo and Kirin) or saké. If you're familiar with the many Benihana restaurants in the United States, you'll feel at home here.

The most economical time to come is for lunch, when a variety of set meals are available, including yaki-udon (Japanese noodles with pork and vegetables), grilled fish, sukiyaki (paper-thin beef simmered with a stock of vegetables), sashimi with Japanese pickles, and a platter of mixed seafood cooked on the grill. All set lunches come with soup, salad, and rice. Dinner is much more expensive but offers a wider variety, from grilled giant shrimp or salmon to grilled steaks. The service, of course, is the best, for which the Japanese are legendary.

MODERATE

MÖVENPICK, Europa-Center. Tel. 262 70 77.
   Cuisine: INTERNATIONAL   **U-Bahn:** Kurfürstendamm or Wittenbergplatz, each about a 3-minute walk.
$ Prices: Entrées 11.50–34 DM ($6.95–$20.60). AE, DC, MC, V.
   Open: Sun–Thurs 8am–midnight, Fri and Sat 8am–1am.

This huge branch of Mövenpick, a Swiss chain of restaurants, is on the second floor of the Europa-Center and is divided into various sections serving different kinds of food. The Backstube, for example, specializes in pizza and quiche and offers seating on a terrace overlooking the inner atrium of the Europa-Center. The more upscale Le Caveau, a wine cellar with more than 100 different vintages from around the world, offers a changing menu that might include shrimp, roast hare, or turkey breast, with most entrées here costing 18 to 34 DM ($10.90 to $20.60). And the largest dining area, called Café des Artistes, offers herring, smoked salmon, pasta dishes, curries, steak, fish, and pork cutlets, as well as a self-service salad bar. One trip through the salad bar with a small plate costs 8.50 DM

($5.15). In summer, there's outdoor seating with views of the Gedächtniskirche at Mövenpick's ground-floor coffeehouse, which sells snacks and desserts.

INEXPENSIVE

KADEWE, Wittenbergplatz. Tel. 212 10 or 24 01 71.
    Cuisine: INTERNATIONAL **U-Bahn:** Wittenbergplatz, less than a 1-minute walk.
$ Prices: 3–20 DM ($1.80–$12.10). Cash only.
    Open: Mon–Fri 9am–6:30pm, Sat 9am–2pm (to 6pm first Sat of the month).

KaDeWe is the popular name for Kaufhaus des Westens, the largest department store on the European continent. Its top attraction, believe it or not, is the huge food emporium on the sixth floor, which has to be seen to be believed—row after row of gourmet foods, including exotic teas and coffees, spices, jams, sweets, vegetables, fruits, and an amazing array of sausages and cuts of pork. In the middle of all these sections are sit-down counters, each specializing in a different type of food. One counter sells pasta dishes, another Asian cuisine, while others sell grilled chicken, salads, oysters, and more. One counter is devoted to the potato alone, which you can order baked or fried in a number of styles. There is also a wine bar and a coffee bar.

ROTER SAND, Kurfürstenstrasse 109. Tel. 213 64 41.
    Cuisine: SEAFOOD **U-Bahn:** Wittenbergplatz, a 3-minute walk.
$ Prices: 8–20 DM ($4.85–$12.10); fixed-price lunches 14.95 DM ($9.05). DC, MC, V.
    Open: Mon–Sat 11am–10pm. **Closed:** Sun and holidays.
Decorated like a boat at sea, with fishermen's nets strung across the ceiling, Roter Sand offers 30 different types of fish—including flounder, salmon, herring, and mackerel—cooked in a variety of ways. Altogether there are 200 items on the menu, most priced under 20 DM ($12.10), although there is lobster if you feel like splurging. You might wish to dine on the Fischtopf Schöne Fischerin, a mixed platter of steamed fish with vegetables and potatoes, or perhaps the Schlemmerfilet Florida, salmon with a curried tropical fruit sauce, along with pineapple and rice. The best deal is the special fixed-price lunch, served only Monday through Friday from 11am to 3pm, which offers a different meal each day—for example, fish soup, followed by fish baked in beer dough and served with a tomato sauce and rice, along with a fruit salad.

BUDGET

EINHORN, Wittenbergplatz 5-6. Tel. 24 63 47.
    Cuisine: VEGETARIAN **U-Bahn:** Wittenbergplatz, a 1-minute walk.
$ Prices: 6.50–9 DM ($3.95–$5.45). Cash only.

Open: Mon–Fri 10am–6pm, Sat 10am–2pm.

⑤ At the north end of Wittenbergplatz, this natural-foods shop offers changing daily specials of ready-made vegetarian dishes, which in the past have included curried risotto with vegetables, spinach cannelloni, vegetarian lasagne, stews, salads, spinach casserole, and vegetarian moussaka. There are tempting fruit juices as well. You can eat at the stand-up counter or take your purchase outside and sit on one of the benches lining the square.

There's another branch located at Mommsenstrasse 2 (tel. 881 42 41), a minute's walk north of the Ku'damm near Knesebeckstrasse, with the same hours.

4. NEAR WILMERSDORFER STRASSE & BAHNHOF CHARLOTTENBURG

In addition to the restaurants listed here, other restaurants within a 10-minute walk of the Wilmersdorfer Strasse shopping lane include Anselmo, Athener Grill, Heinz Holl, and Ciao Ciao described above in "On or Near the Ku'damm."

EXPENSIVE

ALT LUXEMBURG, Pestalozzistrasse 70. Tel. 323 87 30.
Cuisine: NOUVELLE CONTINENTAL   **Reservations:** Imperative. **U-Bahn:** Wilmersdorfer Strasse, less than a 2-minute walk.
$ Prices: Soups and appetizers 13–24 DM ($7.85–$14.55), entrées 35–40 DM ($21.20–$24.25). Cash only.
Open: Tues–Sat 6:30pm–1am (last order 11pm).

★ The tiny Alt Luxemburg, which seats only 25 persons, is considered one of Berlin's top gourmet restaurants because of chef/owner Karl Wannemacher's imaginative dishes. Beautifully decorated in a style reminiscent of the 1800s, with elaborate antique chandeliers, fine pink tablecloths, and mirrors, it makes the perfect place for a romantic tête-à-tête. The service is impeccable yet unobtrusive.

The menu changes with the seasons and according to what's fresh and available. Though the unusual combinations of international spices and foods are at first surprising, they go together so perfectly you'll wonder why you've never had them that way before. Starters have included spinach ravioli with a Roquefort sauce, goose liver with grapes, and curried cream of chicken soup with Japanese shiitake mushrooms. Past entrées have included lobster lasagne, beef filet with pesto, rack of lamb with thyme, and pigeon with a truffle sauce. In any case, you're in for a culinary treat, and there's a wide range of wines to complement your meal.

PONTE VECCHIO, Spielhagenstrasse 3. Tel. 342 19 99.
Cuisine: ITALIAN   **Reservations:** Recommended.   **U-Bahn:**

Bismarckstrasse, less than a 3-minute walk.

$ Prices: Appetizers 10–22 DM ($6.05–$13.35), entrées 29–38 DM ($17.55–$23.05). DC.

Open: Wed–Mon 6:30–11pm.

The light-orange facade of this small and unpretentious-looking eatery belies the delights inside, for Ponte Vecchio ranks as one of the best gourmet Italian restaurants in town. The simple yet pleasant dining room caters to a clientele more interested in what touches their palates than what's on the walls.

The cuisine takes its cues from Tuscany, with only the freshest of ingredients used. For an appetizer, you might try the carpaccio with mozzarella and tomatoes or the seafood with basil. There's always a fresh fish of the day, as well as lamb and veal dishes, or perhaps you'll opt for homemade noodles with a rabbit sauce or gnocchi with ricotta and tomato sauce. The selection of Italian wines is varied and perfect for the dishes on hand.

INEXPENSIVE

TEGERNSEER TÖNNCHEN, Mommsenstrasse 34. Tel. 323-3827.

Cuisine: GERMAN **U-Bahn:** Wilmersdorfer Strasse, about a 4-minute walk.

$ Prices: 9–18 DM ($5.45–$10.90). Cash only.

Open: Daily 11:30am–midnight.

This typical Gaststätte near Bahnhof Charlottenburg specializes in hearty portions of local and Bavarian favorites. Its decor is traditional, with wooden tables and a wooden floor—a perfect match for such dishes as the Berliner Eisbein, Tafelspitz, Bavarian-style Leberkäs, Schweinshaxen, Wurst salad, and Schnitzel. The truly enormous platters consist of the main course plus side dishes (Sauerkraut, vegetables, potatoes).

TY BREIZH, Kantstrasse 75. Tel. 323 99 32.

Cuisine: FRENCH **U-Bahn:** Wilmersdorfer Strasse, about a 4-minute walk.

$ Prices: 5.50–24.50 DM ($3.35–$14.85). Cash only.

Open: Daily 6pm–midnight.

One of the cheapest places in town for French food, the slightly rustic Ty Breizh looks more like a bar or campus pizza parlor than a restaurant specializing in dishes from Brittany. Owner Patrick Mattei also serves as chef, and he has created an appetizer of mushrooms with shrimp and cheese. Other dishes include a casserole of eggplant, paprika, onions, and tomatoes; beef cooked in a rich Burgundy wine sauce with onions, carrots, and butter noodles; omelets; quiches; and crêpes. The fish soup is especially recommended. Diners are serenaded every evening by a guitar player named Richard.

BUDGET

All these budget-priced restaurants and stand-up eateries are located on Wilmersdorfer Strasse, Berlin's main pedestrians-only shopping lane.

DIE BUFFETERIA, Quelle department store, Wilmersdorfer Strasse 50. Tel. 31 51 11.

Cuisine: GERMAN **U-Bahn:** Wilmersdorfer Strasse, a 1-minute walk.

$ Prices: 9–12 DM ($5.45–$7.25). Cash only.

Open: Mon–Fri 9am–6pm (Thurs to 8pm), Sat 9am–2pm (to 6pm first Sat of the month).

Situated on the second floor of Quelle department store, this cheerful cafeteria has a predominantly white interior designed to induce a summertime atmosphere. The overall effect, however, is a bit kitschy, probably because of all those fake plants and all that white latticework. No matter. Die Buffeteria offers a wide variety of daily specials, which might include grilled chicken, steak, pork Gulasch, Schnitzel, curried lamb ragoût, and Sauerbraten. There's also a help-yourself salad bar, as well as a selection of soups, and beer is available. There's even a no-smoking section, rare in Germany's restaurants. Breakfast is served until 11am.

JOSEPH LANGER, Wilmersdorfer Strasse 118. Tel. 31 67 80.

Cuisine: GERMAN **U-Bahn:** Wilmersdorfer Strasse, a 1-minute walk.

$ Prices: 1.40–7 DM (85¢–$4.25). Cash only.

Open: Mon–Fri 9am–6:30pm, Sat 8:30am–2pm (to 6pm first Sat of the month).

Joseph Langer is a butcher shop that also sells simple and inexpensive meals, specializing of course in its own meats. You can order take-out or eat standing up at one of the chest-high tables. The cheapest item on the menu is a pair of Würste for 1.40 DM (85¢), and other offerings include Leberkäs, Gulasch soup, Schnitzel, Eisbein, Boulette, and potato salad.

KARSTADT, Wilmersdorfer Strasse 109-111. Tel. 31 891.

Cuisine: GERMAN **U-Bahn:** Wilmersdorfer Strasse, a 1-minute walk.

$ Prices: 6–15 DM ($3.65–$9.10). Cash only.

Open: Mon–Fri 9am–6pm (Thurs to 8:30pm), Sat 9am–2pm (to 6pm first Sat of the month).

Karstadt is another large department store on Wilmersdorfer Strasse, with an inexpensive restaurant on the fourth floor called simply Restaurant-Café. A waitress will take your order, which may consist of a daily special such as Schnitzel, Rumpsteak, fish filet with rémoulade, chicken fricassee, or spaghetti; most specials start at about 8 DM ($4.85) for a complete meal. There's also a salad bar, and you can order breakfast until 11:30am.

NORDSEE, Wilmersdorfer Strasse 58. Tel. 323 10 44.

Cuisine: SEAFOOD **U-Bahn:** Wilmersdorfer Strasse, a 1-minute walk.

$ Prices: 6–10 DM ($3.65–$6.05). Cash only.

Open: Mon–Fri 9am–7pm, Sat 9am–3pm (to 6:30pm first Sat of the month).

Nordsee is a chain of fast-food fish restaurants that originated in northern Germany. They've made ordering easy, with the menu illustrated on the wall behind the cashier—simply go through the cafeteria line and order one of the dozen choices available, such as fried haddock, herring, fish sticks, or fish soup. There's also take-out service, including all kinds of fish sandwiches starting at around 2 DM ($1.20).

ROGACKI, Wilmersdorfer Strasse 145-146. Tel. 341 40 91.
  Cuisine: GERMAN **U-Bahn:** Bismarckstrasse, a 1-minute walk.
$ Prices: 2–8 DM ($1.20–$4.85). Cash only.
  Open: Mon–Fri 9am–6pm, Sat 8am–2pm.

Another butcher shop that sells ready-to-eat meals that can be eaten at chest-high tables, Rogacki devotes most of its considerable space to retail, with glass cases displaying all kinds of meats, Würste, fish, cheeses, breads, and more. Walk toward the back left corner of the shop, where the self-service counter offers a great variety of dishes at prices that must surely be among the lowest in Berlin. No wonder the place has been around for more than 60 years and is still going strong. Entrées may include pig's knuckle, fish, grilled chicken, Wurst, salads, stews. And there are changing daily menus. Located about a 7-minute walk north of the pedestrian shopping section of Wilmersdorfer Strasse, between Bismarckstrasse and Zillestrasse, Rogacki has a picture of a blue fish on its facade.

5. NEAR HARDENBERGSTRASSE & THE TECHNICAL UNIVERSITY

Hardenbergstrasse leads northwest from Bahnhof Zoo, past the Technical University to Ernst-Reuter-Platz, Bismarckstrasse, and Strasse des 17. Juni. Because of the many students in the area, there are a number of inexpensive restaurants here. Keep in mind, too, that Savignyplatz and its immediate surroundings are never more than a 10-minute walk from Hardenbergstrasse; there you'll find a number of restaurants in all price categories described above under "On or Near the Ku'damm." These include Carmer's, Florian, Paris Bar, Friesenhof, San Marino, Shell, Jahrmarkt, Korfu, and Ashoka.

INEXPENSIVE

CAFÉ HARDENBERG, Hardenbergstrasse 10. Tel. 312 33 30.
  Cuisine: GERMAN/INTERNATIONAL **U-Bahn:** Ernst-Reuter-Platz, less than a 3-minute walk.
$ Prices: 8–14 DM ($4.85–$8.50). Cash only.
  Open: Daily 9am–midnight.

★ Less than a 10-minute walk from Bahnhof Zoo, and across the street from the Technical University, this popular café is always packed with students and people who work nearby. Decorated with museum posters, plants, and ceiling fans, it serves as a coffeehouse, a restaurant, and, in the evening, a bar. In summer, there are tables and chairs outside. Classical music is played through the sound system until 4pm, after which music of the 20th century takes over. It's a good place for a meal, since portions are hearty and the menu includes an interesting range of dishes that change daily. Your choice can range from spaghetti or a huge Greek salad to an omelet, dolmades, pork chops, or chili con carne.

BUDGET

CIAO ITALIA, Goethestrasse 84. Tel. 313 76 67.
   Cuisine: ITALIAN   **U-Bahn:** Ernst-Reuter-Platz, a 5-minute walk.
$ **Prices:** 7–10 DM ($4.25–$6.05). Cash only.
   Open: Mon–Sat 9am–midnight.

Ⓢ It would be easy to walk right by this tiny place and never know that it harbored a counter with a variety of pasta dishes, along with a few tables and chairs where you can eat your goodies. That's because it actually is a shop, with walls unceremoniously lined with packages of noodles and bottles of wine. There's hardly room for diners, but people in the know come here for some of the cheapest and best pasta in town, which may range from tortellini and ravioli to rigatoni and lasagne. After selecting a pasta at the counter, diners can then choose one of four sauces: tomato, mushroom, gorgonzola, or meat. There are also olives for sale, and wine by the glass. Because this place is so small, try to eat during the off hours. You'll find it at the corner of Goethe and Knesebeck streets, about a 5-minute walk north of Savignyplatz or a 10-minute walk north of the Ku'damm.

IHRE FRISCH BACKSTÜBE, Knesebeckstrasse 12. Tel. 31 06 00.
   Cuisine: GERMAN   **U-Bahn:** Ernst-Reuter-Platz, about a 5-minute walk.
$ **Prices:** 2–6 DM ($1.20–$3.65). Cash only.
   Open: Mon–Sat 6:30am–6:30pm, Sun noon–6:30pm.
Located catty-corner from Ciao Italia (above), this bakery also has a self-service counter serving good take-out or eat-in food. There are several varieties of breads and cakes, of course, as well as pizza by the slice, sandwiches, and a changing menu of warm dishes, which may range from smoked pork chops to Leberkäs and Sauerkraut. The dining area is cheerful.

MENSA, Technische Universität, Hardenbergstrasse 34.
   Cuisine: GERMAN   **U-Bahn:** Ernst-Reuter-Platz, a few minutes' walk.

$ Prices: 2.70–4 DM ($1.65–$2.40). Cash only.
Open: Mon–Fri 11:15am–2:30pm.

Ⓢ A student cafeteria of the Technical University, the Mensa has a self-service restaurant on the top floor that will serve fixed-price meals to anyone, students and nonstudents alike. Simply walk through the ground floor of the Mensa (past the ticket booths selling cheaper meals to students only) and then follow the signs for *Restaurant* up the stairs. Pick up a tray and choose from one of the changing daily menus, complete meals that may range from Gulasch stew or curried rice to liver or a vegetarian ragoût. Although the dining area has that unmistakable cafeteria look and feel to it, this is one of the cheapest places in Berlin for a complete meal. It's located about a 10-minute walk from Bahnhof Zoo.

6. IN EAST BERLIN

In addition to the establishments listed here, there are several fine hotel restaurants described in the "Hotel Dining" section later in this chapter. In addition, several of the bars listed in the nightlife section serve food.

EXPENSIVE

APHRODITE, Schönhauser Allee 61. Tel. 448 17 07.
   Cuisine: NOUVELLE GERMAN   **Reservation:** An absolute necessity. **U-Bahn:** Schönhauser Allee, less than a 5-minute walk.
$ Prices: Fixed-price dinners 40 and 45 DM ($24.25–$27.25). Cash only.
   Open: Tues–Sat 4pm–midnight.

★ This was one of the first privately owned restaurants to open in Berlin (predating even the November 1989 revolution) and was an instant success. A long, narrow dining hall with chandeliers and stucco details on the walls, as well as candles on each table and white tablecloths, it has a reputation good enough to pull in diners from all corners of Berlin, making it imperative to make a reservation in advance. East Berliners dress up in their finest to come here, and you'll probably want to do the same.

The handwritten menu offers two fixed-price menus, which change monthly. The less expensive one is a four-course dinner, which may include an appetizer of carpaccio or tuna with a mousse of trout, followed by sweet-and-sour soup, pork chops baked in a crispy dough and served with vegetables, and ice cream. Since there isn't much choice, you may wish to inquire beforehand about the menu, but my guess is that anything offered will be a treat. Hopefully, Aphrodite is an indication of things to come in East Berlin.

RESTAURANT EPHRAIM-PALAIS, Poststrasse 16, Nikolaiviertel. Tel. 217 13 164 or 217 13 296.
  Cuisine: GERMAN/CONTINENTAL **Reservations:** Imperative. **U-Bahn:** Klosterstrasse, about a 7-minute walk.
$ Prices: Appetizers and soups 5–15 DM ($3.05–$9.10), entrées 15–60 DM ($9.10–$36.35). Cash only.
  Open: Daily 11am–midnight.

Situated in the Nikolaiviertel (Nikolai Quarter) of East Berlin just off Alexanderplatz near the Rathaus, this very fine restaurant is decorated like a palace. In fact, it's an exact replica of Ephraim-Palais, built for a man named Veitel Ephraim who worked as court jeweler to Frederick II. Rococo inside and out, with an ornate facade and shimmering chandeliers in dining halls that resemble a nobleman's drawing rooms, it recalls an atmosphere of yesterday, with waiters dressed in black coat and tie. A classy place, so dress accordingly. The menu changes weekly, but always includes selections of fish, steak, veal, and pork, all traditionally cooked in ways you'll find familiar.

RESTAURANT MOSKAU, Karl-Marx-Allee 34. Tel. 279 28 69.
  Cuisine: RUSSIAN **Reservations:** A must for dinner, recommended for lunch. **U-Bahn:** Schillingstrasse, a 1-minute walk.
$ Prices: Appetizers and soups 5–15 DM ($3.05–$9.10), entrées 15–50 DM ($9.10–$30.30). Cash only.
  Open: Daily 11am–11pm.

About a 10-minute walk from Alexanderplatz on one of East Berlin's main thoroughfares, this large restaurant is located in a modern building but still manages to evoke an old-world atmosphere. A stylish place with flowers, white lacy curtains, and attentive waiters, it's considered one of Berlin's premier Russian restaurants. At dinner, patrons are treated to live piano and violin music. The same building also houses a bar with international shows, plus a Tanzcafé (dance café), open in the evenings.

  The specialties of the restaurant are soups such as borscht and soljanka, while entrées include duck breast, stuffed pork cutlet, beef Stroganoff, fish, chicken Kiev, and roast lamb. And who could resist Russian vodka?

MODERATE

ERMELER HAUS, Märkisches Ufer 10. Tel. 279 36 17.
  Cuisine: GERMAN/CONTINENTAL **U-Bahn:** Märkisches Museum, a few minutes' walk.
$ Prices: 15–35 DM ($9.10–$21.20). Cash only.
  Open: Daily 11am–midnight.

This ornate, rococo-style house, once the private residence of a merchant, has been one of Berlin's best-known restaurants for more than two decades. Facing a canal and located about a 15-minute walk southwest of Alexanderplatz, it's actually two restaurants in one. In the basement you'll find a rustic pub-style place with wooden tables serving hearty platters of typical German fare, including pork cutlets

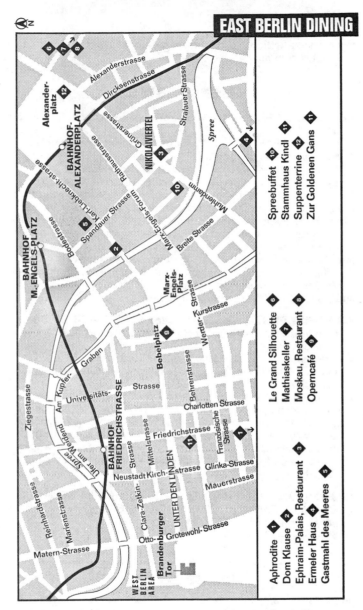

Aphrodite 1
Dom Klause 2
Ephraim-Palais, Restaurant 3
Ermeler Haus 4
Gastmahl des Meeres 5

Le Grand Silhouette 6
Mathiaskeller 7
Moskau, Restaurant 8
Opercafé 9

Spreebuffet 10
Stammhaus Kindl 11
Suppenterrine 12
Zur Goldenen Gans 11

and Eisbein, at reasonable prices. Or you may prefer the much finer wine restaurant up on the first floor; its fish and seasonal international dishes are at slightly higher prices. On the ground floor there's also an elegant café, where in the afternoon you can relax to the sound of the violin. In the evening from 7pm to midnight, Tuesday through Saturday, the café turns into a dance hall for middle-aged Berliners, who come to dance to records popular in their youth. On Friday and Saturday nights, the first-floor restaurant also has dancing. Because this is one of Berlin's most popular spots for a night out, be sure to make a reservation.

INEXPENSIVE

GASTMAHL DES MEERES, Spandauer Strasse 4. Tel. 213 32 86.
    Cuisine: SEAFOOD   **U-Bahn** or   **S-Bahn:** Alexanderplatz.
$ Prices: 11–18 DM ($6.65–$10.90). Cash only.
    Open: Mon–Sat 11am–midnight, Sun 11am–4pm.
Easily recognizable by its large stained-glass facade, Gastmahl des Meeres specializes in a wide variety of fresh fish, with a menu that changes daily according to what's available. This usually includes trout, carp, flounder, herring, and mackerel, prepared in several styles. Because of the restaurant's convenient location on the corner of Karl-Liebknecht-Strasse between Alexanderplatz and Museumsinsel (Museum Island), there are often queues for a table. If it's full, you might try the Korallenbar in the basement, a combination bar/restaurant with slightly higher prices. It doesn't open until 4pm, and it's closed on Mondays and Tuesdays.

MATHIASKELLER, Karl-Marx-Allee 91. Tel. 436 21 89.
    Cuisine: HUNGARIAN   **U-Bahn:** Marchlewskistrasse, about a 3-minute walk.
$ Prices: 6.50–13 DM ($3.95–$7.85). Cash only.
    Open: Lunch Fri–Sun 11:30am–3pm; dinner daily 6pm–midnight.
Located in the basement of Haus Budapest, this Hungarian restaurant has a friendly staff, plus live music every night except Monday. Brightly decorated in red and black, it offers a very piquant goulash soup, as well as such favorites as paprika chicken, crispy roast duck, trout, pork medallions, and roast beef. Since the place is a good 20-minute walk from Alexanderplatz, you'll probably want to take the U-Bahn.

OPERNCAFÉ, Unter den Linden 5. Tel. 200 02 56.
    Cuisine: GERMAN/CONTINENTAL   **S-Bahn:** Friedrichstrasse, about a 10-minute walk.
$ Prices: 7–23 DM ($4.25–$13.95). Cash only.

IMPRESSIONS

In the Berlin cafés and restaurants the busy time is from midnight on till three. Yet most of the people who frequent them are up again at seven. Either the Berliner has solved the great problem of modern life, how to do without sleep, or, with Carlyle, he must be looking forward to eternity.
    —JEROME K. JEROME, 1900

Think of the man who first tried German sausage.
    —JEROME K. JEROME, 1889

Open: Daily 11am–midnight.

There are two restaurants up on the second floor of East Berlin's most famous coffeehouse (see "Coffeehouses" below). The Grill-restaurant and the Weinrestaurant both offer the same menu, which includes fricassee of chicken with mushrooms, grilled chicken, duck, Eisbein, pork cutlet, steak, and a ragoût with cheese and hollandaise. I personally prefer the Weinrestaurant because it's a bit more formal, but there is very little difference between the two. You may find yourself glad for a seat in either, since this is a popular place. The ground floor café serves snacks and desserts, with outdoor seating in the square.

BUDGET

SPREEBUFFET, Spree Ufer, Nikolaiviertel. Tel. 217 13 331.
   Cuisine: GERMAN   **U-Bahn:** Klosterstrasse, about a 7-minute walk.
$ Prices: 6–10 DM ($3.65–$6.05). Cash only.
   Open: Tues–Sun 10am–7pm.

This simple cafeteria, with an outdoor sign that reads *SB Restaurant*, is located in the renovated Nikolaiviertel (Nikolai Quarter) on the bank of the Spree River. In nice weather, you may wish to order a beer and sausages from its open-air counter and sit at one of the outdoor tables. Otherwise, there's an indoor cafeteria line where you can pick up simply prepared fare such as salads, soups, stews, and noodle dishes. Not a lot of choice, but this is one of the cheapest eating establishments in the area.

SUPPENTERRINE, Alexanderplatz 2. Tel. 212 40 32.
   Cuisine: GERMAN   **S-Bahn** and   **U-Bahn:** Alexanderplatz.
$ Prices: 2–4 DM ($1.20–$2.40). Cash only.
   Open: Mon–Fri 10am–8pm, Sat 9am–3pm.

Conveniently situated in the heart of East Berlin right on Alexanderplatz, this simple place specializes in one-pot stews, called *Eintöpfe* in German. Diners sit at U-shaped counters, while those waiting for seats simply stand against the wall until places become vacant. The stews change frequently, but may include Linseneintopf (lentil stew), Hungarian Gulasch, Sauerkraut soup, potato soup, or Serbian bean soup. Just around the corner from the restaurant in an adjoining room is a bar popular with workers in the area.

7. IN DAHLEM

MODERATE

ALTER KRUG DAHLEM, Königin-Luise-Strasse 52. Tel. 832 50 89.

Cuisine: GERMAN   **U-Bahn:** Dahlmen-Dorf, about a 2-minute walk.

$ Prices: Appetizers and soups 8–16 DM ($4.85–$9.70), entrées 15–37 DM ($9.10–$22.40). DC, MC, V.

Open: Mon–Wed, Fri and Sat noon–midnight, Sun noon–10pm.

This pleasant German restaurant—convenient if you're visiting the many museums in Dahlem (to reach the restaurant, turn left out of the U-Bahn station instead of right as you do for the museums)—is decorated in typical Teutonic fashion, with a low, open-beamed ceiling, ceramic-tile heater in the middle of the dining hall, cheerful yellow tablecloths, and candles on each table. In summer there's outdoor seating in the backyard garden. The menu includes such favorites as turkey breast, trout, salmon, veal Schnitzel, beef Stroganoff, pork chops, and lamb cutlets. The huge salads are meals in themselves. Since the restaurant also serves as a retailer of wines from all over Germany, it keeps a large stock on hand. If you're interested in a specific wine from a specific region—Baden, Württemberg, Franken, Mosel, Saar, Rheingau, or Rheinhessen—you might strike it lucky here.

8. NEAR SCHLOSS CHARLOTTENBURG

INEXPENSIVE

LUISEN-BRÄU, Luisenplatz 1. Tel. 341 93 88.

Cuisine: GERMAN   **Bus:** 9 from Bahnhof Zoologischer Garten or Kurfürstendamm to Schloss Charlottenburg, then a half-minute walk.

$ Prices: 8–20 DM ($4.85–$12.10). Cash only.

Open: Daily 11am–midnight.

What better place to round off a day of museum sightseeing than at a brewery—this one conveniently located southeast of Schloss Charlottenburg, at the corner of Spandauer Damm. Nice, cheerful, and rustic, it has large windows and paneled walls, with the primary decoration provided by stainless-steel tanks of beer brewing at one end of the room. Customers sit at long wooden tables, and since you're expected to sit wherever there's an empty seat, the close contact with strangers makes it easy to strike up conversations, especially after the downing of a few beers. A small glass of the brew costs 2.60 DM ($1.55). As for the food, it's served buffet style, with the price of meats dependent on the weight of the slice you order, just as in a butcher shop. Slices of Schweinebraten, Kasseler Rippenspeer, Leberkäs, Boulette, and Schweinshaxen are priced in 100-gram increments. There are also stews and salads, but if all you want is a beer, that's perfectly acceptable in a brewery. In summer there's outdoor seating.

9. NEAR RATHAUS SCHÖNEBERG

Both these restaurants are convenient if you're visiting Rathaus Schöneberg.

INEXPENSIVE

MASKERA, Koburger Strasse 5. Tel. 784 12 27.
Cuisine: VEGETARIAN **U-Bahn:** Rathaus Schöneberg, about a 5-minute walk.
$ Prices: 11.50–28 DM ($6.95–$16.95). Cash only.
Open: Daily 4pm–1am (food served from 5pm).

Opened back in 1972, this simple vegetarian restaurant is firmly entrenched in Berlin's alternative scene, evident from the placards and posters advertising yoga classes, natural childbearing, and other health-related services on its public bulletin board. Maskera is run by a German-Italian-Dutch cooperative whose goal is to introduce vegetarian cooking to an ever larger public, which it does by using such familiar European staples as vegetables, grains, milk products and eggs (and thus it is not vegetarian in the strictest sense of the word). The grains for its breads, pizzas, and noodles are ground daily on a stone mill. Specialties of the house include whole-meal pizzas, homemade whole-meal noodles, vegetable soufflé, and tofu creations. Since dishes are made to order, dine here when you have time to enjoy it.

BUDGET

KASINO BEIM SENATOR FÜR WIRTSCHAFT UND VERKEHR, Martin-Luther-Strasse 105. Tel. 784 77 24.
Cuisine: GERMAN **U-Bahn:** Rathaus Schöneberg, about a 4-minute walk.
$ Prices: Fixed-price lunches 4.80–6 DM ($2.90–$3.65). Cash only.
Open: Mon–Fri 11:30am–2pm.

Down the street from the Rathaus Schöneberg is the administration building for trade and industry (look for the sign on the front door that says *Senatsverwaltung für Wirtschaft*). Up on the fifth floor is a cafeteria for building employees, but it's open to the general public as well. Take the elevator and then follow the sign that says *Zur Kantine* (it won't look as if there's a restaurant when you step out of the elevator). Popular with young and old alike, this cantine offers two set meals a day, as well as one stew for 2.75 DM ($1.65). The menu changes daily, but past meals have included Schweinebraten with red cabbage and potatoes, stuffed cabbage rolls with potatoes, Gulasch with mushrooms and noodles, and grilled trout with salad and potatoes.

10. NEAR NOLLENDORFPLATZ

BUDGET

ZUM AMBROSIUS, Einemstrasse 14. Tel. 261 29 93.
   Cuisine: GERMAN   **U-Bahn:** Nollendorfplatz, about a 5-minute walk.
$ Prices: 7–15 DM ($4.25–$9.10). Cash only.
   Open: Daily 11:30am–11:30pm.

Ⓢ   Zum Ambrosius is a real working-class pub, or Gaststätte, simple and unpretentious, where servings are monstrous enough to satisfy even the most voracious appetites. On the corner of Einemstrasse and Kurfürstenstrasse, the place has been here for more than 50 years, dishing out such Berliner specialties as Eisbein with puréed peas, Sauerkraut, and potatoes; Schnitzel; Schlachteplatte (blood and liver sausage with Sauerkraut); Schweinebraten; Leberknödl; Sülze with rémoulade, salad, and grilled potatoes; Leberkäs; and Bauernfrühstück (an omelet, with potatoes, sausage, and onions). Most platters are priced under 11 DM ($6.65). In summer there's dining outdoors.

ZUR NOLLE, above Nollendorfplatz U-Bahn station, Nollendorfplatz. Tel. 216 75 46.
   Cuisine: GERMAN   **U-Bahn:** Nollendorfplatz, above the station.
$ Prices: 6–14 DM ($3.65–$8.50). Cash only.
   Open: Wed–Mon 11am–7pm.

This restaurant/bar is right above the U-Bahn station, in a flea market called Die Nolle, which spreads over the length of a defunct upper platform. Zur Nolle occupies one end of the platform, with seating on a large terrace and even in some old train compartments on the tracks. A good place for some refreshment after antiques hunting, it serves such dishes as Boulette with bread, Kasseler Braten, Schweinebraten, Brathering, and Sülze with bread, along with such daily specials as chicken breast served with mushrooms and rice, Hungarian goulash, tortellini with spinach and ham, and quiche. The best time to come is on Sunday from noon to 6pm, when there's live Dixieland jazz—but be sure to make a reservation beforehand for this popular event.

11. IN KREUZBERG

INEXPENSIVE

GROSSBEERENKELLER, Grossbeerenkeller 90. Tel. 251 30 64.
   Cuisine: GERMAN.   **U-Bahn:** Möckernbrücke, less than a 5-minute walk.

$ Prices: 12–29 DM ($7.25–$17.55). Cash only.
Open: Mon–Fri 4pm–2am, Sat 6pm–2am. **Closed:** Sun and holidays.

There used to be hundreds of places like this in Berlin before World War II—simple, smoky bars peopled by the famous, the infamous, stars, artists, and politicians. Most of these bars were destroyed in the war, but Grossbeerenkeller survived and is now more than a century old, evident in its aged wooden ceiling and walls, which are hardly visible because of the photos of theater personalities who have been here. Theater-goers still stop in for a late-night meal, dining on the good home-style cooking for which this basement establishment is famous: simple and inexpensive dishes such as Berliner Wurst salad with grilled potatoes, Leberkäs, and Bauernfrühstück, as well as Schnitzel, Rumpsteak, fish, and Sülze. If you want to dine at the Grossbeerenkeller later than 7pm, you would be wise to make a reservation.

HENNE, Leuschnerdamm 25. Tel. 614 77 30.
Cuisine: CHICKEN **Reservations:** Imperative. **U-Bahn:** Moritzplatz, an 8-minute walk.
$ Prices: 3–10 DM ($1.80–$6.05). Cash only.
Open: Wed–Sun 7pm–midnight.

One of the things that used to make Henne unique was its location smack beside the Wall. But even though the Wall is history, the restaurant is no less popular, for it turns out what is probably Berlin's best grilled chicken (*Henne* means hen), with deliciously crispy skin. In fact, that's the only thing served, barring side orders of potato salad and Kraut salad. The beer's good too, especially the dark Klosterschwarzbier, and the ambience is even better. The place is packed with everyone from students to professionals in business suits; reservations are an absolute necessity. The restaurant itself looks ancient, with brown spotted walls, a clock that runs a few hours late, antlers everywhere, an elaborate wooden bar, and against one wall, small wooden barrels that used to hold grog, raspberry juice, and other unlikely concoctions. The whole place reminds me of some long-neglected hunting lodge. Incidentally, behind the bar hangs a photo of John F. Kennedy, who was invited to Henne during his Berlin trip. He didn't eat here, but he did send a letter of apology.

12. ELSEWHERE IN BERLIN

VERY EXPENSIVE

ROCKENDORF'S RESTAURANT, Düsterhauptstrasse 1. Tel. 402 30 99.
Cuisine: FRENCH **Reservations:** A necessity.
Directions: A 10-minute taxi ride from city center.
$ Prices: Fixed-price lunches 93–105 DM ($56.35–$63.65);

fixed-price dinners 170–210 DM ($103–$127.25). AE, DC, MC, V.

Open: Tues–Sat noon–2 and 7–midnight.

⭐ Rockendorf's is reputedly the best and most expensive restaurant in all of Berlin. Proof that this could well be true lies in the parking lot outside—it's jam-packed with Mercedeses, Porsches, and Jaguars. Occupying the first floor of a restored Jugendstil villa, the restaurant can be entered only after ringing the front-door bell, whereupon diners are ushered upstairs. Plush yet understated, this is where Berlin's top echelon have their business luncheons or come for a romantic evening. The service, of course, is the best that money can buy.

The kitchen is under the direction of the restaurant's namesake, chef Siegfried Rockendorf. He offers only complete meals, which range from three to six courses at lunch; there are both a six-course menu and a nine-course menu at dinner. Rockendorf has such an unblemished record that diners are comfortable leaving everything to him. A handwritten bill of fare (in German) changes every day, with an emphasis on the seasons, including wild game in winter. Lunch may start off with asparagus with truffles, followed in succession by flounder in curry butter with wild rice; rack of lamb with thyme, artichokes, and tomatoes; and a Grand Marnier parfait and petits fours. Dinner is even more elaborate, and may include the likes of pigeon breast with Périgord truffles; deer with cranberries and a purée of brussels sprouts; or lobster lasagne with mussels in a cognac sauce.

EXPENSIVE

TAFELRUNDE, Nachodstrasse 21. Tel. 211 21 41.
  Cuisine: GERMAN **Reservations:** Recommended, especially on weekends and before Christmas. **U-Bahn:** Spichernstrasse, less than a 5-minute walk.
$ Prices: Fixed-price dinner 65.50 DM ($39.65). Cash only.
  Open: Daily 6pm–midnight.

Dining as it was in the Middle Ages—that's the theme of the Tafelrunde (Round Table). Diners are given only a special knife, just as in the good old days, and are expected to eat with their fingers. Bibs are passed out just in case. The simple dining halls, in the spirit of the times, have only long wooden tables and chairs, although the building itself is modern. It's about a 15-minute walk south of the Ku'damm, or only one stop away by U-Bahn.

Only one fixed meal is served, changing several times a month and centering on different themes, with entertainment provided by the staff. Usually a seven-course meal, it starts with a drink from a cow's horn, loaves of bread, soup, and appetizers. These are followed by a main course such as Spiessbraten (shish kebab) or Spanferkel (suckling pig), a surprise dish, and cheese and fruit.

MODERATE

BLOCKHAUS NIKOLSKOE, Nikolskoer Weg, Wannsee. Tel. 805 29 14.

Cuisine: GERMAN **S-Bahn:** Wannsee station, then a bus bound for Pfaueninsel to Nikolskoe stop.

$ Prices: 15–30 DM ($9.10–$18.20). DC, MC, V.

Open: Summer, Fri–Wed 10am–10pm; winter, Fri–Wed 10am–8pm.

Generations of Berliners have eaten at this rustic log cabin, perched on a wooded hill with sweeping views of Havel Lake. The origins of the cabin, with its carved wooden eaves, date back to 1819, when Friedrich Wilhelm III had it built in Russian style as a surprise for his daughter, Charlotte, married to a Russian prince who later became Tsar Nicholas I. The entire dining room is of unfinished wood, from the walls and ceiling to the floor and furniture; a ceramic-tiled heater (*Kachelofen*) warms customers on wintry days. (If the cabin looks suspiciously new, that's because it is—the original was destroyed by a fire in 1984, and this one is a faithful copy.) The hearty German fare includes large portions of Schnitzel, Eisbein, steak, fish, Hungarian goulash, and daily specials. In summer you may wish to dine on the terrace overlooking the lake. The only disadvantage: Blockhaus Nikolskoe is a bit isolated and difficult to reach. The bus that travels between Wannsee station and the restaurant leaves only once an hour, even less frequently in winter. From April through October, your best bet is to take one of the excursion boats that ply the Havel from Wannsee station to the Pfaueninsel stop, from which it's about a 10-minute walk. Along the footpath you'll pass Peter-Pauls-Kirche, a Russian Orthodox church built in the 1830s.

13. SPECIALTY DINING

HOTEL DINING

ON OR NEAR THE KU'DAMM

BELLE EPOQUE, Savoy Hotel, Fasanenstrasse 9–10. Tel. 31 10 30.

Cuisine: FRENCH **Reservations:** Recommended.

U-Bahn: Bahnhof Zoologischer Garten, a 3-minute walk; Kurfürstendamm, a 4-minute walk.

$ Prices: Appetizers 16–23 DM ($9.70–$13.95), entrées 20–39 DM ($12.10–$23.65). AE, DC, MC, V.

Open: Daily noon–11:30pm.

Light, airy, and elegant, with crystal chandeliers hanging from the high ceilings, the Belle Epoque looks turn of the century but is actually new. Piano music serenades diners in the evenings, making it a popular place for dinner before or after attending one of the many theaters in the area. The cuisine is light and healthful, with an emphasis on seasonal changes. You might opt for a salad with mushrooms, avocados, and grapefruit, or an appetizer of pike pâté with broccoli and salmon. Main courses include tender roast chicken, prepared with mushrooms and steamed chicory and covered

---

(F) FROMMER'S COOL FOR KIDS
Restaurants

Jimmy's Diner *(see p. 106)* Is your teenager bugging you for a hamburger or some "real" food? Head for this '50s-style diner, which offers hamburgers, sandwiches, chicken, spaghetti, and Mexican food. The diner's clientele, mainly Berlin teenagers striving for just the right look in punk, leather, or '50s clothing, will keep you all entertained as you dine.

Piccola Taormina Tavola Calda *(see p. 107)* One of the cheapest places in town for pizza, which you can order take-out by the slice or eat at one of the simple wooden tables. Also spaghetti, lasagne, and risotto dishes.

Zitadelle *(see p. 225)* Older kids love the drama of this place—a medieval setting in a 700-year-old fortress in Spandau, where customers even eat with their fingers. Expensive, but an evening you won't forget.

Alter Markt in the Hotel Schweizerhof *(see p. 130)* A good place for Sunday brunch, with special prices for kids. There's live jazz for adults, and for children there's a special children's corner, with toys, balloons, and other surprises.

---

with flaky pastry; breaded veal with fresh herbs, zucchini, and spinach noodles; lamb cutlet with basil sauce, spinach, and cornmeal pancakes; grilled salmon with asparagus, morels, hollandaise, and potatoes; fried sole with marinated salmon and capers; and breast of duck in orange sauce with morello cherries, kenya beans, and potato pancakes. Leave room for dessert, which might be fresh fruit flambée with black-currant sorbet, or marinated figs over gooseberry mousse with black-currant ice cream.

BERLINER STUBE, Steigenberger Hotel, Los-Angeles-Platz 1. Tel. 210 80.
  Cuisine: GERMAN **Reservations:** Not necessary. **U-Bahn:** Kurfürstendamm, a 2-minute walk.
$ **Prices:** Appetizers and soups 5–20 DM ($3.05–$12.10), entrées 12–35 DM ($7.25–$21.20). AE, DC, MC, V.
  Open: Daily noon–3pm and 6–11:30pm.

Designed to resemble an old-style Berliner pub, this rustic eatery specializes in typical German home-cooked meals. The English menu makes ordering easy, with selections ranging from smoked eel and roasted herring to lamb stew, Königsberger Klopse (meatballs in a caper sauce), knuckle of pork, and steak. There are several fish choices, from poached halibut to roasted salmon steak. You may wish to take advantage of the special lunch, which changes daily and offers a complete meal for less than 18 DM ($10.90).

PARK RESTAURANT, Steigenberger Hotel, Los-Angeles-Platz 1. Tel. 210 80.
   Cuisine: NOUVELLE FRENCH **Reservations:** Recommended, especially on Fridays. **U-Bahn:** Kurfürstendamm, a 2-minute walk.
$ Prices: Appetizers and soups 11–30 DM ($6.65–$18.20), entrées 30–52 DM ($18.20–$31.50). AE, DC, MC, V.
   Open: Tues–Sun 6pm–midnight.

The Steigenberger's premier restaurant, the spacious and modern Park is decorated in a soothing mauve color scheme. The menu, an interesting array of nouvelle French cuisine, offers many steak and seafood choices. The popular Friday night champagne dinner, a six-course meal, includes as much bubbly as you can drink for 125 DM ($75.75). There's piano music nightly, and an adjoining cocktail bar opens at 5pm for happy hour.

KEMPINSKI GRILL, Bristol Hotel Kempinski, Kurfürstendamm 27. Tel. 88 43 40.
   Cuisine: GERMAN/FRENCH **Reservations:** A necessity.
   U-Bahn: Uhlandstrasse, a 1-minute walk.
$ Prices: Appetizers and soups 12–29 DM ($7.25–$17.55); fixed-price lunch 45 DM ($27.25), fixed-price dinner 115 DM ($69.70). AE, DC, MC, V.
   Open: Mon–Sat noon–3pm and 6pm–2am.

Long an old standby, the Kempinski Grill gives pleasure with both its superb service and its fine cuisine. A small and intimate restaurant, with seating for only 45 guests, plus a small bar, it boasts an open grill where diners can observe the chefs at work; however, many of the dishes are prepared at table. The menu changes weekly, but examples of past dishes include a terrine of trout with lobster sauce, a lobster salad with a champagne vinaigrette, consommé of tomatoes with cockles, médaillons of veal with kidneys, and rack of lamb with cabbage, brussels sprouts, carrots, and potato au gratin. Especially good are the fixed-price lunches and dinners.

IN EAST BERLIN

East Berlin's finest restaurants are hotel restaurants. These are among the best.

DOM KLAUSE, Palasthotel, Karl-Liebknecht-Strasse 5. Tel. 241 22 68.
   Cuisine: GERMAN **Reservations:** Recommended.
   S-Bahn: Alexanderplatz, less than a 10-minute walk.
$ Prices: Appetizers and soups 3–25 DM ($1.80–$15.15), entrées 14.50–43 DM ($8.80–$26.05). AE, DC, MC, V.
   Open: Daily 11am–midnight.

Anyone can feel at home in this comfortable German restaurant, conveniently located near Museumsinsel (Museum Island) and with a view of the Berliner Dom. There's even an English menu. Dom Klause serves traditional German fare, including pickled knuckle of pork with "mushy" peas (obviously a dictionary translation), Sauerkraut, and boiled potatoes; roast lamb; rump of beef with raisin sauce; roast chicken; trout; and pike perch. There's outdoor dining in summer, with tables set up beside the Spree River.

LE GRAND SILHOUETTE, Grand Hotel, Friedrichstrasse 158-164. Tel. 209 23 253.

    Cuisine: FRENCH   **Reservations:** A necessity. **S-Bahn:** Friedrichstrasse.

$ Prices: Appetizers 16–28 DM ($9.70–$16.95), entrées 27–85 DM ($16.35–$51.50). AE, DC, MC, V.

    Open: Daily noon–4pm and 6:30pm–1am.

Ever since the Grand Hotel opened in 1987, Le Grand Silhouette has reigned as undisputed champion of fine cuisine in East Berlin and as one of the top restaurants in Eastern Europe. Situated on the hotel's bright and airy top floor, it has Jugendstil decor from the turn of the century. Guests usually begin their culinary journey with a predinner cocktail at the adjoining bar, where they can look over the menu and make their choices. Then it's on to one of the widely spaced tables in a bi-level dining area. Note how each table has a different place setting. Plates range from hand-painted one-of-a-kind items to those with gilded etchings; even the napkins are different, from their color and style to the way they're arranged. Common to each table, however, are orchids, a reoccurring motif throughout the Grand Hotel. From 9pm, a small band plays gentle, listenable tunes, and there's also a small dance floor.

From the English menu, diners can choose from such hors d'oeuvres as smoked fish, Baltic salmon, and iced tenderloin of beef. Entrées include calves' sweetbreads, fried duck liver, scallops in champagne on a bed of spinach, halibut filet in a cress cream, and lamb, veal, steak, and pheasant breast in a morel cream with truffles. Desserts include various mousses and soufflés, and the extensive wine list encompasses 300 different vintages from around the world. If you don't see something on the menu, chances are it can be made for you. The staff is very accommodating—the manager assured me that the restaurant stays open until the last guest is ready to leave, even if that means staying open through the night. Any takers?

STAMMHAUS KINDL, Grand Hotel, Friedrichstrasse 158-164. Tel. 209 23 253.

    Cuisine: GERMAN   **Reservations:** Not necessary.

    S-Bahn: Friedrichstrasse.

$ Prices: Appetizers 10–14 DM ($6.05–$8.50), entrées 16–53 DM ($9.70–$32.10). AE, DC, MC, V.

    Open: Daily 10am–midnight.

Under the management of the Grand Hotel, this German-style pub with brass fixtures has its own entrance on Friedrichstrasse. You may be able to find a table here when other restaurants are full. It serves typical German food, including Eisbein, Schweinshaxen in a red-wine sauce, Schnitzel, and Gulasch. And of course, there's beer to wash everything down.

ZUR GOLDENEN GANS, Grand Hotel, Friedrichstrasse 158-164. Tel. 209 23 246.

    Cuisine: GERMAN **Reservations:** A must. **S-Bahn:** Friedrichstrasse.

$ Prices: Appetizers 21–28 DM ($12.70–$16.95), entrées 23–53 DM ($13.95–$32.10). AE, DC, MC, V.

Open: Mon–Fri noon–midnight, Sat and Sun 11am–midnight.

Its name translates as the Golden Goose, and that's the specialty of this place—roast goose with Thuringian potato salad, along with other Thuringian dishes (including fish). Located one floor up from street level, the dining room is decorated like a rustic country inn, with exposed dark-wood beams and stark-white walls. Windows overlook Friedrichstrasse below. This place is so popular that it's impossible to eat here without reservations; sometimes it's booked solid weeks in advance.

DINING WITH A VIEW

PANORAMA 37, Hotel Stadt Berlin, Alexanderplatz. Tel. 219 43 47.

Cuisine: FRENCH   **Reservations:** A must.   **S-Bahn:** Alexanderplatz.

$ Prices: Appetizers and soups 7.50–21.70 DM ($4.55–$13.15), entrées 17.80–29 DM ($10.80–$17.55). AE, DC, MC, V.

Open: Daily noon–midnight.

Thirty-seven floors up and almost in the exact center of East Berlin, this French restaurant is a great place from which to watch the day fade and the lights of night take over. Its menu includes frogs' legs, escargots, filet of beef, crab ragoût, trout, chicken breast, and chateaubriand. A bar, also on the 37th floor and open at 10pm, is a romantic spot to conclude a night high over the town.

DINING CLUSTERS

As mentioned at the beginning of this chapter, the city's greatest concentration of restaurants centers around the Ku'damm, but nowhere are they more numerous than in the nearby **Europa-Center.** Easy to spot because of the Mercedes-Benz star that crowns its roof, this huge complex contains a number of German and international eateries—Japanese, Swiss, French, fast food. **I-Punkt,** is on a top floor, while **Mövenpick** coffeehouse on the ground floor spills over onto Breitscheidplatz with tables and colored umbrellas.

FAST FOOD & IMBISSE

An *Imbiss* is a food stall or a tiny hole-in-the-wall where take-out food is available or customers eat standing up at chest-high counters. There are several such places up and down the Ku'damm where sausages or cans of beer are sold for about 2.50 DM ($1.50). Many sell side dishes to accompany them, including french fries and potato salad. There are also Imbisse in the Tiergarten park, and at Berlin's many markets. The Turkish Market in Kreuzberg, for example, sells Turkish fast food and specialties in addition to the usual sausages. And during my last visit to the weekend market on Strasse des 17. Juni, I found stalls selling everything from Turkish pizzas to sausages, chili con carne, and hamburgers. Check the shopping chapter for more information on markets.

In addition, several inexpensive locales described above in the restaurant section serve take-out food or are actually Imbisse. These include **Asia-Quick** (Chinese), **Einhorn** (vegetarian), **Joseph Langer** (German), **Karavan** (Turkish), **Nordsee** (fish), **Orient** (Middle Eastern), **Piccola Taormina Tavola Calda** (Italian), and **Rogacki** (German). For exact page numbers, refer to the "Restaurants by Cuisine" section at the end of this chapter.

SUNDAY BRUNCH/BUFFET BREAKFAST

Many hotels and pensions in Berlin include breakfast in their rates. However, in case yours doesn't, or you're hungry again by lunchtime, you might want to take advantage of what has become a Berlin tradition, the Sunday brunch. Not surprisingly, the most elaborate brunches are those served at Berlin's best hotels. Extremely popular are those that also provide entertainment, usually Dixieland jazz (called *Frühschoppen*).

ALTER MARKT, Hotel Schweizerhof, Budapester Strasse 21-31. Tel. 269 60.
   Cuisine: BUFFET BRUNCH   **Reservations:** Recommended.
   U-Bahn: Bahnhof Zoologischer Garten, about a 5-minute walk.
$ Prices: Fixed-price brunch 39 DM ($23.65) for adults, 19.50 DM ($11.80) for children 6 to 12, free for children up to 6. AE, DC, MC, V.
   Open: Sunday 11:30am–2:30pm.   **Closed:** July and Aug.

A huge space, the Alter Markt is designed to look like an outdoor market and even has an outdoor terrace. The buffet table is generously laid out with everything from croissants and rye bread to scrambled eggs, smoked ham, Muesli, fruit yogurt, and Swiss tortes and desserts. A jazz band sets the tone, and for the little ones there's a children's corner with toys, balloons, and other surprises. A good place for the entire family.

BRISTOL BAR, Bristol Hotel Kempinski, Kurfürstendamm 27. Tel. 88 43 40.
   Cuisine: BUFFET BRUNCH   **Reservations:** Not necessary.
   U-Bahn: Uhlandstrasse, a 1-minute walk.
$ Prices: Fixed-price brunch 44 DM ($26.65) for adults, 22 DM ($13.35) for children up to 12. AE, DC, MC, V.
   Open: Sunday 11am–2pm.
The businessperson's Sunday brunch is served in the very masculine Bristol Bar, with comfortable leather seats and low tables. The lavish buffet spread has everything from breads and sausages to eggs, ham, fruit, and desserts. A civilized and dignified way to start a Sunday.

EIERSCHALE, Rankestrasse 1. Tel. 882 53 05.
   Cuisine: BUFFET BREAKFAST   **Reservations:** None taken, but get there early.   **U-Bahn:** Kurfürstendamm, about a 1-minute walk.
$ Prices: Fixed-price brunch 10.70 DM ($6.50). Cash only.
   Open: Breakfast served daily 8am–2pm.

Right off the Ku'damm across the street from the Gedächtniskirche, this popular music house offers a breakfast brunch every day, which includes breads, croissants, marmalade, Würste, cheeses, eggs (soft-boiled, scrambled, or fried), ham, salad, and cereal. On Sundays it's especially nice, with jazz bands playing from 10am through much of the day.

ZUR NOLLE, above Nollendorfplatz U-Bahn station. Tel. 216 75 46.
   Cuisine: GERMAN   **Reservations:** A must.   **U-Bahn:** Nollendorfplatz.
$ Prices: 3.50–7.50 DM ($2.10–$4.55). Cash only.
   Open: Sunday 11am–7pm.

Zur Nolle is a bar/restaurant with a unique location on an upper platform of Nollendorfplatz station. The platform, no longer used for transportation, is also home of Die Nolle flea market, with vendors selling their wares from old railway cars. At any rate, the liveliest day of the week is Sunday, when a Dixieland jazz band plays from noon to 6pm for those who have had the foresight to make reservations at this popular place. The pub is pleasant, spread along a covered terrace with large windows that can be opened on fine days. The food is German, and includes Berliner Boulette, Kasseler Braten, Schweinebraten, and herring, as well as daily specials.

COFFEEHOUSES

The afternoon coffee break is a national custom. Germans not only drink coffee but put away large portions of cakes and pastries. Here are some of the best places to indulge.

If you're on a budget go to one of the chains that sell both the brew and the beans for an inexpensive cup of coffee. **Tschibo** is one such chain, offering a cup of coffee for 1.20 DM (70¢) and an espresso for 1 DM (60¢), along with a few choices in cakes and sandwiches. You can drink it standing up at one of the chest-high tables. Two convenient locations are at 11 Kurfürstendamm, across from the Gedächtniskirche, and at Wilmersdorfer Strasse 117. They're open Monday through Friday from 9am to 6:30pm and on Saturday from 9am to 2pm (to 6pm the first Saturday of the month).

EINSTEIN, Kurfürstenstrasse 58. Tel. 261 50 96.
   U-Bahn: Nollendorfplatz, about a 3-minute walk.
$ Prices: Coffee from 3 DM ($1.80), cocktails and long drinks from 11 DM ($6.65). Cash only.
   Open: Daily 10am–2am.
Einstein probably wouldn't mind lending his name to this student café, located in a beautiful high-ceilinged town house dating from the 1920s, with waiters in black suits and bow ties. Henny Porten, one of Germany's first silent film stars, lived here. Popular with Berlin's younger generation, it's a good place for either coffee or alcoholic drinks, and breakfast is served until 2pm. In summer there's seating for as many as 180 persons outside. Einstein is on Kurfürstenstrasse (not to be confused with the Ku'damm), north of Nollendorfplatz.

CAFÉ IM LITERATURHAUS, Fasanenstrasse 23. Tel. 882 54 14.

U-Bahn: Uhlandstrasse, a 1-minute walk.
$ Prices: Coffee from 3 DM ($1.80). Cash only.
Open: 10am–1am.

Just off the Ku'damm in a neighborhood of restored turn-of-the century villas, art galleries, and the Käthe-Kollwitz-Museum (next door), you'll find this refined oasis—a café above a bookstore. In summer you can sit outside amidst the greenery of a garden. Breakfast is served until 1pm to a decidedly artsy crowd; also available are salads and snacks, plus such desserts as Apfel strudel with vanilla sauce, rice pudding with purée of kiwi, and Rote Grütze.

CAFÉ KRANZLER, Kurfürstendamm 18-19. Tel. 882 69 11.

U-Bahn: Kurfürstendamm, less than a 1-minute walk.
$ Prices: Coffee from 3 DM ($1.80). AE, DC, MC, V.
Open: Daily 8am–midnight.

✪ There used to be many cafés in Berlin, but most were destroyed during World War II, taking with them a way of life that has all but vanished in today's more hectic world. One of the few to have survived the ravages of the war is Café Kranzler, one of Berlin's most famous coffeehouses. Founded in 1825 and formerly on Unter den Linden, it's now in a modern building occupying a prime spot on the Ku'damm and is one of the city's premier people-watching spots—especially in summer, when it becomes a sidewalk café. In winter Café Kranzler still makes a nice place to sit because of the huge floor-to-ceiling windows. In addition to breakfasts and snacks, it offers cakes and tortes, including Sachertorte.

LEYSIEFFER, Kurfürstendamm 218. Tel. 882 78 20.

U-Bahn: Uhlandstrasse or Kurfürstendamm, each less than a 2-minute walk.
$ Prices: Coffee from 3 DM ($1.80). AE, DC, MC, V.
Open: Mon–Sat 9am–8pm, Sat and holidays 10am–8pm.

Almost across the street from Café Kranzler is this small café in what once served as the Chinese embassy. The ground floor is a shop selling bonbons, chocolates, cakes, and marmalades, while the coffee shop upstairs resembles an art gallery, with a black-and-white tiled floor, an ornate stucco ceiling, and pictures on the wall by the owner's sister. The place is best known for its cakes, including an exotic fruit cake and a butter cake with almonds. Some people rave about its Rote Grütze, cooked fruits with a vanilla sauce, a specialty of northern Germany. The miniature-size balcony has room for only a lucky few, right above the Ku'damm.

CAFÉ MÖHRING, Kurfürstendamm 213. Tel. 881 20 75.

U-Bahn: Uhlandstrasse, less than a 1-minute walk.
$ Prices: Coffee from 3 DM ($1.80). Cash only.
Open: Daily 7am–midnight.

✪ When Café Möhring first opened here on the Ku'damm back in 1898, it was out in the countryside. Now, of course, it sits on some of the most expensive property in Berlin. (It was rebuilt after a fire burned it to the ground in 1973.) In addition to cakes and coffees, including the spiked variety, it offers daily specials, from soups and salads to main courses.

There are two other Café Möhrings on the Ku'damm, one at no. 163, near Adenauerplatz, and the other across from the Gedächtniskirche at no. 234. The latter, which opened in 1977, took over a preexisting coffeehouse and restored it to its former glory, including a turn-of-the-century facade that was renovated according to old documents and photographs.

OPERNCAFÉ, Unter den Linden 5. Tel. 200 02 56.

S-Bahn: Friedrichstrasse, about a 10-minute walk.

$ Prices: Coffee from 2.40 DM ($1.45). Cash only.

Open: Daily 11am–7pm.

Located on one of Berlin's most famous boulevards is one of its most famous coffeehouses, the Operncafé. It occupies part of a palace originally built in 1733, destroyed during World War II, and then painstakingly and lovingly restored. Although rather austere in comparison to the grand coffeehouses of, say, Vienna, the place still exudes a bit of the Old World, especially if you can find a seat outside underneath the trees of this pretty square, lined with buildings from another era. You can snack on ice cream or other desserts, or if you wish, eat a substantial meal at one of the two restaurants up on the first floor.

LATE-NIGHT DINING

If hunger strikes after midnight, there are a number of restaurants open to 2am, some even later. The following places, described above in detail, are all within walking distance of the Ku'damm. For exact page numbers, turn to the "Restaurants by Cuisine" section at the end of this chapter. In addition, many bars listed in the nightlife chapter remain open until the wee hours.

Expensive restaurants that are open to 3am include **Florian** (Continental), **Fofi's Estiatorio** (Greek), and **Lutter & Wegner** (German/Continental). **Paris Bar** (French) is open to 2am.

Moderately priced restaurants near the Ku'damm with late hours include **Bovril** (Continental), open to 2am; **Ciao Ciao** (Italian), open to 2am Sunday through Thursday and to 3am on Friday and Saturday nights; and **Grung Thai** (Thai), open to 3am.

If you're searching for an inexpensive restaurant, try **Korfu** (Greek), open to 2am, or **Orient** (Middle Eastern), to 3am. Budget restaurants open late are **Ashoka** (Indian), open to 2am; **Athener Grill** (Greek and Italian), to 4am during the week and to 5am on weekends; and **Jimmy's Diner** (American/Mexican), open to 4am during the week and to 6am on Friday and Saturday nights.

PICNIC FARE & WHERE TO EAT IT

All department stores have large food departments with counters serving prepared meats, salads, and take-out food. Two of the largest are **KaDeWe** (Kaufhaus des Westens), on Wittenbergplatz (tel. 21 210), with a huge food department on the sixth floor; and **Wertheim,** 231 Kurfürstendamm (tel. 88 20 61), with a food section in the basement. You can buy everything from cheese, bread, fruit, and wine to Leberkäs, grilled chicken, and casseroles. Both food departments are open Monday through Friday from 9am to 6pm (KaDeWe to 6:30pm) and on Saturday from 9am to 2pm (to 6pm the first Saturday of each month). In addition, restaurants listed above under "Fast Food and Imbisse" sell take-out foods that may be perfect for an afternoon picnic.

And where to eat your goodies? The largest and most convenient green space in the center of Berlin is the Tiergarten, a park located just northwest of Bahnhof Zoo. It stretches all the way to the Brandenburger Tor, with ponds, woods, meadows, and trails throughout. Another option is Loretta's Garden, 89 Lietzenburger Strasse, one block south of the Ku'damm near Knesebeckstrasse. It's a beer garden (admittedly a tourist-oriented one), complete with a Ferris wheel. Open in the summer months from 10am to 1am daily, it allows customers to bring their own food.

RESTAURANTS BY CUISINE

Cuisine and Restaurant	Rating
AMERICAN	
Jimmy's Diner (p. 106)	B
SUNDAY BRUNCH/BUFFET BREAKFAST	
Alter Market (p. 130)	
Bristol Bar (p. 130)	
Eierschale (p. 130)	
Zur Nolle (p. 131)	
CHICKEN	
Henne (p. 123)	I
CHINESE	
Asia-Quick (p. 106)	B
Chung (p. 100)	M
CONTINENTAL	
Alt Luxemburg (p. 110)	E
Bovril (p. 99)	M
Carmer's (p. 92)	VE
Restaurant Ephraim-Palais (p. 116)	E
Ermeler Haus (p. 116)	M
Florian (p. 95)	E
Heinz Holl (p. 97)	E
Lutter & Wegner (p. 97)	E
Operncafé (p. 118)	I
CZECHOSLOVAKIAN	
Zlata Praha (p. 99)	E
FRENCH	
Belle Epoque (p. 125)	E
Le Grand Silhouette (p. 128)	VE
Kempinski Grill (p. 127)	VE
Restaurant le Paris (p. 97)	E
Panorama 37 (p. 129)	M

Cuisine and Restaurant	Rating
Paris Bar (p. 98)	E
Park Restaurant (p. 127)	VE
Rockendorf's Restaurant (p. 123)	VE
Ty Breizh (p. 111)	I

GERMAN

Alter Krug Dahlem (p. 119)	M
Aphrodite (p. 115)	E
Berliner Stube (p. 126)	M
Blockhaus Nikolskoe (p. 124)	M
Die Buffeteria (p. 112)	B
Club Culinare (p. 104)	I
Dom Klause (p. 127)	M
Dorfgasthaus (p. 100)	M
Ermeler Haus (p. 116)	M
Restaurant Ephraim-Palais (p. 116)	E
Friesenhof (p. 101)	M
Gasthaus Meineke (p. 104)	I
Grossbeerenkeller (p. 122)	I
Café Hardenberg (p. 113)	I
Hardtke (p. 101)	M
Heinz Holl (p. 97)	E
Ihre Frisch Backstübe (p. 114)	B
Jahrmarkt (p. 104)	I
Joseph Langer (p. 112)	B
Karstadt (p. 112)	B
Kasino beim Senator für Wirtschaft und Verkehr (p. 121)	B
Kempinski Grill (p. 127)	VE
Luisen-Bräu (p. 120)	I
Lutter & Wegner (p. 97)	E
Mensa (p. 114)	B
Operncafé (p. 118)	I
Rogacki (p. 113)	B
Spreebuffet (p. 119)	B
Stammhaus Kindl (p. 128)	M
Suppenterrine (p. 119)	B
Tafelrunde (p. 124)	E
Tegernseer Tönnchen (p. 111)	I
Zum Ambrosius (p. 122)	B
Zur Goldenen Gans (p. 128)	M
Zur Nolle (p. 122)	B

GREEK

Athener Grill (p. 106)	B
Fofi's Estiatorio (p. 96)	E
Korfu (p. 105)	I
Taverna Plaka (p. 103)	M

HUNGARIAN

Mathiaskeller (p. 118)	I
Zlata Praha (p. 99)	E

Cuisine and Restaurant	Rating
INDIAN	
Ashoka (p. 106)	B
Kalkutta (p. 105)	I
INTERNATIONAL	
Café Hardenberg (p. 113)	I
KaDeWe (p. 109)	I
Mövenpick (p. 108)	M
Shell (p. 103)	M
ITALIAN	
Anselmo (p. 91)	VE
Ristorante da Antonio (p. 92)	VE
Athener Grill (p. 106)	B
Ciao Ciao (p. 100)	M
Ciao Italia (p. 114)	B
Mario (p. 98)	E
Piccola Taormina Tavola Calda (p. 107)	B
Ponte Vecchio (p. 110)	E
San Marino (p. 102)	M
Ristorante Tavola Calda (p. 98)	E
JAPANESE	
Daitokai (p. 108)	E
Fukagawa (p. 96)	E
KOSHER	
Restaurant in Jüdischen Gemeindehaus (p. 102)	M
MEXICAN	
Jimmy's Diner (p. 106)	B
MIDDLE EASTERN	
Orient (p. 105)	I
RUSSIAN	
Restaurant Moskau (p. 116)	E
SEAFOOD	
Gastmahl des Meeres (p. 118)	I
Nordsee (p. 112)	B
Roter Sand (p. 109)	I
THAI	
Grung Thai (p. 101)	M
TURKISH	
Istanbul (p. 102)	M
Karavan (p. 107)	B
VEGETARIAN	
Einhorn (p. 109)	B
Maskera (p. 121)	I
Shell (p. 103)	M

Note: VE = Very Expensive, E = Expensive, M = Moderate, I = Inexpensive, B = Budget

CHAPTER 6

WHAT TO SEE & DO IN BERLIN

It would be worth coming to Berlin for its museums alone, so impressive and diverse are they. From Egyptian art treasures to contemporary art, from musical instruments to traditional costumes and furniture, Berlin offers something for everyone. Further, many of its more than 100 public museums are free, and they attract more than two million visitors annually. I can't imagine being bored here even for a minute.

Rather, the problem is just the opposite: There are so many choices that they may seem bewildering—compounded by the fact that Berlin's museum treasures were divided between East and West after World War II. Both East and West Berlin set about developing their own Egyptian museums, Islamic art museums, European art museums, and history museums, to name only a few. All of these still exist today, and it is not easy to rank them, particularly since so many have at least a few items that catapult them into the must-see category. Perhaps the city will consider merging some of its collections, once the more pressing problems posed by unification have been addressed.

But even though Berlin has an awesome number of museums, don't despair. The city is surprisingly compact, making it an easy place to explore. What's more, most of its major museums and attractions are clustered in four distinct parts of the city, all conveniently reached by an efficient public transportation system. Visitors can see quite a bit of what the city has to offer in just a few days.

SUGGESTED ITINERARIES

To help you get the most out of your visit, here are some suggested itineraries to guide you to the most important attractions. Since the dining, sightseeing, and nightlife chapters are all arranged according

- By the year 1700, nearly one Berliner in five was of French extraction.
- In the 1920s the city boasted 35 theaters, several opera houses, more than 20 concert halls, and as many as 150 daily and weekly newspapers.
- Founded in 1844, Berlin's Tiergarten zoo housed 10,000 animals in 1939; only 91 animals survived the war.
- From 1949 until the Wall went up in 1961, approximately 3 million East Germans fled their country.
- Thirty percent of West Berlin is forests, rivers, and lakes, and there are 485 miles of hiking trails and biking paths.
- Berlin is closer to Poland (only 60 miles away) than it is to any city in West Germany.
- Berlin claims to have more students, dogs, (200,000) and local rock groups (1,000) than any other city in Europe.
- West Berlin has 6,000 restaurants and 5,000 pubs and bars.

to geographic locations, it should be no problem to tailor these itineraries to your own choices in restaurants, attractions, and after-dark entertainment. Have fun!

IF YOU HAVE 1 DAY

Day 1 Get up early and head straight to Dahlem, where you'll find half a dozen of Berlin's finest museums. (*Note:* Most museums are closed on Monday.) Most important of these is the Gemäldegalerie (Picture Gallery), with its masterpieces from the 13th to the 18th century, including works by Dürer, Brueghel, Botticelli, Raphael, Rubens, and Rembrandt. Since time is precious, concentrate on the artists you're most interested in. If you're still in Dahlem at lunchtime, you might wish to dine on traditional German cuisine at Alter Krug Dahlem. If you're on a budget or in a hurry, there's a thatch-roofed Imbiss right across the street from the subway station, selling Würste, coffee, and beer.

From Dahlem, head for Schloss Charlottenburg (Charlottenburg Palace) and its surrounding museums. Just southeast of the palace is the Luisen-Bräu brewery, another good spot for lunch. At the palace itself, visit the Knobelsdorff Flügel (New Wing) and the Schinkel Pavilion for a look at how Prussian royalty lived. Be sure, too, to see the famous bust of Queen Nefertiti in the Ägyptisches Museum (Egyptian Museum), located across the street from the palace.

Before the day ends, head for the Brandenburger Tor (Brandenburg Gate) (bus 69 from Bahnhof Zoo), built in the 1780s as the grand finishing touch to Berlin's most famous boulevard, Unter den Linden. After Berlin became a divided city, the gate (as well as the boulevard) ended up under East Berlin's jurisdiction and was inaccessible to West Berliners, making it a poignant symbol of Germany's division. After the November 1989 revolution in East Berlin and the subsequent fall of the Wall, it was here that many Berliners gathered to rejoice. Today visitors continue to seek out the Brandenburger Tor, which still crowns the start of Unter den Linden. Take a stroll down this thoroughfare, stopping off for a coffee at the celebrated Operncafé.

Finish off the day with a leisurely evening stroll along the Ku'damm, Berlin's showcase avenue with its many shops and restaurants. Relax over coffee at one of the many coffeehouses, or order a drink at one of the numerous bars near the Ku'damm; if it's summer, try to get a seat outdoors. And then start planning your next trip to Berlin.

IF YOU HAVE 2 DAYS

Day 1   Devote your entire morning to Dahlem, as described above, first visiting the Gemäldegalerie. Add to it one or two of the other museums that most interest you. The Museum für Deutsche Volkskunde (Museum of German Ethnology) has an excellent display of ethnic and historical items once in common use, including simple peasant furniture and household items. There are also fine museums of Asian art and one of the world's largest general ethnological museums. In the afternoon, head for Charlottenburg, where in addition to the palace and the Ägyptisches Museum, there's also the Antikenmuseum (Museum of Greek and Roman Antiquities), the Museum für Vor- und Frühgeschichte (Museum of Pre- and Early History), and the wonderful Bröhan Museum with its art deco and Jugendstil collection.

Day 2   Go to East Berlin. Start with a stroll down Unter den Linden and a look at the Brandenburger Tor, then visit the outstanding Pergamon Museum on Museumsinsel (Museum Island), with its incredible Pergamon Altar, Market Gate of Miletus, and Babylonian Processional Street leading to the Gate of Ishtar. If you have time, add the Museum für Deutsche Geschichte (Museum of German History), the Nationalgalerie (National Gallery), or the Bode Museum. Finish the day with a walk to Alexanderplatz, which was once considered the heart of East Germany's capital, and the nearby Nikolaiviertel (Nikolai Quarter), a small neighborhood of restored buildings housing several pubs and restaurants.

IF YOU HAVE 3 DAYS

Days 1 and 2   Spend Days 1 and 2 as outlined above.

Day 3   On Day 3, head for the Tiergarten museum complex (south of the Tiergarten park), a newly developed center for European art, where you'll find the Neue Nationalgalerie (New National Gallery). It houses German and European artists of the 19th and 20th centuries. Nearby are the Kunstgewerbe Museum (Museum of Applied Arts), with its collections dating from the Middle Ages to the present day, and the Musikinstrumenten Museum (Museum of Musical Instruments).

Spend the rest of the day according to your own special interests: the Berlin Museum (in Kreuzberg) for more about the history of this fascinating city; the Käthe-Kollwitz Museum (near the Ku'damm) with its powerful drawings by one of Berlin's best-known artists; the Bauhaus-Archiv and the Hansaviertel (Hansa Quarter) for architectural buffs; Die Nolle, the Ku'damm, and Wilmersdorfer Strasse for shopping. In the evening, try to attend a performance at the Deutsche Opera or, if you understand German, one of the several theaters, or enjoy a rock, jazz, or blues concert at one of the city's many live-music houses.

IF YOU HAVE 5 DAYS OR MORE

Days 1–3   Spend Days 1–3 as outlined above. In addition, if you're in Berlin on a Saturday or Sunday, be sure to schedule in a trip to the flea market held every weekend on Strasse des 17. Juni near the Tiergarten park. It offers antiques, curios, and junk, as well as arts and crafts from Berlin's enterprising young artists. On Tuesday or Friday, try to include a visit to the Turkish Market (in Kreuzberg) for a fascinating insight into another aspect of Berlin's varied population.

Day 4   Take an excursion to Wannsee or Havel, where you can swim or take a pleasure boat and spend a relaxing day. Alternatives include one of the suggested walking tours in the next chapter, an excursion to Köpenick or Müggelsee, or visiting those museums you haven't yet had time for.

Day 5   Head for Potsdam with its palace and park of Sanssouci.

---

1. THE TOP ATTRACTIONS

Berlin has four major museum centers. Dahlem is the largest, with its famous Gemäldegalerie, Museum für Deutsche Volkskunde, and many museums of non-European art. Not to be outdone is Museumsinsel (Museum Island), the island in the middle of the Spree River, so laden with treasures from the Pergamon Museum and other major collections that I'm surprised it isn't sinking. Charlottenburg boasts the Schloss Charlottenburg and museums of antiquities. And finally, Berlin's newest museum complex is in a precinct called Tiergarten, a region still under construction that will eventually be the city's center for European art.

Because Berlin's major museums are conveniently located in these four clusters, it makes sense to cover Berlin section by section. In each section, I've listed the most important attractions first.

MUSEUMS IN DAHLEM

You can reach Dahlem in about 20 minutes from the city center by taking U-Bahn 2 to the Dahlem-Dorf station. From the station, signs point the way to the various museums, most of which are a 5-minute walk away. The Gemäldegalerie and museums for sculpture, ethnology, and East Asian, Islamic, and Indian art are all located in a huge sprawling complex with entrances on either Arnimallee or Lansstrasse.

Note that several of the Dahlem museums will eventually find new homes in the Tiergarten arts complex during the 1990s. The Kupferstichkabinett (Museum of Prints and Drawings) has already closed and will reopen its doors in Tiergarten by late 1992 (check with the Berlin tourist office for the exact opening). Next to move will be the Gemäldegalerie in 1995, followed by the Skulpturengalerie at the turn of the century. Thus, Tiergarten will be the new center for European art, while Dahlem will continue to house collections of non-European art.

GEMÄLDEGALERIE (Picture Gallery), Arnimallee 23-27. Tel. 830 11.

⭐ Based on the royal collections and added to through the years, the Gemäldegalerie is considered by many to be Berlin's top art museum. It offers a comprehensive survey of European painting from the 13th to the 18th century, with more than 1,500 works in its possession. Only half of these are now on display—a shortcoming that will be remedied when the gallery moves into new and larger quarters in the Tiergarten precinct.

The museum's holdings are arranged historically and systematically, by schools and by periods. Included are works by German, Flemish, Dutch, Netherlandish, Italian, French, English, and Spanish artists, including important works by Botticelli, Raphael, Dürer, Cranach, Holbein, Titian, El Greco, Brueghel, Rubens, Vermeer, Velázquez, Gainsborough, Goya, and Murillo. The Rubens collection is outstanding, but the crowning glory of the museum is probably its 20 or so paintings by Rembrandt, one of the world's largest holdings by this master. Look for his self-portrait, and, one of my favorites, his portrait of Hendrickje Stoffels, his common-law wife (the intimacy of their relationship is reflected in her gaze at the painter). The famous and striking *Man with the Golden Helmet* is no longer attributed to Rembrandt.

Other notable paintings include Botticelli's *Venus*, Dürer's portrait of a Nürnberg patrician, and Hans Holbein's portrait of the merchant Georg Gisze. Brueghel the Elder's *The Netherlands Proverbs* contains the enaction of more than a hundred adages and idioms. Lucas Cranach's *The Fountain of Youth* depicts old women being led to the fountain, swimming through it, and then emerging young and beautiful. Note that apparently only women need the bath—men in the painting regain their youth through relations with younger women.

Since the museum is large, you will probably want to concentrate on your particular areas of interest. The ground floor is devoted to German, Netherlandish, and Italian art from the 13th through the 16th century, as well as to French and English paintings of the 18th century. The first floor is where you'll find French, Flemish, and Dutch 17th-century paintings, Spanish works of art, and Italian paintings of the baroque and rococo periods. Pick up a map of the museum, as well as a pamphlet in English.

Admission: Free.

Open: Tues–Fri 9am–5pm, Sat and Sun 10am–5pm. **Closed:** Mon, Jan 1, Tues after Easter and after Whitsunday, May 1, and Dec 24, 25, and 31. **U-Bahn:** Dahlem-Dorf.

SKULPTURENGALERIE (Sculpture Gallery), Arnimallee 23-27. Tel. 830 11.

⭐ The gallery contains approximately 1,200 works of European sculpture, dating from the early Christian and Byzantine periods to the end of the 18th century. Most notable are its works from the Italian Renaissance and German Gothic periods, including carvings by one of Germany's most famous artists, Tilman Riemenschneider. Extending along two floors, the gallery also displays wooden religious figurines, ivories, marble reliefs, and bronzes.

Admission: Free.

Open: Tues–Fri 9am–5pm, Sat and Sun 10am–5pm. **Closed:** Mon, Jan 1, Tues after Easter and after Whitsunday, May 1, and Dec 24, 25, and 31. **U-Bahn:** Dahlem-Dorf.

MUSEUM FÜR VÖLKERKUNDE (Ethnological Museum), Lansstrasse 8. Tel. 830 11.

⭐ One of the world's largest ethnological museums, it contains a half million objects from around the world, ranging from everyday household objects to fine gold jewelry to spears and cult artifacts.

Particularly fascinating are the watercraft from the Pacific region, including life-size boats from Tonga, Samoa, the Marshall Islands, and Micronesia. There are also original dwellings and facades from the Pacific islands, including a men's clubhouse from Palau and a hut from New Guinea. Equally impressive is the museum's fine collection of pre-Columbian artifacts, especially its gold objects and Peruvian antiquities. Other departments center on Buddhist art in China, the nomadic cultures of Mongolia, shadow puppetry and the marionette theaters of Asia, folk music from around the world, ceremonial masks, and African sculpture.

Admission: Free.

Open: Tues–Fri 9am–5pm, Sat and Sun 10am–5pm. **Closed:** Mon, Jan 1, Tues after Easter and after Whitsunday, May 1, and Dec 24, 25, and 31. **U-Bahn:** Dahlem-Dorf.

MUSEUM FÜR DEUTSCHE VOLKSKUNDE (Museum of German Ethnology), Im Winkel 6-8. Tel. 8390 12 87 or 83 20 31.

Whereas the Museum für Völkerkunde (above) contains objects relating to people from around the world, this ethnological museum concentrates on items relating to the German-speaking people in Central Europe, from the 16th century to the present day—with an emphasis on everyday rural folk culture before and during the early stages of the Industrial Revolution. Devoted to past generations of middle- and working-class Germans who were skilled in making almost everything they needed, it provides an interesting contrast to the extravagance of Schloss Charlottenburg and lifestyle of Germany's ruling class.

On the ground floor is a wonderful collection of peasant furniture, including beds, chests, and cupboards. A display called "Furniture as Dowry" explains that items of furniture were one of the

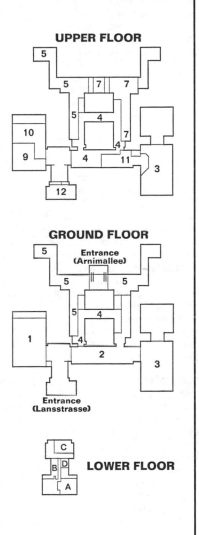

DAHLEM MUSEUMS

TOP FLOOR
(not shown)

UPPER FLOOR

3 Museum für Völkerkunde
  (South Seas)
4 Skulpturengalerie
5 Gemäldegalerie
7 Museum für Völkerkunde
  (Africa)
9 Museum für Islamische Kunst
10 Museum für Ostasiatische
  Kunst
11 Museum für Völkerkunde
  (Southeast Asia)
12 Special exhibitions

GROUND FLOOR

1 Museum für Indische Kunst
2 Museum für Völkerkunde
  (America)
3 Museum für Völkerkunde
  (South Seas)
4 Skulpturengalerie
5 Gemäldegalerie

LOWER FLOOR

A Lecture Room
B Young People's Museum
C Cafeteria
D Museum for the Blind

UPPER FLOOR

GROUND FLOOR

Entrance
(Arnimallee)

Entrance
(Lansstrasse)

LOWER FLOOR

most important things in a young woman's dowry and were passed down from generation to generation as heirlooms. The clothing section is equally fascinating, with everything from shawls and bonnets to bridal gowns and hats. Other displays contain cooking, baking, and eating and drinking utensils, including those made of stoneware, porcelain, pewter, and glass.

The first floor is devoted to displays demonstrating various

household tasks: turning flax into linen thread, knitting and crocheting, weaving, and lacemaking. Life today is certainly easier, but does that make it better? As you look at all these objects made lovingly by hand and compare them with their factory-produced counterparts, you may well question the price of progress. At any rate, this is a museum well worth a visit. Note that it is not connected to the other museums in Dahlem; follow the signs from the subway station.
Admission: Free.
Open: Tues–Fri 9am–5pm, Sat and Sun 10am–5pm. **Closed:** Mon, Jan 1, Tues after Easter and after Whitsunday, May 1, and Dec 24, 25, and 31. **U-Bahn:** Dahlem-Dorf.

MUSEUM FÜR INDISCHE KUNST (Museum of Indian Art), Lansstrasse 8. Tel. 830 11 or 830 13 61.

Quite simply, this is the most significant collection of Indian art in Germany, its displays covering a period of almost 4,000 years and including items from not only India but Nepal, Tibet, Burma, Thailand, and Indonesia. Objects range from prehistoric terra-cotta and stone sculptures of Buddhist, Jainist, and Hindu divinities to finely crafted miniatures, ivories, and murals. Of special note is the **Turfan Collection** of famous 6th- to 10th-century frescoes depicting Buddhist legends. The museum is also famous for its art from the Buddhist cave-monasteries along what was once the legendary Silk Road in Central Asia. In addition, be on the lookout for the 9th-century stone sculpture of the god Siva and his wife, considered a masterpiece of Nepalese art.
Admission: Free.
Open: Tues–Fri 9am–5pm, Sat and Sun 10am–5pm. **Closed:** Mon, Jan 1, Tues after Easter and after Whitsunday, May 1, and Dec 24, 25, and 31. **U-Bahn:** Dahlem-Dorf.

MUSEUM FÜR ISLAMISCHE KUNST (Museum of Islamic Art), Lansstrasse 8. Tel. 830 11 or 830 13 92.

All Islamic countries are represented in this important collection of carpets, sculptures, examples of Arabic script, pottery, glass, jewelry, miniatures, and other applied arts from the 8th to the 18th century. The museum begins with representative selections of the finest in Islamic art; subsequent rooms follow its chronological development through the ages. Highlights include a Koran parchment from the 9th century, enameled Syrian glassware, and Turkish carpets from the 16th and 17th centuries.
Admission: Free.
Open: Tues–Fri 9am–5pm, Sat and Sun 10am–5pm. **Closed:** Mon, Jan 1, Tues after Easter and after Whitsunday, May 1, and Dec 24, 25, and 31. **U-Bahn:** Dahlem-Dorf.

MUSEUM FÜR OSTASIATISCHE KUNST (Museum of Far Eastern Art), Lansstrasse 8. Tel. 830 11 or 830 13 61.

Chinese, Korean, and Japanese art from 3000 B.C. to the present is on display here, including woodcuts, paintings, bronzes, ceramics, lacquerware, and sculptures. The first of its kind in Germany when it was established in 1906, the museum offers a fine overview of Far

FROMMER'S FAVORITES

BERLIN EXPERIENCES

A Stroll Along the Ku'damm No trip to Berlin would be complete without a leisurely stroll down the Ku'damm, the city's showcase boulevard.

Café Life Cafés are where people meet friends, discuss the day's events, read the newspaper, or just sit at a sidewalk table and watch the never-ending parade.

A Picnic in the Tiergarten The Tiergarten in the heart of the city, home of the Berlin Zoo and Aquarium, is laced with hiking paths that skirt ponds and cut through meadows, a good place for a picnic or a leisurely walk.

Browsing the Market at Strasse des 17. Juni The best flea market in the city has a wide variety of antiques, curios, and junk, as well as handcrafted items such as jewelry and clothes. Food stalls sell sausages, drinks, and Turkish fast food, giving the market a festive atmosphere. Held Saturdays and Sundays only.

An Afternoon at the Turkish Market Berlin has a large Turkish population, and nowhere is this more evident than in Kreuzberg, where you'll find this colorful and bustling market on Tuesday and Friday afternoons. Exotic spices, clothing, and Turkish fast food are sold here. You'll think you've landed in Istanbul.

A Lazy Day at the Beach Europe's largest inland beach is at Wannsee, which boasts a children's playground, shops, and restaurants. A great place to while away a fine summer's day—and if you wish, you can swim au naturel.

An Evening with the Berlin Philharmonic Orchestra Don't miss the chance of hearing one of the world's great orchestras at the fabulous Philharmonic Hall.

Pub Crawling 'til Dawn There are no mandatory closing hours for bars in Berlin, which means you can celebrate all night long. And if you do stay out all night, there are café/bars ready to serve you breakfast in the wee hours.

A Sunday Jazz Brunch Sunday brunch is very much in vogue in Berlin, and there are a number of places that offer a tempting buffet of goodies. Even more popular are those that offer live jazz as well, such as the Alter Markt at the Hotel Schweizerhof, the Eierschale, and Zur Nolle.

Eastern decorative and religious art. Of note are a 17th-century lacquered Chinese imperial throne with mother-of-pearl inlays, the collection of Japanese woodblock prints, and Japanese and Chinese paintings and scrolls. Because the paintings and scrolls are fragile, displays change every three months and center on different themes. On one of my visits, for example, there was a special exhibition of 18th- and 19th-century woodblock prints depicting foreigners (who, despite their rounded eyes, still look rather Asian). Another special print exhibition was devoted to Japanese women during the four seasons.

Admission: Free.

Open: Tues–Fri 9am–5pm, Sat and Sun 10am–5pm. **Closed:** Mon, Jan 1, Tues after Easter and Whitsunday, May 1, and Dec 24, 25, and 31. **U-Bahn:** Dahlem-Dorf.

BRÜCKE-MUSEUM, Bussardsteig 9. Tel. 831 20 29.

Located on a quiet dead-end street at the edge of the Grünewald is this museum dedicated to members of Die Brücke (The Bridge), a group of artists established in Dresden in 1905 and credited with introducing expressionism to Germany. Works on display include Erich Heckel's *Man in His Younger Years,* Emil Nolde's *Vacation Guests,* Max Pechstein's *Fishing Boat,* and Ernst Ludwig Kirchner's *Street, Berlin.*

Admission: 3.50 DM ($2.10) for adults, 1.50 DM (90¢) for students and children.

Open: Wed–Mon 11am–5pm. **U-Bahn:** Dahlem-Dorf, about a 15-minute walk. **Bus:** 50.

SIGHTS IN CHARLOTTENBURG

Most of the museums described in this section are located on the corner of Schlossstrasse and Spandauer Damm. Other sights in Charlottenburg borough, including the Käthe-Kollwitz-Museum and the Gedächtniskirche, are described later under "More Attractions."

SCHLOSS CHARLOTTENBURG (Charlottenburg Palace), Spandauer Damm. Tel. 32 09 11.

⭐ Schloss Charlottenburg, now considered Berlin's most beautiful baroque building, started out as something far less grand.

Constructed in the 1690s as a small residence for Sophie Charlotte, wife of the future Friedrich I, it was later greatly expanded into a palace fit for kings. Indeed, it served as the summer residence of almost all Prussian kings from Friedrich I to Friedrich Wilhelm IV, and today it contains objects spanning the periods from the baroque to Biedermeier.

The first thing that catches your eye as you approach the front of the palace is the equestrian statue of the Great Elector standing in the forecourt. Considered a treasure of baroque art, it was cast in one piece to a design by Andreas Schlüter in 1700. To protect the statue during World War II, it was sunk to the bottom of Tegel Harbor; it found a new home here in 1952.

The central section of the palace, topped with a dome and a

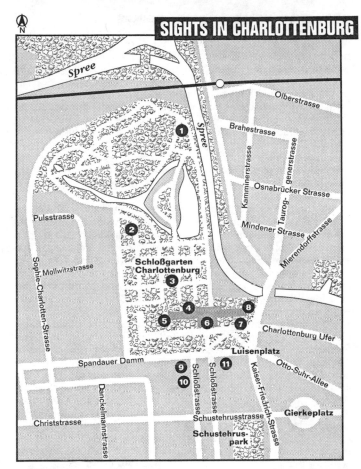

Spree

Olberstrasse

Brahestrasse

Spree

Kamminerstrasse

Taurog-generstrasse

Osnabrücker Strasse

Osnabrücker Strasse

Mindener Strasse

Mierendorffstrasse

Pulsstrasse

**Schloßgarten
Charlottenburg**

Sophie-Charlotten-Strasse

Sophie-Mollwitzstrasse

Charlottenburg Ufer

Luisenplatz

Spandauer Damm

Schloßstrasse

Kaiser-Friedrich-Strasse

Otto-Suhr-Allee

Dankelmannstrasse

Gierkeplatz

Christstrasse

Schustehrusstrasse

**Schustehrus-
park**

clock, takes in the **Historical Apartments,** which served as the private living quarters of Sophie Charlotte and her husband. Containing rich furnishings, including a priceless Chinese porcelain cabinet and lacquered furniture, the apartments can be visited only on guided tours conducted solely in German. You might want to check to see whether the influx of foreign visitors has prodded the authorities into

offering tours in English. Otherwise, unless you speak German, you're better off skipping the Historical Apartments and heading instead for the **Knobelsdorff-Flügel** (New Wing), located to the right as you face the apartments.

On the ground floor of the Knobelsdorff-Flügel are more royal living quarters, where visitors can wander at will through rooms charmingly decorated in styles from the romantic and Biedermeier periods, including furniture, paintings, and porcelain. Upstairs you'll find the Golden Gallery with its gold-and-green ornamentation—a ballroom considered one of the most impressive examples of German rococo—and the state dining hall. Be sure too to walk through the Galerie der Romantik, a collection of paintings from the German romantic period.

Next head for the **Schinkel Pavilion,** located at the far east end of the palace behind the Knobelsdorff-Flügel. A small and delightful summer house built in 1825 in the style of an Italian villa by Karl Friedrich Schinkel, one of Berlin's most respected architects, it has small and cozy rooms, each one differently decorated with sculptures, examples of applied arts, and paintings from the early 19th century. There are also drawings, sketches, and paintings by the amazing Schinkel, who was an accomplished artist in addition to being an architect.

As with most European palaces, a **park** stretches behind Schloss Charlottenburg. First laid out in 1697 in French style and transformed into an English garden in the first half of the 19th century, it was destroyed in World War II and subsequently restored to its baroque form. Besides the Schinkel Pavilion, it contains two other important structures. The **Mausoleum,** located at the west end of the park, holds the tombs of Queen Luise, Friedrich Wilhelm III, Kaiser Wilhelm I, and Kaiserin Augusta. It was built in 1810 according to the designs of Schinkel, and with its Doric columns resembles an ancient temple. The **Belvedere,** located at the far end of the park near the Spree River, is a former teahouse that now contains Berlin porcelain of the 18th and 19th centuries.

Admission: Combination ticket covering all the above, 6 DM ($3.65) for adults, 3 DM ($1.80) for students and children; for the Schinkel Pavilion, Knobelsdorff-Flügel, or Belvedere, 2.50 DM ($1.50) each for adults, 1.50 DM (90¢) each for students and children; for the Mausoleum, 50 pfennigs (30¢) for adults, 25 pfennigs (15¢) for students and children; Galerie der Romantik, free.

Open: Tues–Sun 10am–5pm. **Closed:** Mausoleum closed Nov–Mar. **Bus:** 9, 54, 62, or 74 to Charlottenburger Schloss. **U-Bahn:** Sophie-Charlotte-Platz or Richard-Wagner-Platz, both about a 10-minute walk.

ÄGYPTISCHES MUSEUM (Egyptian Museum), Schloss-strasse 70. Tel. 320 91 261 or 32 09 11.

Just across the street from Schloss Charlottenburg is this collection illustrating Egyptian cultural history. Originally constructed in the 1850s as barracks for the royal bodyguards, the building now houses Berlin's most famous art object—**Queen Nefertiti** (called *Königin Nofretete* in German). She's up on the first floor, in a dark room all to herself. Created more than 3,300 years ago and unearthed in 1912 by a team of German archeologists, the bust never left the sculptor's studio but, rather, served as a model for all further portraits of the queen.

In adjoining rooms are smaller likenesses of Nefertiti's husband, King Ahkenaton, and her daughter, Princess Meritaton. Look also for Queen Tiyi, Akhenaton's mother, remembered for her shrewdness in politics. Other items in this amazing museum include burial cult objects, a mummy, sarcophagi, a papyrus collection, tools used in everyday life, and the Kalabasha Gate.

Admission: Free.

Open: Mon–Thurs 9am–5pm, Sat and Sun 10am–5pm. **Closed:** Fri, Jan 1, Maundy Thursday, May 1, and Dec 24, 25, and 31. **Bus:** 9, 54, 62, or 74 to Charlottenburger Schloss. **U-Bahn:** Sophie-Charlotte-Platz or Richard-Wagner-Platz, each about a 10-minute walk.

ANTIKENMUSEUM (Museum of Greek and Roman Antiquities). Schlossstrasse 1. Tel. 320 91 215 or 32 09 11.

Standing directly across from the Ägyptisches Museum and also originally designed as barracks, the Antikenmuseum contains Greek, Etruscan, and Roman pottery, ivory carvings, glassware, jewelry, wood and stone sarchophagi, and small statuettes in marble. Particularly outstanding are the Attic red-figure vases of the 5th century, with their depictions of everyday life in ancient Greece and the world of the gods. But the most impressive collections are in the basement Schatzkammer (Treasury), with its silver collection and its exquisite jewelry from about 2000 B.C. to late antiquity.

Admission: Free.

Open: Mon–Thurs 9am–5pm, Sat and Sun 10am–5pm. **Closed:** Fri, Jan 1, Maundy Thursday, May 1, and Dec 24, 25, and 31. **Bus:** 9, 54, 62, or 74 to Charlottenburger Schloss. **U-Bahn:** Sophie-Charlotte-Platz or Richard-Wagner-Platz, each about a 10-minute walk.

MUSEUM FÜR VOR- UND FRÜHGESCHICHTE (Museum of Pre- and Early History). Spandauer Damm. Tel. 320 91 233 or 32 09 11.

This museum, in the west wing of Schloss Charlottenburg (to the left if you're facing the palace, outside the palace gate), is dedicated to the history of mankind from the Old Stone Age through the Bronze Age and late Iron Age, illustrated with objects from prehistoric Europe and the Near East. Arranged in chronological order, the displays start with Paleolithic cave paintings and idols and continue with sections devoted to the creation of written language; the beginning of agriculture; metalworking; Trojan antiquities; and items relating to the pre-Roman Iron Age and the early Germanic tribes. Also included are glass, pottery, jewelry, and coins of the Roman provinces, as well as archeological finds from the Spandau district of Berlin. Spandau was first settled in the 7th century by Slavic people and remains Berlin's most extensively researched archeological site.

Admission: Free.
Open: Mon–Thurs 9am–5pm, Sat and Sun 10am–5pm.
Closed: Fri, Jan 1, Maundy Thursday, May 1, and Dec 24, 25, and 31. **Bus:** 9, 54, 62, or 74 to Charlottenburger Schloss. **U-Bahn:** Sophie-Charlotte-Platz or Richard-Wagner-Platz, each about a 10-minute walk.

BRÖHAN MUSEUM, Schlossstrasse la. Tel. 321 40 29.

⭐ Located right next to the Antikenmuseum, this privately owned museum—the only one in the Charlottenburg complex—is named after Professor Karl Bröhan, who started the collection housed here. He began gathering art nouveau (Jugendstil) and art deco pieces at a time when others thought they were worthless and were throwing them away. With approximately 1,600 objects dating from 1889 to 1939, including exquisite vases, glass, furniture, silver, sculptures, and paintings, the museum ranks as one of the finest of its kind in the world.

Pieces are beautifully arranged, with most rooms resembling period salons rather than museum galleries. Outstanding is the porcelain collection, including KPM Berlin, Meissen, and Royal Copenhagen, as well the turn-of-the-century buffet created by Hector Guimard (1867–1942), who also designed the cast-iron entranceways of the Paris Métro. Also on display: glass by Emile Gallé, Bohemian iridescent glass, paintings by a group of artists known as the Berlin Secession, silver objects by Viennese artist Josef Hoffmann, and magnificent furniture crafted by Jacques-Émile Ruhlmann. In short, it's a joy to walk through the airy rooms filled with the graceful motifs of art nouveau and art deco. Don't miss it.

Admission: 3 DM ($1.80) for adults, 1.50 DM (90¢) for students.
Open: Tues–Sun 10am–6pm. **Bus:** 9, 54, 62, or 74 to Charlottenburger Schloss. **U-Bahn:** Sophie-Charlotte-Platz or Richard-Wagner-Platz, each about a 10-minute walk.

MUSEUMS ON MUSEUMSINSEL

The four museums described here, located in East Berlin on Museumsinsel (Museum Island), comprise the city's oldest museum complex. Construction began in the 1820s under the direction of Friedrich Wilhelm III, who wished to make available to the viewing public the art treasures that had been collected by the royal family. Through the next century, and particularly under the guidance of museum director Wilhelm von Bode, there was a determined effort to rival the other great museums of Europe, especially those of Paris, London, Madrid, and Vienna. The many German archeologists sent out into the field brought back important artifacts from Persia, Greece, and Egypt, and the museums developed outstanding collections.

After World War II, many works originally displayed here ended up in Dahlem, Charlottenburg, and the Tiergarten museum complex. However, Museumsinsel is still world-renowned for its ancient

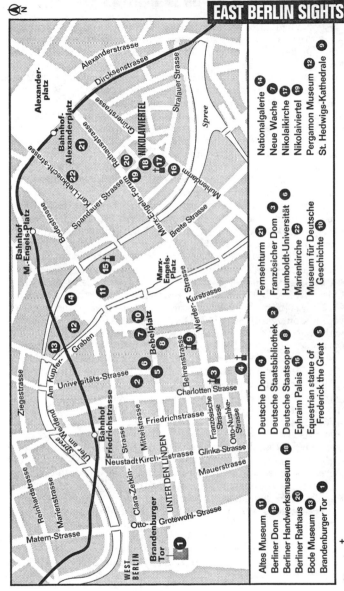

EAST BERLIN SIGHTS

Nationalgalerie ⑭
Neue Wache ⑦
Nikolaikirche ⑰
Nikolaiviertel ⑲
Pergamon Museum ⑫
St. Hedwigs-Kathedrale ⑨

Fernsehturm ㉑
Französischer Dom ③
Humboldt-Universität ⑥
Marienkirche ㉒
Museum für Deutsche Geschichte ⑩

Deutsche Dom ④
Deutsche Staatsbibliothek ②
Deutsche Staatsoper ⑧
Ephraim Palais ⑯
Equestrian statue of Frederick the Great ⑤

Altes Museum ⑪
Berliner Dom ⑮
Berliner Handwerksmuseum
Berliner Rathaus ⑳
Bode Museum ⑬
Brandenburger Tor ①

Church ✝◼

architectural and sculptural wonders, particularly the Pergamon Altar.

For museums in East Berlin in addition to those listed here, refer to the "More Attractions" section.

PERGAMON MUSEUM, Kupfergraben, Museumsinsel. Tel. 220 03 81.

★ Named after its most treasured possession, the Pergamon Altar, this is essentially a museum of architecture, the first of its kind when it opened in 1930. Its collection of Greek and Roman antiquities ranks among the world's best, and it also contains Near Eastern and Asian art, Islamic art, and German folk art. Along with the Gemäldegalerie in Dahlem and the Ägyptisches Museum in Charlottenburg, it is one of Berlin's most visited.

The **Pergamon Altar**, a huge and magnificent Hellenistic structure dating from 160–180 B.C., occupies a hall of its own directly behind the museum's main entryway. Coming from a town that now belongs to Turkey, it was dedicated to Zeus and Athena. A 7-foot frieze along the base of the altar depicts the struggle of the Greek gods against the giants (Zeus and Athena are to be seen in the eastern frieze, across from the steps).

In an adjoining room is the Roman Architecture Hall, where you'll find another one of the museum's major treasures, the **Market Gate of Miletus.** Erected around A.D. 120, this two-story Roman gate provided access to a public market, but was also large enough to contain a few shops as well. Entering the next room, you'll come upon the museum's third architectural gem, the dazzling **Babylonian Processional Street,** which leads to the **Gate of Ishtar.** Originally 990 feet long and twice as wide as reconstructed here, the street was used for religious processionals during the reign of Nebuchadnezzar II (605–562 B.C.); it is bordered by walls decorated with lions in stride, against a striking blue background. The gate itself is of blue and ochre tiles, decorated with fanciful bulls and dragons.

Upstairs are the collections of Asian and Islamic art, including Chinese pottery from the Stone Age to the beginning of this century, as well as significant pieces of Chinese sculpture. The Japanese department contains ceramics and porcelain, lacquerware, and woodblock prints by one of Japan's foremost artists, Hokusai (1760–1849). The highlight of the Islamic department is the Facade from Mschatta, a desert palace begun in the 8th century but never completed. Note the intricate designs carved in its walls, not unlike the designs of an elaborate carpet. Carpets, too, are a part of the museum's collection, many from the 13th, 14th, and 15th centuries.

Note that the museum is entered via a bridge off a lane called Kupfergraben, behind and to the left of Das Alte Museum.

Admission: 1.05 DM (65¢) for adults, 50 pfennigs (30¢) for children.

Open: Daily 10am–6pm (on Mon and Tues open only for those sections of the museum containing the Pergamon Altar, the Market Gate of Miletus, and the Gate of Ishtar). **S-Bahn:** Marx-Engels-Platz or Friedrichstrasse, each less than a 10-minute walk.

BODE MUSEUM, Bodestrasse 1-3 (entrance on Monbijoubrücke), Museumsinsel. Tel. 220 03 81.

Named after the former director responsible for bringing famous works of art to Museumsinsel, this is actually several museums housed in one. Here you'll find the **Egyptian Museum** with its **Papyrus Collection,** the **Early Christian and Byzantine Collection,** the **Museum for Primeval and Early History,** the **Sculpture Collection,** and the **Picture Gallery.**

On the ground floor you'll find the Egyptian Museum, considered one of the world's best with its lively presentation of the life and times of the Pharaohs. The Early Christian and Byzantine Collection gives an overview of early Christian art in Rome and the Byzantine Empire, and includes a valuable 6th-century mosaic from the Church of San Michele in Ravenna and a collection of ikons. The Picture Gallery, many of whose masterpieces ended up in Dahlem following World War II, nevertheless has German and Netherlandish works from the 15th and 16th centuries; Dutch, Flemish, French, and English paintings from the 17th and 18th centuries; and Italian works. The Bode Museum also boasts a Coin Cabinet, its more than half a million coins, medallions, and seals making up one of the largest and most important such collections in the world.

Admission: 1.05 DM (65¢) for adults, 50 pfennigs (30¢) for children.

Open: Wed–Sun 10am–6pm. **S-Bahn:** Marx-Engels-Platz or Friedrichstrasse, each less than a 10-minute walk.

NATIONALGALERIE (National Gallery), Bodestrasse, Museumsinsel. Tel. 220 03 81.

Taking up where the Picture Gallery of the Bode Museum leaves off, the Corinthian-style Nationalgalerie contains paintings and sculptures from the 19th and early 20th centuries, mainly by German and French artists. Among them are Gottfried Schadow, Adolph von Menzel, Edgar Degas, Paul Cézanne, and Auguste Rodin. Of special note are the German expressionist and impressionist departments on the upper floor, with works by Max Liebermann, Max Slevogt, Ernst Ludwig Kirchner, Emil Nolde, Oskar Kokoschka, and Käthe Kollwitz.

Admission: 1.05 DM (65¢) for adults, 50 pfennigs (30¢) for children.

Open: Wed–Sun 10am–6pm. **S-Bahn:** Marx-Engels-Platz, about a 5-minute walk; Friedrichstrasse, about a 10-minute walk.

DAS ALTE MUSEUM (Old Museum), Museumsinsel (entrance on Lustgarten). Tel. 220 03 81 or 22 04 20.

Built according to plans by Karl Friedrich Schinkel and considered one of his greatest works, this museum was the first constructed on Museumsinsel—and is the first one you see if you approach the island from Unter den Linden. Easily recognized by its 18 Ionic columns, it offers changing exhibitions devoted mainly to the art of ancient times. A former exhibition, for example, centered on "The World of the Etruscans."

Admission: 1.05 DM (65¢) for adults, 50 pfennigs (30¢) for children.

Open: Wed–Sun 10am–6pm. **S-Bahn:** Marx-Engels-Platz, about a 5-minute walk; Friedrichstrasse, about an 8-minute walk.

MUSEUMS IN TIERGARTEN

The precinct known as Tiergarten includes the city's largest and oldest park of the same name, the Hansaviertel (Hansa Quarter) north of the park, the zoo, and an area stretching south of the park designated as the city's newest cultural center. This last, with the

Philharmonie in the middle, is home of the Neue Nationalgalerie, the Kunstwerbe Museum, and the Musikinstrumenten Museum. Once additional construction is completed throughout the next decade, it will also house several museums now in Dahlem: the Gemälde-galeries, the Skulpturengalerie, and the Kupferstichkabinett (Museum of Prints and Drawings). In fact, the Kupferstichkabinett is scheduled to open in its new Tiergarten quarters by the end of 1992. Check with the Berlin Tourist Information Office for exact details.

NEUE NATIONALGALERIE (New National Gallery), Potsdamer Strasse 50. Tel. 266 26 63 or 2666.

The first museum to open in the Tiergarten cultural area, the Neue Nationalgalerie is called "new" to distinguish it from East Berlin's much older Nationalgalerie on Museumsinsel. In fact, it owes its core collection to the latter, since it received more than 600 artworks from the older museum after World War II. A starkly modern building designed by architect Mies van der Rohe and built in the 1960s, it's set in a vast square surrounded by a sculpture garden. Featuring art of the 19th and 20th centuries, it shows changing exhibitions on the ground floor, while a lower floor houses the permanent collection.

Highlights are works by Adolph von Menzel (1815–1905)—the world's largest collection of this Berlin artist—and works by Monet, Manet, Pissarro, Renoir, Beckmann, Corinth, Klee, Picasso, Kokoschka, Kirchner, and Dali. With the galleries covering art from preimpressionism and realism to impressionism, expressionism, modern classicism, and surrealism, there's great variety in this small, bright, and airy museum—one of my Berlin favorites. If you aren't familiar with German artists of the past century, this is a good introduction.

Admission: Free to permanent collection; temporary exhibits average 4 DM ($2.40).

Open: Tues–Fri 9am–5pm, Sat and Sun 10am–5pm. **Closed:** Mon, Jan 1, Tues after Easter and after Whitsunday, May 1, Dec 24, 25, and 31. **U-Bahn:** Kurfürstenstrasse, then bus 48 or 83. **Bus:** 29 from the Ku'damm.

KUNSTGEWERBE MUSEUM (Museum of Applied Arts), Tiergartenstrasse 6. Tel. 266 29 02.

A 5-minute walk from the Nationalgalerie and located next door to the Philharmonie, this modern red-brick museum is devoted to European applied arts from the early Middle Ages to the present day: glassware, porcelain, beer steins, tableware, measuring instruments, and more. Particularly outstanding is the collection of medieval goldsmiths' works, including the *Guelph Cross* and the *Domed Reliquary,* among the richest ecclesiastical treasures in any German museum; an 8th-century piece associated with Charlemagne; and the baptism bowl of Emperor Barbarossa. The *Lüneburg Town Hall Silver Plate,* another priceless treasure, consists of 32 vessels and implements in gold-plated silver. There are also displays of Venetian glass, early Meissen porcelain, and Jugendstil vases and other objects. The bottom floor is devoted to changing exhibits of contemporary

crafts and product design, from typewriters to teapots and furniture.
Admission: Free.
Open: Tues–Fri 9am–5pm, Sat and Sun 10am–5pm. **Closed:**
Mon, Jan 1, Tues after Easter and after Whitsunday, May 1, Dec 24,
25, and 31. **U-Bahn:** Kurfürstenstrasse, then bus 48 or 83. **Bus:** 29
from the Ku'damm.

**MUSIKINSTRUMENTEN MUSEUM (Museum of Musical
Instruments), Tiergartenstrasse 1. Tel. 25 48 10.**
   A small gray building in the shadow of the larger Philharmonie,
the Musikinstrumenten Museum reopened in its new Tiergarten
home in 1984. The collection, which originated in 1888, suffered
greatly during World War II, with a loss of more than 3,000 pieces
out of a 4,000 total. The past decades have seen so many new
acquisitions, however, that the museum once again boasts a healthy
collection of European musical instruments from the 16th century to
the present day, with valuable pieces from the Renaissance and
baroque periods. Included are spinets, clavichords, violins, trumpets,
flutes, alpenhorns, harps, zithers, guitars, and the now-forgotten glass
harmonica, for which Mozart and others wrote compositions.
Admission: Free.
Open: Tues–Fri 9am–5pm, Sat and Sun 10am–5pm. **Closed:**
Mon, Jan 1, Tues after Easter and after Whitsunday, May 1, Dec 24,
25, and 31. **U-Bahn:** Kurfürstenstrasse, then bus 48 or 83. **Bus:** 29
from the Ku'damm.

2. MORE ATTRACTIONS

NEAR THE KU'DAMM

**KAISER-WILHELM GEDÄCHTNISKIRCHE (Kaiser Wil-
helm Memorial Church), Breitscheidplatz. Tel. 24 50
23.**
   This church, which marks the beginning of the Ku'damm, would
be difficult to overlook. In fact, almost a half century after the end of
World War II, it comes as something of a surprise to see the skeletal
ruins of a war-damaged steeple in the heart of modern Berlin. But lest
we forget the horrors of war, the Gedächtniskirche was left as a
bombed-out shell of its former self. The church dates from 1895, and
today it contains a small museum with displays related to war and
destruction. Beside it, in striking contrast, stands a newer, octagonal
church with a hexagonal tower. Designed by Professor Egon
Eiermann and completed in 1961, it's made of blue glass plates from
Chartres. In the true Berliner style of nicknaming everything in sight,
the new church is referred to as the "powderbox and lipstick."
Admission: Free.

Open: Ruined church open Tues–Sat 10am–6pm, Sun 11am–6pm; new church open daily 9am–7:30pm. Services held Sun and holidays 10am and 6pm; short services Mon–Fri 1, 5:30, and 6pm. Organ concerts Sat 6pm. **U-Bahn:** Kurfürstendamm or Bahnhof Zoologischer Garten, each about a 1-minute walk.

KÄTHE-KOLLWITZ-MUSEUM, Fasanenstrasse 24. Tel. 882 52 10.

Just south of the Ku'damm, this small but significant museum displays the powerful, gripping drawings and sketches of Käthe Kollwitz (1867–1945). A Berliner, Kollwitz was a genius who captured the human emotions of her subjects, from the tenderness mothers feel toward their children to the despair and grief caused by poverty and oppression. Don't miss the opportunity to see her works—their power will stay with you long afterward.

Admission: 6 DM ($3.65) for adults, 3 DM ($1.80) for students.

Open: Wed–Mon 11am–6pm. **U-Bahn:** Uhlandstrasse, a 1-minute walk.

EUROPA-CENTER, Tauentzienstrasse.

With the star emblem of Mercedes-Benz like a beacon atop its roof, the Europa-Center is a mammoth, 22-story building in the heart of Berlin just a minute's walk from the Gedächtniskirche, the Ku'damm, and Bahnhof Zoo. It houses mainly offices, but also contains restaurants, shops, pubs, cabarets, a hotel, a casino, and the Berlin tourist office. There's even a public bath and sauna facility, called Thermen, which also includes a swimming pool, steam baths, and a fitness room (refer to the "Sports & Recreation" section later in this chapter). The Europa-Center's top floor is a sightseeing platform, open daily from 9am to midnight (in winter from 10am), where for 3 DM ($1.80) you have a view of all Berlin. Of most interest to tourists, however, is *Multivision Berlin* (first floor), an hour-long program relating seven centuries of Berlin's history on a 70-foot screen. Shows are held daily between 9am and 1:30pm, and admission is 8 DM ($4.85).

Admission: Free to Europa-Center. **U-Bahn:** Kurfürstendamm or Bahnhof Zoologischer Garten, each about a 2-minute walk.

IMPRESSIONS

This place recalls to the beholder at every step, the image, genuis, and the actions of the reigning Sovereign. . . . If however, Berlin strikes by its regularity and the magnificence of its public buildings, it impresses not less forcibly with a sentiment of melancholy.
—Sir N. W. Wraxall, 1779

Berlin is all show, a forced place, having little commerce, and less content; no smiling faces—no mediocrity, that happiest of all conditions.
—Captain John Dundas Cochrane, 1824

IN KREUZBERG

BERLIN MUSEUM, Lindenstrasse 14. Tel. 2586 28 39.

Housed in an impressive yellow-and-white baroque building (1735) that once served as the Supreme Court, the Berlin Museum is dedicated to the city's history. Using furniture, toys, porcelain, paintings, newspaper clippings, and other artifacts, it relates the story of life here since the 17th century, with particular emphasis on the 18th and 19th centuries. Displays highlight the living standards of Berlin's bourgeoisie, and there is a fine collection of Biedermeier furniture. Jugendstil art is also shown. In chronological progression, the museum depicts life in the 1920s under the Weimar Republic, and later under the Nazis and during World War II. Unfortunately, most explanations are in German only, but you can still learn a lot here. One room devoted to Jewish religious artifacts soberingly reveals that of the 60,000 Jews living in Berlin in 1939, 50,000 were taken to concentration camps. Since the museum lacks sufficient room, the Jewish displays continue in the Martin-Gropius-Bau, described below.

For refreshment after touring the museum, drop by the museum's Alt-Berliner Weissbier Stube, an old Berlin–style pub, where a special wheat beer is served.

Admission: 3.50 DM ($2.10) for adults, 1.50 DM (90¢) for students.

Open: Tues–Sun 10am–10pm. **U-Bahn:** Hallesches Tor, then bus 41 or a 10-minute walk. **Bus:** 29 from the Ku'damm to Charlottenstrasse stop, then a 10-minute walk.

MARTIN-GROPIUS-BAU, Stresemannstrasse 110. Tel. 25 48 60.

The Martin-Gropius-Bau, beautiful inside and out, was designed by architect Martin Gropius in 1881. It houses two museums: Berlinische Galerie and the Jewish department of the Berlin Museum. The **Berlinische Galerie,** the city's museum for modern art, photography, and architecture, features changing exhibitions and a permanent display, with an emphasis on art of the 20th century. Though most of its works are by contemporary Berlin artists, it also shows international art.

Admission: Permanent exhibition 6 DM ($3.65) for adults, 3 DM ($1.80) for children; temporary exhibitions cost extra.

Open: Tues–Sun 10am–8pm. **U-Bahn:** Kochstrasse, about a 5-minute walk. **S-Bahn:** Anhalter Bahnhof, about a 5-minute walk.

MUSEUM HAUS AM CHECKPOINT CHARLIE, Friedrichstrasse 44. Tel. 251 10 31.

This small but important museum opened soon after the Berlin Wall went up in 1961, with the sole purpose of documenting the grisly events that were taking place because of the Wall. Even though the Wall and Checkpoint Charlie (once a major border check for foreigners entering East Berlin) are now relics of the past, the museum will continue showing photographs, items used in escapes (a hot-air balloon, cars with hidden compartments), and newspaper clippings. Its display on nonviolent revolutions includes information on Mahatma Gandhi, Lech Walesa, and the peaceful 1989 upheaval in East Germany. More than any other Berlin museum, this one manages to convey most vividly the drama of life in the city during the Cold War, especially those decades when everyone lived in the shadow of the Wall.

Admission: 4 DM ($2.40) for adults, 3 DM ($1.80) for students.
Open: 9am to 10pm daily. **U-Bahn:** Kochstrasse, a few minutes' walk.

IN EAST BERLIN

MUSEUM FÜR DEUTSCHE GESCHICHTE (Museum of German History), Unter den Linden 2. Tel. 200 05 91 or 200 09 41.

Originally built in the 17th century as an arsenal for the Prussian army, this museum traces the history of Germany from prehistoric times to 1949. After the revolution of 1989, those displays relating to postwar East Germany were shut down—to be redesigned in light of new developments. A rewriting of history, as it were. The other displays, however, have been left intact, presenting a decidedly socialist point of view: farmers' uprisings against oppressive feudal lords, class struggles, the "fall of feudalism and the rise of capitalism," "imperialist" World War I. Unfortunately, explanations are in German only, but it's worth wandering through for the museum's unique perspective.

Admission: 1.05 DM (65¢) for adults, 50 pfennigs (30¢) for children.
Open: Mon–Thurs 9am–6pm, Sat and Sun 10am–5pm. **S-Bahn:** Friedrichstrasse, less than a 10-minute walk.

MÄRKISCHES MUSEUM, Am Köllnischen Park 5. Tel. 270 05 14.

Whereas the museum described above concerns itself with the history of Germany, this one concentrates on the history of Berlin. Displays include prehistoric archeological finds, beginning with the Stone Age; models of the city around 1500, when it consisted of two villages called Berlin and Cölln; and paintings, glassware, porcelain (including KPM Berlin), wrought-iron furniture, and other items produced through the ensuing centuries. There's also a special section dedicated to Berlin theater, with photographs and pictures of famous actors, actresses, and directors.

Admission: 1.05 DM (65¢) for adults, 50 pfennigs (30¢) for children.
Open: Wed–Fri 10am–6pm, Sat and Sun 10am–5pm. **U-Bahn:** Märkisches Museum, a few minutes' walk.

OTTO-NAGEL-HAUS, Märkisches Ufer 16-18. Tel. 279 14 02.

Situated on the banks of a canal, this small museum features proletarian and antifascist artwork. Though there are some changing displays, it is primarily devoted to Otto Nagel and his contemporaries. In his paintings, the Berlin-born Nagel (1894–1967) realistically portrayed the city's working class of the 1920s and 1930s, with no attempt at glorification. A very interesting museum.

Admission: 50 pfennigs (30¢).
Open: Sun–Thurs 10am–6pm. **S-Bahn:** Märkisches Museum, a few minutes' walk.

IN ZEHLENDORF

MUSEUMSDORF DÜPPEL, Clauertstrasse 11. Tel. 802 66 71.

Open in summer only, this open-air reproduction of a medieval village features thatch-roofed houses and live demonstrations of woodworking, baking, weaving, and other household chores. Explanations are in German only, but coming here makes a pleasant trip in fine weather. Good for a family outing.

Admission: 3 DM ($1.80) for adults, 1 DM (60¢) for children.
Open: May–beginning of Oct, Sun and holidays 10am–5pm (enter before 4pm), Thur 3–7pm (enter by 6pm). **Bus:** 3 to Lindenthaler Allee/Ecke Clauertstrasse; 18 to Potsdamer Chaussee/Ecke Lindenthaler Allee; or 50 to Berlepschstrasse/Ecke Ludwigsfelder Strasse.

---

3. ZOOS, PARKS & GARDENS

Many visitors are surprised to learn that the city limits encompass a large area of woods and lakes. During the decades when West Berlin was surrounded by East Germany and the Wall, its green spaces and water—accounting for a full 30% of its total 190 square miles—served as an important emotional escape valve for urban dwellers in need of nature. The most popular destinations for a day's outing continue to be Grünewald forest and Havel and Wannsee lakes. For more information on these destinations, refer below to the sections on "Organized Tours" and "Sports & Recreation."

THE TIERGARTEN, from Bahnhof Zoo to Brandenburger Tor.

Berlin's most convenient park, as well as its largest, is the Tiergarten park. Approximately 1.86 miles long and a half mile wide, it stretches east from Bahnhof Zoo all the way to the Brandenburger Tor. Originally used as a hunting reserve and then as the elector's private park, the Tiergarten was opened to the public at the end of the 19th century. Largely destroyed in World War II, it suffered further damage when Berliners used most of its trees for fuel during the long cold winters. Today trees have been replanted, and it's one of the most popular places in the city for picnics, jogging, sunbathing, and strolling. In addition to ponds, streams, a rose garden, and an English-style garden, it also contains the Zoologischer Garten (Berlin Zoo), located in the massive park's southwest corner (for more information on the zoo, refer below to "Cool for Kids").

BOTANISCHER GARTEN (Botanical Garden), Königin-Luise-Strasse 6-8, Dahlem. Tel. 83 00 60.

Berlin's Botanischer Garten was laid out at the turn of the century and boasts 104 acres and 18,000 species of plants. Its 16 greenhouses contain plants from all continents and environments, from rain forests to deserts. Outdoor beds are arranged geographically, so that visitors can wander through landscapes that resemble the Alps, Japan, the Himalayas, South Africa, North America, and other regions. There's also a garden of medicinal plants, as well as a garden for the visually handicapped, where visitors can smell and touch the plants. The small Botanisches Museum displays the history and usage of various plants.

Admission: 2.50 DM ($1.50) for adults, 1.20 DM (70¢) for students and children; Botanisches Museum, free.

Open: Botanischer Garten open daily Nov–Feb 9am–4pm, Mar and Oct 9am–5pm, April and Sept 9am–7pm, May–Aug 9am–8pm. Greenhouses open daily Nov–Feb 10am–3:15pm, Mar and Oct 9am–4:15pm, Apr–Sept 9am–5:15pm. Botanisches Museum open Tues–Sun 10am–5pm. **S-Bahn:** Botanischer Garten.

ZOOLOGISCHER GARTEN (Berlin Zoo), Budapester Strasse 32 and Hardenbergplatz 8 (tel. 261 11 01).

One of Europe's best, founded in 1844 and located just a short walk from the Ku'damm or Bahnhof Zoo, it is home to more than 11,000 animals of almost 2,000 species. Probably the best-known and most-beloved resident is BaoBao, the panda, but other popular animals include the camels, kangaroos, antelopes, lions, tigers, and monkeys. There's also a birdhouse with 720 species. The adjacent **Aquarium** has a collection of more than 6,000 fish, reptiles, and amphibians.

Admission: A combination ticket, allowing entrance to both the zoo and the aquarium, costs 11.50 DM ($6.95) for adults, 10 DM ($6.05) for students, 6 DM ($3.65) for children. Tickets for the zoo only are 7.50 DM ($4.55) for adults, 6.50 DM ($3.95) for students, and 4 DM ($2.40) for children.

Open: Daily in summer from 9am to 6:3pm and in winter from 9am to 5pm.

U-Bahn: Bahnhof Zoo, just a few minutes' walk away.

---

4. COOL FOR KIDS

TOP ATTRACTIONS

Ethnological Museum (Museum für Völkerkunde) (see p. 142) One of the largest ethnological museums in the world, with a fascinating display of boats, canoes, masks, dwellings, weapons, clothing, and other fascinating items. Fun and educational.

Museum Haus am Checkpoint Charlie (see p. 157) This museum documents the decades of the Berlin Wall, and on display are vehicles used in daring escapes, including cars with hidden compartments and a hot-air balloon. With its many photographs, it is one of the best places to show your child what Berlin during the Cold War was all about.

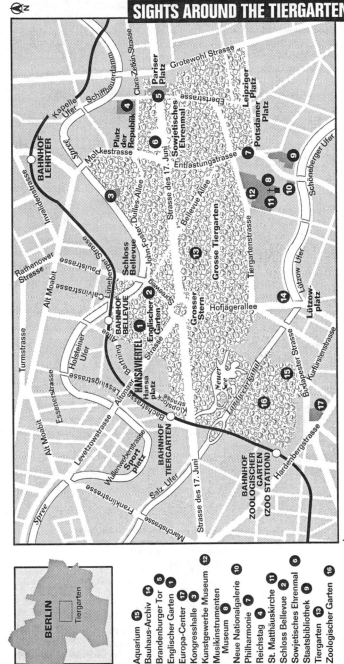

SIGHTS AROUND THE TIERGARTEN

BERLIN

Tiergarten

✝ Church

Museumsdorf Düppel in Zehlendorf (*see page 159*), is a re-created open-air medieval village complete with thatch-roofed houses and live demonstrations of woodworking, baking, weaving, and other occupations.

PARKS, THE ZOO & THE BEACH

Zoologischer Garten and Aquarium (*see p. 160*) Who can resist BaoBao the panda, as well the monkeys, the lions, and the camels? The Berlin Zoo, founded in 1844, houses more than 11,000 animals of all kinds. Fun for the entire family, it's only minutes from the Ku'damm.

Botanischer Garten (*see p. 159*) Show your child that cocoa grows on trees or that there are such things as insect-eating plants. The Botanical Garden, laid out at the turn of the century, also has a special area for the visually handicapped, who are encouraged to smell and touch the plants.

Tiergarten (*see p. 159*) The park, located right in the heart of Berlin, is another good spot for an outing.

Wannsee Beach (*see p. 165*) A day at the beach is always fun, and children can enjoy a playground here (complete with slides) as well as the swimming.

ENTERTAINMENT

At **Europa-Center** (*see p. 156*) older kids might enjoy *Multivision Berlin,* an hour-long film on the history of Berlin.

Grips, Altonaer Strasse 22 (tel. 391 40 04), the undisputed champion of children's theater in Berlin, is famous throughout Germany, with shows that appeal to kids aged 7 and up. Its highly praised performances are designed for different age groups, including older children. If your child doesn't understand German, try to attend one of the productions meant for a young age group, where there's lots of action and the plot is easy to follow.

Berliner Kammerspiele, Alt-Moabit 99 (tel. 391 55 43), has programs appealing mainly to young children. Check the *Berlin Programm* for information on current performances, times, and prices.

---

5. SPECIAL-INTEREST SIGHTSEEING

FOR THE ARCHITECTURE LOVER

Because Berlin suffered such widespread destruction during World War II, the city is conspicuously devoid of the architectural gems that grace many other European cities. One notable exception is **Schloss Charlottenburg,** described above under "Top Attractions" as Berlin's most beautiful baroque structure.

In addition, some buildings remain that were designed by Karl

Friedrich Schinkel (1781–1841), one of Berlin's best-known architects. Among his surviving works are the **Schinkel Pavilion** on the grounds of Schloss Charlottenburg, the **Altes Museum** on Museum Island, and the **Schlossbrücke** (renamed the Marx-Engels-Brücke), which connects Unter den Linden and Marx-Engels-Platz in East Berlin.

The bulk of Berlin's architecture, however, dates back only a few decades. The most famous modern buildings are those in the **Hansaviertel** (Hansa Quarter), which stretches along the northern border of the Tiergarten park. The quarter consists primarily of housing projects, from one-family dwellings to apartment buildings, along with two churches, a library, and a school. The Hansaviertel resulted from a 1957 international gathering of 50 leading architects (from more than 20 countries), who were asked to design a community for Berliners still homeless as a result of World War II. Famous architects who participated included Walter Gropius, Alvar Aalto, Pierre Vago, Oscar Niemeyer, and Werner Düttmann. For orientation, be sure to consult the outdoor map of the Hansaviertel, which lists each building and its architect; the closest subway station is Hansa station. Incidentally, Le Corbusier's design was of such proportions that it was built in the western end of the city near the Olympiastadion (Olympic Stadium). It's Berlin's largest housing project, with 530 apartments.

Another place of interest to architecture fans is the **Bauhaus-Archiv,** Klingelhöferstrasse 13-14 (tel. 261 16 18 or 254 00 233). Located in a light, airy building designed by Walter Gropius, it is dedicated to preserving both the ideals and artifacts relating to the Bauhaus school of design. The Bauhaus, founded by Gropius in Weimar in 1919 and disbanded in Berlin in 1933, revolutionized the teaching of architecture and industrial design through its emphasis on aesthetics.

The Bauhaus-Archiv contains a museum, an extensive collection of documents, and a library. The museum's permanent collection includes architectural models, designs, paintings, drawings, and applied arts that adhere to Bauhaus principles, including the work of Gropius, Hannes Meyer, Ludwig Mies van der Rohe, Marcel Breuer, and Ludwig Hilberseimer. Also shown are paintings and drawings by Herbert Bayer, Lyonel Feininger, Johannes Itten, Wassily Kandinsky, Paul Klee, Laszlo Moholy-Nagy, Georg Muche, and Oskar Schlemmer. Note, however, that items on permanent display are sometimes removed to make way for temporary special exhibitions, relating to the Bauhaus.

The Bauhaus-Archiv, which can be reached by taking bus 2, 9, 16, or 24 to Lützowplatz, is open Wednesday through Monday from 11am to 5pm. Admission is 3.50 DM ($2.10) for adults and 1.50 DM (90¢) for students. On Mondays, admission is free.

FOR VISITING AMERICANS

More than 100 streets, boulevards, and squares are named after Americans, testimonial to the close ties Berlin has had through the years with the United States. Most famous of all is probably **John-F.-Kennedy-Platz,** the square in front of Rathaus Schöneberg. It was from here that Kennedy gave his famous "Ich bin ein Berliner" speech on June 26, 1963, just months before he was assassinated. **Rathaus Schöneberg** (tel. 7831) remains of interest to Americans because of its huge Freedom Bell, modeled after the U.S. Liberty Bell, Sundays only, from 10am and 3:30pm (follow the signs that say *Zum Turm*). In the tower you'll also find display cases devoted to the history of the bell, including some of the 16 million signatures of Americans who pledged their support by signing the "Declaration of Freedom" (the bulk of the signatures are kept in a vault in the tower). At any rate, you have to climb a lot of steps to reach the tower, but the view from the top is grand. To reach Rathaus Schöneberg, take U-4 to the U-Bahn station of the same name, from which it's a minute's walk.

Other streets and places named after Americans include **Truman Plaza, Clayallee** (named in honor of Gen. Lucius Clay for his part in the Berlin Airlift of 1948–49), and the **John F. Kennedy School** (part of the Berlin school system but staffed by both American and German teachers).

---

6. ORGANIZED TOURS

In light of the many changes taking place in Berlin because of reunification, tour companies are redesigning their offerings. In particular, trips to the environs are expected to increase greatly, so be sure to inquire for updated schedules.

BUS TOURS

With the aid of this book, you shouldn't have to spend money on a tour. However, you may wish to take one upon arrival in Berlin simply for orientation and for identifying the highlights. You can then return to the sights that interest you and enjoy them at leisure.

There are a number of tour companies in Berlin, with most of their buses departing from the Ku'damm area. Oldest and largest of these is **Severin + Kuhn,** Kurfürstendamm 216 (tel. 883 10 15), which is open daily from 9am to 7pm. A 2-hour tour of Berlin costs 22 DM ($13.35), while a 4-hour evening nightclub tour costs 95 DM ($57.55), including two drinks.

If you're in Berlin for several days, you may wish to join Severin + Kuhn on its day trip to historic Potsdam, favored residency of Prussian royalty, where you'll visit Frederick the Great's rococo palace, Sanssouci, and its surrounding gardens. You'll also visit Schloss Cecilienhof, former home of the crown prince and his family. It was here that the 1945 Potsdam Agreement was signed by the Allied Powers following World War II. Days, times, and prices vary according to the season—in summer a 9-hour tour costs 109 DM ($66.05), including lunch. For more information, contact Severin + Kuhn.

Other companies with similar tours and prices include **Berolina,** whose buses depart from the corner of the Kurfürstendamm and Meinekestrasse (tel. 883 31 31 or 881 68 57), and **Berliner Bären Stadtrundfahrt,** Rankestrasse 35 (tel. 213 40 77).

BOAT TRIPS

The Spree, a river that winds its way through the heart of Berlin, serves as a popular waterway for boat trips throughout the year. Excursions of 2, 3, and 4 hours are offered by **Horst Duggen** (tel. 394 49 54), with departures directly in front of the Kongresshalle north of the Tiergarten park (take bus 69 or 83 to the Kongresshalle stop). The 4-hour trip, which costs 10 DM ($6.05) for adults and 5 DM ($3.05) for children, travels along the Spree past Schloss Charlottenburg all the way to Zitadelle Spandauer (fortress) and back.

If you're in Berlin from April to the end of October, you can also climb aboard one of the many boats plying the waters of Havel and Wannsee lakes. One of the most popular trips is from Wannsee (near the U-Bahn station) to Pfaueninsel and back, operated by **Stern and Kreisschiffahrt** (tel. 810 00 40 or 803 87 50).

7. SPORTS & RECREATION

With approximately 6,000 sports grounds, 70 gyms, 60 indoor and outdoor public swimming pools, as well as numerous bowling alleys, tennis courts, and other facilities, Berlin offers a wide range of activities for the sports-minded visitor. If you'd rather watch than participate, check *Berlin Programm* for a day-by-day account of spectator events, from ice hockey and soccer to basketball and table tennis.

SWIMMING

In summer both Berliners and visitors flock to **Wannsee,** site of Europe's largest lake beach. On a warm sunny day, as many as 20,000 people will take advantage of its facilities, which include a children's playground, slides, and a terrace with shops and restaurants. And if you wish you can rent one of those huge basketlike beach chairs common to northern Germany, which help shield against wind as well as sun. The beach—open May through September, daily from 7am to 8pm—costs 3 DM ($1.80) for adults and 1.50 DM (90¢) for children. To reach it, take the S-Bahn to Nikolassee. Incidentally, don't be surprised to see topless bathing. Wannsee even has a section devoted to nude bathing.

If it's winter, try one of the numerous indoor public pools. **Stadtbad Charlottenburg,** Krumme Strasse 9 and 10 (tel. 343 03 241 or 343 03 214), is open daily, with times varying because of swimming lessons, etc.; so call beforehand. Otherwise, ask at your hotel front desk for the nearest public bath. If you're staying at one of the larger, more expensive hotels, you may even have free access to a swimming pool and fitness center.

Although it's expensive, you may wish to indulge in the hot baths 32). Open Monday through Saturday from 10am to midnight and on Sunday from 10am to 9pm, it charges 24 DM ($14.55) for 3 hours, which includes use of a thermal swimming pool (with an outdoor lane), saunas, steam room, fitness room, TV room, table-tennis room, and a sunning terrace with 150 lounge chairs. Also available are a solarium, massage facilities, and even a restaurant. Again, bathing is mixed, and in European style, most visitors go in the buff.

STROLLING AROUND BERLIN

Even though Berlin is a large city, most of its sights, shops, restaurants, and attractions are concentrated in specific neighborhoods, making the city easy to explore on foot.

The first two recommended strolls begin in the vicinity of the Gedächtniskirche and the Europa-Center, which means that you could cover both in a day's walk. Similarly, you could also combine the second two strolls in a daylong tour if you have the stamina. From my experience, visitors usually prefer walking wherever possible, simply because it is sometimes easier than figuring out which bus to take and because it allows them to see something of the city en route. Natives, more likely to jump on the subway or bus, are often astounded at the great distances visitors are prepared to walk. How often have you been told by a native, "It's too far to walk," only to discover that it's actually only a 10- or 20-minute hike?

WALKING TOUR 1 — Along the Ku'damm

Start: Kaiser-Wilhelm Gedächtniskirche on Breitscheidplatz.

Finish: Wertheim department store, 231 Kurfürstendamm, near Joachimstaler Strasse.

Time: Allow approximately 2 hours, not including museum and shopping stops.

Best Times: Weekdays, when shops are open; or the first Saturday of the month, when shops stay open until 6pm.

Worst Times: Tuesdays, when both the Käthe-Kollwitz-Museum and the Ku'damm Karree antiques market are closed; or Sundays, when all shops are closed.

The Kurfürstendamm is Berlin's most famous boulevard, home of the city's most expensive shops, hotels, restaurants, bars, and nightclubs. No visit to Berlin would be complete without at least one stroll down the Kurfürstendamm, affectionately called the Ku'damm by Berliners, who are also apt to complain about their beloved boulevard. It's too crowded with tourists, they say, and there are too many bad restaurants out to make a buck. But that doesn't stop them from coming here, especially when the weather's warm and they can sit at one of the outdoor cafés to watch the passing parade. And what a parade it is: tourists from around the world, street performers, shoppers, punks, bejeweled women. Never a dull moment on the Ku'damm.

By the way, the Ku'damm stretches 2½ miles, but don't worry—we'll cover only the more important half of it, with excursions into the most interesting side streets along the way. It's a loop stroll, ending up across the street from where it begins.

FROM THE GEDÄCHTNISKIRCHE TO SAVIGNYPLATZ It would be difficult to miss the:

1. **Kaiser-Wilhelm Gedächtniskirche** on Breitscheidplatz, so out of place does this ruined church look beside the modern high-rises that surround it. Left as a reminder of World War II, it marks the beginning of the Ku'damm.

    West of the Gedächtniskirche on Breitscheidplatz is the:

2. **American Express office,** Ku'damm 11, as well as:

3. **Tschibo coffee shop,** where you can drink a cup of coffee for 1.20 DM (70¢), standing up at one of its chest-high counters. Walking past Tschibo along the north side of the Ku'damm, you'll soon come to:

4. **Café Kranzler,** Ku'damm 18, one of Berlin's most famous coffee shops and a favored spot for people-watching at its sidewalk tables. Nearby is:

5. **KPM,** Ku'damm 26a, a shop that deals in the exquisite porcelain of the Königliche Porzellan-Manufaktur, one of Berlin's most famous products with a history dating back more than 200 years.

    The next intersection is Fasanenstrasse, and if you turn right here and walk past the Bristol Kempinksi Hotel, within a minute you'll come to:

6. **Zille Hof,** Fasanenstrasse 14, a jumble of junk stalls underneath the S-Bahn tracks. Who knows, you might find a treasure here among the crowded and dusty shelves laden with plates, glasses, pots and pans, books, clothing, and odds and ends. If nothing else, its entryway is worth a photograph.

    Back on the Ku'damm, continue heading west one block to the corner of Uhlandstrasse. Here, in the median that runs in the middle of the Ku'damm, you'll notice a futuristic-looking row of lights. Believe it or not, it's a:

7. **Clock,** and here's how it works. Every light of the top row represents 5 hours; the lights beneath it each represent 1 hour; the third row stands for 5 minutes; and the bottom-row lights each represent 1 minute. If you count them all together, they'll tell you the exact time. Thus, if you had two lights on the top row, followed by one light in the next row, three lights on the third, and then two, it would be 11:17am. If you still have

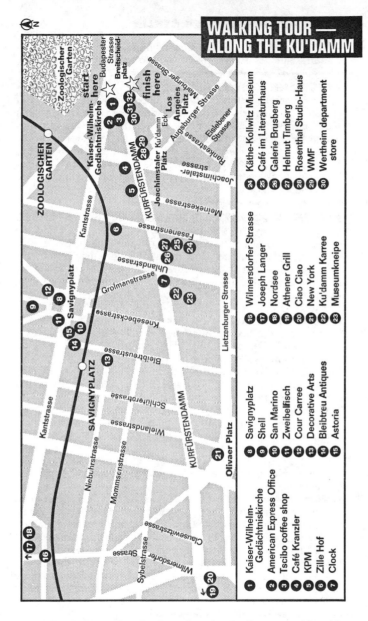

start here · **finish here**

1. Kaiser-Wilhelm-Gedächtniskirche
2. American Express Office
3. Tscibo coffee shop
4. Café Kranzler
5. KPM
6. Zille Hof
7. Clock
8. Savignyplatz
9. Shell
10. San Marino
11. Zweibelfisch
12. Cour Carree
13. Decorative Arts
14. Bleibtreu Antiques
15. Astoria
16. Wilmersdorfer Strasse
17. Joseph Langer
18. Nordsee
19. Athener Grill
20. Ciao Ciao
21. New York
22. Ku'damm Karree
23. Museumkneipe
24. Käthe-Kollwitz Museum
25. Café im Literaturhaus
26. Galerie Brusberg
27. Helmut Timberg
28. Rosenthal Studio-Haus
29. WMF
30. Wertheim department store

difficulty, consider the fact that the Berliners consider this **a** child's game.

Continue walking west along the Ku'damm one more block to Knesebeckstrasse, where you should turn right. Within a 5-minute walk you'll find yourself on:

8. Savignyplatz, a grassy square lined with restaurants, bars, and turn-of-the-century apartment buildings. This is where you'll find some of Berlin's interesting nightlife, including trendy bars and restaurants, so you might want to return here after dark.

REFUELING STOPS **9. Shell,** on the north end of Savignyplatz at Knesebeckstrasse 22, is popular with young residents of the area, particularly for its international dishes, including light meals and vegetarian selections. Nearby is **10. San Marino,** Savignyplatz 12, an Italian pizzeria with outdoor seating in the square. If all you want is a drink, try **11. Zwiebelfisch,** Savignyplatz 7-8, open from noon to 6am, or **12. Cour Carrée,** Savignyplatz 5, recommended for its outdoor seating in the shade of spreading vines.

FROM SAVIGNYPLATZ TO WILMERSDORFER STRASSE

Begin from Savignyplatz's southwest corner, where you'll find the overhead tracks of the S-Bahn. Beneath the arches of the tracks are a few interesting shops, bars, and restaurants, including a boutique (devoted to lamps) and an inexpensive Greek eatery. At the end of the passage is Bleibtreustrasse, home to three interesting art deco shops. Take a left and walk one short block to the corner of Niebuhrstrasse, where you'll find:

13. Decorative Arts, a shop that specializes mainly in glass and furniture from the Jugendstil period to the 1920s and 1930s.

If you backtrack and walk farther north on Bleibtreustrasse, within minutes you'll come to two more shops.

14. Bleibtreu Antiques, at Kantstrasse and Bleibtreustrasse, sells Biedermeier furniture, Jugendstil and art deco jewelry, and a wide selection of lamps and glass. Likewise:

15. Astoria, across the street at Bleibtreustrasse 50, deals in lamps, statues, jewelry and some furniture, including antiques and reproductions. Take note that all three art deco shops are open only in the afternoon.

You're now on the corner of Bleibtreustrasse and Kantstrasse. Head west for approximately 10 minutes, until you reach:

16. Wilmersdorfer Strasse. This is Berlin's main pedestrian shopping lane, where in quick succession you'll find such large department stores as Karstadt, Quelle, and Hertie. There are also a number of smaller shops and boutiques, as well as several restaurants. If you're tired or decide to spend the rest of the day shopping, you can return to your hotel by taking the subway from Wilmersdorfer Strasse station. Otherwise, take advantage of the many fast-food restaurants in the area, or head back down to the Ku'damm.

REFUELING STOPS There are a number of inexpensive eateries on Wilmersdorfer Strasse, including cafeterias and restaurants in the three department stores listed above. For a quick standup meal, try **17. Joseph Langer,** Wilmersdorfer Strasse 118, a butcher shop that also sells simple meals and Würste. Across the street is **18. Nordsee,** Wilmersdorfer Strasse 58, a fast-food fish restaurant.

If you prefer a more relaxed and less hectic environment where you can linger over a meal or drink, head for **19. Athener Grill,** Ku'damm 156, near Adenauerplatz. This cafeteria sells both Greek and Italian food, from moussaka to pizza. next door is **20. Ciao Ciao,** a popular Italian restaurant with outdoor seating.

A popular watering hole in the area is **21. New York,** Olivaer Platz 15, where Berlin's trendy youth gather throughout the day and late into the evening.

FROM ADENAUERPLATZ TO JOACHIMSTALER STRASSE ON THE KU'DAMM Walking back in the direction of the Gedächtniskirche, this time on the south side of the Ku'damm, you'll again pass a number of shops. This, after all, is Berlin's classiest shopping street. Note the many freestanding display cases along the sidewalk, advertising the wares of nearby shops. If it were evening, you'd notice wares of a different sort being offered, since the Ku'damm has long been a favored spot for the ladies of the night (prostitution, by the way, is legal in Germany).

Our first stop on this leg of our journey is the:

22. Ku'damm Karree, located at Ku'damm 207 near Knesebeckstrasse. There are a number of clothing and accessory shops on the ground floor of this shopping center, but of particular interest is the antiques market up on the first floor, where you'll find jewelry, clothing, furniture, old records, books, glassware, and bric-a-brac. Next to the market is a pub called:

23. Museumsknelpe, another good place to stop for a drink.

Just 2 minutes farther east on the Ku'damm brings you to Fasanenstrasse, where you should turn right. This is where you'll find the:

24. Käthe-Kollwitz-Museum, located at Fasanenstrasse 24 and one of my favorite museums in Berlin. A Berliner, Kollwitz was a genius in capturing human emotions in her portraits of the people around her; she deserves more worldwide recognition for her works. Beside the museum is a charming coffee house,

25. Café im Literaturhaus, where you can linger over a cup of coffee in its outside garden or, in winter, in its greenhouse.

For more look at art, this time by contemporary artists, stop by:

26. Galerie Brusberg, located near Uhlandstrasse at Ku'damm 213. The gallery, up on the second floor, represents such famous names as Salvador Dali, Bernhard Dörries, Max Ernst, Joan Miró, and Pablo Picasso, as well as lesser-known artists. Entry is free, so it's worth a spin through. Next door, at Ku'damm 214, is:

27. Helmut Timberg, a shop specializing in Meissen and Dresden porcelain. Just a minute's walk away is another smart boutique, the:

28. Rosenthal Studio-Haus, Ku'damm 226, which sells porcelain, Boda crystal, and Rosenthal porcelain. Ordinary and not-so-ordinary cookware and tableware are featured at:

29. WMF, Ku'damm 229, a well-known chain throughout Germany. Finally, end your tour at:

30. Wertheim department store, Ku'damm 231, convenient for stocking up on sundry items, film, or a souvenir of Berlin.

FINAL REFUELING STOPS In the **31. basement of Wertheim department store,** next to the food department, is an informal and casual cafeteria with various counters devoted to different foods, from salads and stews to chicken and beer. Just around the corner from Wertheim is **32. Eierschale,** Rankestrasse 1, a popular bar with live jazz in the evenings. In fact, there are so many bars and restaurants in the area that it would take a whole book to describe them—which is what the dining and entertainment chapters are all about. You're on your own to decide which place is best for you.

WALKING TOUR 2 — Along
Tauentzienstrasse & Nollendorfplatz

Start: Europa-Center on Tauentzienstrasse.

Finish: Nollendorfplatz or Winterfeldtplatz.

Time: Allow approximately 1 hour, not including stops along the way.

Best Times: Wednesday and Saturday mornings, when the Winterfeldtplatz market takes place.

Worst Times: Sundays, when shops are closed, or Tuesdays, when the flea market Die Nolle is closed.

This stroll takes in some of Berlin's most important shopping destinations and attractions, including the Europa-Center, the Berlin Zoo, the huge KaDeWe department store, and the flea market above Nollendorfplatz station. Begin your exploration at the Europa-Center, located between Budapester Strasse and Tauentzienstrasse.

FROM THE EUROPA-CENTER TO WITTENBERGPLATZ

1. Europa-Center, easy to spot from far away because of the Mercedes-Benz star at its top, is 22 stories high and contains offices, a hotel, more than 100 shops and restaurants, a movie theater, cabarets, a casino, and an observation platform on the top floor. In the main atrium on the ground floor is a strange-looking contraption, measuring 42 feet high. It's a clock, showing the time by way of colored water passing through pipes, and is known as the Fliessenden Uhr (the "Running Clock"; get it?). A good introduction to Berlin and its history is available by watching *Multivision Berlin,* an hourlong program up on the first floor. Be

BERLIN

Tauentzien-
strasse

1. Europa-Center
2. Zoologischer Garten and Aquarium
3. Thermen
4. Kaufhaus des Westens
5. KaDeWe's food emporium
6. Einhorn
7. Postmuseum Berlin
8. Die Nolle
9. Winterfeldtplatz
10. Die Nolle
11. Slumberland
12. Café Sidney

sure to stop off at the Berlin tourist office, located in the Europa-Center but with its own separate entryway on Budapester Strasse, for maps and brochures on sightseeing.

Also on Budapester Strasse, across the street from the Europa-Center, is the:

2. Zoologischer Garten (Berlin Zoo) and **Aquarium,** Budapester Strasse 32. Founded in 1844, it boasts more than 11,000 animals, including a panda. From the zoo, walk to the right side of the Europa-Center, where you'll immediately see Nürnberger Strasse. At Nürnberger Strasse 7, you'll see the entrance to the:

3. Thermen, a huge bathing facility that includes a thermal swimming pool (with an outdoor lane), saunas, steam room, sunning terrace, and fitness room. At the end of the block is Tauentzienstrasse, busy with traffic. Cross the street and take a left, where you'll pass one clothing boutique after the other. Prices are cheap and the styles are young and fun, and since most are open-fronted shops it may be difficult to refrain from the temptation of giving the sales racks a once-over. If you can resist, however, within minutes you'll find yourself at Wittenbergplatz, home of:

4. Kaufhaus des Westens, popularly called **KaDeWe.** It's the star of this walk, and not to be missed is its huge food department up on the sixth floor. It makes American grocery stores look like dime stores, so complete and lavish are its shelves of gourmet foods. There are more than 1,000 different kinds of sausages alone. A true culinary adventure.

REFUELING STOPS The **5. KaDeWe's food emporium** on the sixth floor is also a good place to eat. Spread throughout are separate counters with stools, each specializing in a different food or drink. Choose from counters selling salads, pastas, potato dishes, grilled chicken, wines, and much more. If you wish, you can order take-out and eat your goodies on one of the benches on Wittenbergplatz. Another good place for take-out food, especially if you're vegetarian, is **6. Einhorn,** Wittenbergplatz 5-6, located at the opposite end of the square from KaDeWe. A natural foods shop, it also offers daily specials ranging from vegetarian lasagne or spinach casserole to vegetarian moussaka.

FROM WITTENBERGPLATZ TO NOLLENDORFPLATZ OR WINTERFELDTPLATZ Tauentzienstrasse terminates at Wittenbergplatz, and its continuation on the opposite side of the square is Kleiststrasse. The first intersection is An der Urania, a wide street divided by a median. If you're interested in postal systems, take a left here for the:

7. Postmuseum Berlin, An der Urania 15 (tel. 21 28 201). It relates the history of Prussian postal delivery, describes Berlin's postal system, and displays stamps. Admission is free, and it's open Monday through Thursday from 9am to 5pm and on Saturday and Sunday from 10am to 5pm.

If it's shopping that makes your heart beat faster, carry on down Kleiststrasse another 7 minutes or so till it ends at Nollendorfplatz. In the middle of this huge square is Nollendorfplatz station, and above the station is where you'll find:

8. Die Nolle. Spread along an upper platform no longer used for transportation, this antiques flea market offers everything from books and jewelry to porcelain and dolls. Many of the stalls are located inside old railway cars. If it's Wednesday or Saturday morning, you'll want to continue your tour by walking south from Nollendorfplaz on Maassenstrasse for about 5 minutes until you reach:

9. Winterfeldtplatz, site of a twice-weekly produce market and lively with native Berliners.

FINAL REFUELING STOPS At one end of Die Nolle flea market is a pub called **10. Zur Nolle,** a cheerful place with antiques hanging from the ceiling and a patio that extends out along the platform. If you've terminated your tour on Winterfeldtplatz, two bars worth checking out are **11. Slumberland** and **12. Café Sidney,** both on Winterfeldtplatz and open to the wee hours of the morning.

WALKING TOUR 3 — Tiergarten Park
& the Hansaviertel

Start: Tiergarten S-Bahn station.

Finish: Reichstag building.

Time: Allow approximately 1½ hours, not including stops along the way.

Best Times: Saturdays and Sundays, when the market on Strasse des 17. Juni takes place.

Worst Times: There are no bad days for this tour.

Take this stroll when you're tired of museums and want to spend the day out of doors. It takes you through the Tiergarten park all the way to the Brandenburger Tor (Brandenburg Gate), with several interesting stops along the way. If you really want to make an outing of it, pack a picnic lunch. There aren't many possibilities for refreshment on this walk.

FROM TIERGARTEN S-BAHN STATION TO THE SIEGESSÄULE   If it's the weekend, head straight for the:
1. **Flea market near Tiergarten station** (you can see the market from the station's platform) on Strasse des 17. Juni. This is one of my favorite places to shop in all of Berlin, not only because of all the antiques but also because of the crafts section, where young people sell jewelry, drawings, clothing, and other things they've made. I've picked up some great gifts here for friends back home. The crafts section is separated from the antiques stalls by a bridge and a large stone gate—don't miss it.

REFUELING STOPS   There are a number of **2. food stalls** (called Imbisse) mixed in with the antiques at the market on Strasse des 17. Juni, where you can eat everything from sausage and french fries to Turkish pizza and beer. If you'd rather sit down (exhausted from all that shopping), backtrack under the elevated platform of the S-Bahn station, where on the east side you'll find a small white building called the **3. Berlin Pavilion** on Strasse des 17. Juni. There's a small café here, with tables outside in summer. Another good thing to know is that there are toilet facilities here you can use for free.

If there's no market, you'll exit from the Tiergarten S-Bahn station and head east (east is easy—simply walk in the direction of that huge column rising from the middle of the street in the distance). Almost immediately to your left, past the Berlin Pavilion, is a street called Klopstock. Turn left on Klopstock, where you'll soon find yourself in the midst of the:
4. **Hansaviertel (Hansa Quarter).** This is area that was designed by 50 architects from more than 20 countries, each architect designing one building in his own style. Most were apartment buildings, since Berlin was still suffering from a housing crunch after World War II. At any rate, on your right as you walk north on Klopstock you'll see a map of the area, keyed

to the various buildings and their designers. Building 22 by Alvar Aalto, by the way, won the competition. A blue, green, and white apartment house, it will be to your right as you continue walking north on Klopstock.

Within minutes after passing the Aalto building, you'll reach Hansaplatz. Take a right onto Altonaer Strasse (which brings you back to Strasse des 17. Juni—you can see that column again) and on your left you'll soon glimpse the:

5. Englischer Garten (English Garden). It's part of the grounds of Schloss Bellevue (Bellevue Palace), built in 1785 as a summer residence for Frederick the Great's youngest brother and now serving as the private residence of the German president whenever he's in Berlin. The Englischer Garten, reconstructed after the war with donations from England, is open to the public when the president is not in Berlin.

After passing the Englischer Garten, within a few minutes you will find yourself back on Strasse des 17. Juni, at a huge roundabout called:

6. Grosser Stern (which translates as "Great Star," because of the many roads leading away from it). Note the beautiful gas lamps surrounding the Grosser Stern. Berlin still has 40,000 gas lamps, as well as 100 full-time employees whose job it is to clean them and make sure they're still burning. In the middle of the traffic circle is a huge column, called the:

7. Siegessäule (Victory Column). Erected in the 1870s, it commemorates three victorious wars—against Denmark in 1864, against Austria in 1866, and against France in 1870–71. More than 220 feet high, it's topped by a gilded goddess of victory. From April to mid-November, visitors can climb the 290 steps of a spiral staircase to an observation platform 157 feet high, from where they are rewarded with views of the city.

FROM THE SIEGESSÄULE TO THE REICHSTAG From the Grosser Stern and its Siegessäule, continue walking east on Strasse des 17. Juni in the direction of the Brandenburger Tor, which you can see far in the distance. Rather than walk along the boulevard, I suggest you enter the:

8. Tiergarten park at your right and take one of the paths there leading toward the gate. Blessed with ponds, wide grassy fields, and wooded areas, the Tiergarten is Berlin's largest park, stretching approximately 1.86 miles from Bahnhof Zoo all the way to the Brandenburger Tor. You might wish to stop somewhere here for your picnic.

If you don't stop along the way, it takes about 20 minutes to walk from the Siegessäule to the Brandenburger Tor. Just before reaching the gate, you'll see the:

9. Sowjetisches Ehrenmal (Soviet Memorial) to your left on Strasse des 17. Juni. Constructed of marble from Hitler's chancellery, it was erected after World War II as a memorial to the Soviet army and is guarded by two Russian soldiers.

And here we are at the:

10. Brandenburger Tor. Built by Carl Gotthard Langhans in

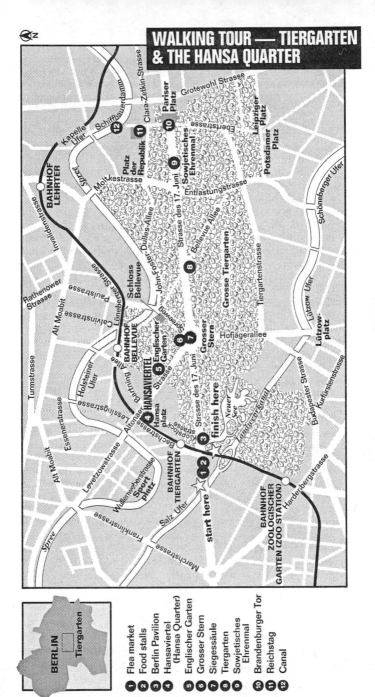

WALKING TOUR — TIERGARTEN & THE HANSA QUARTER

BERLIN — Tiergarten

1. Flea market
2. Food stalls
3. Berlin Pavilion
4. Hansaviertel (Hansa Quarter)
5. Englischer Garten
6. Grosser Stern
7. Siegessäule
8. Tiergarten
9. Sowjetisches Ehrenmal
10. Brandenburger Tor
11. Reichstag
12. Canal

1788–91 as the west entrance onto Under den Linden, it is topped by the famous Quadriga created by Johann Gottfried Schadow and consisting of the goddess of peace in a chariot pulled by four steeds; the Quadriga was severely damaged in World War II but has since been restored. After the Wall went up in 1961, the Brandenburger Tor became inaccessible from West Berlin, making it a symbol of a divided Berlin. After the November 1989 revolution, it was here that many Berliners, from both East and West, gathered to rejoice and to dance together on top of the Wall. I myself witnessed part of the celebration in the months that followed, as people from around the world chiseled at the Wall for a piece of history. At the end of February 1990, the East German government began tearing down the Wall in anticipation of a united Germany. Finally, for the first time in decades, people could pass freely from Strasse des 17. Juni past the Brandenburger Tor to Unter den Linden in East Berlin.

To the left of the Brandenburger Tor is a large, solemn-looking building, the:

11. **Reichstag** (Parliament). Completed in 1894 in Neo-Renaissance style to serve the needs of Bismarck's united Germany, the building had its darkest hour on the night of February 17, 1933, when a mysterious fire broke out. The Nazi government blamed the German Communist Party for setting the flame, and used the incident as an excuse to arrest Communist party members and other enemies of the Nazis and to abolish such basic democratic rights as freedom of the press. Damaged in World War II, the Reichstag was restored with the exception of its dome. Since 1971, part of it has been used for an exhibition called "Fragen an die deutsche Geschichte" (Questions Concerning German History), with displays relating to German history from 1800 to the Cold War. In the wake of reunification, however, it's questionable whether the exhibition will continue; in any case, it's always been in German only.

Behind the northeast corner of the Reichstag is a:

12. **canal** that once formed part of the border between the two Berlins. East German soldiers, armed with guns and binoculars, used to keep watch from a guard tower here, a sight that always caused me anxiety even though I was on the lucky side of the Wall. There is a row of white crosses here, remembering some people who were not so fortunate and who lost their lives as they attempted to flee to the West.

At the north end of the Reichstag is a bus stop; bus 69 goes back to the Europa-Center.

WALKING TOUR 4 — East Berlin

Start: Unter den Linden at the Brandenburger Tor.

Finish: Nikolaiviertel.

Time: Allow approximately 2 hours, not including stops along the way.

Best Times: Weekdays, when restaurants aren't as crowded.

Worst Times: Mondays and Tuesdays, when some museums are closed.

This stroll brings you through what used to be the heart of old Berlin before World War II, later serving as East Germany's capital. From the historic boulevard Unter den Linden, you'll pass Museumsinsel (Museum Island), home of some of Berlin's great museums, and end your tour at the Nikolaiviertel (Nikolai Quarter), a restored neighborhood of restaurants and pubs.

FROM BRANDENBURGER TOR TO MARX-ENGELS-BRÜCKE

This tour starts in front of Brandenburger Tor, which marks the west end of:

1. **Unter den Linden.** The Elector used to pass this way on his journey to the Tiergarten to hunt, and by 1675 this was a paved road. In the centuries that followed, it was the lifeline of old Berlin, the city's most fashionable and liveliest boulevard. Today, after decades of amputation by the Wall at the Brandenburger Tor, Unter den Linden is once again a lively and crowded thoroughfare, the center of a reunited Berlin. From here you have a view of the front of Brandenburger Tor, topped by the Quadriga. Unter den Linden stretches 7/10 mile, from the Brandenburger Tor to Marx-Engels-Brücke.

   With the Brandenburger Tor behind you, walk east on Unter den Linden, shaded with lime trees (Unter den Linden means "under the lime trees"). After a couple of blocks, you'll reach:

2. **Friedrichstrasse,** an important thoroughfare. On your right will be the Grand Hotel, one of Berlin's foremost hotels, built in a turn-of-the-century style. This, in fact, is where Berlin's grand old buildings begin, most built in the 1800s and painstakingly restored. From Friedrichstrasse, continue walking east on Unter den Linden, on your left passing the neobaroque:

3. **Deutsche Staatsbibliothek** (National Library; formerly Prussian State Library), containing over five million volumes, and the neoclassical:

4. **Humboldt-Universität** (Humboldt University), where Hegel and the Brothers Grimm taught. In the median in front of the university is an:

5. **equestrian statue of Frederick the Great.** To the right of the statue is the:

6. **Altes Palais** (Old Palace), built in the 1830s to serve as living quarters for the emperor and now part of Humboldt University. Our first actual stop, however, is the:

7. **Neue Wache** (New Guardhouse), located on Unter den Linden on your left just past the statue of Frederick the Great. Easy to

spot with its columns resembling those of a Greek temple, it was designed by architect Karl Friedrich Schinkel in 1816–18 and today serves as a memorial to victims of fascism and militarism. Inside is an eternal flame, which burns for the Unknown Soldier and Unknown Resistance Fighter. A ceremonial changing of the guards takes place on Wednesdays at 2:30pm, with abbreviated versions taking place daily at 2:30pm.

Beside the Neue Wache is the:

8. Museum für Deutsche Geschichte (Museum of German History) at Unter den Linden 2. Built in the 17th century as an arsenal for the Prussian army, today it serves as a museum tracing the history of Germany from prehistoric times to 1949. It's unique in its socialist interpretations, giving emphasis to class struggles and farmers' uprisings against an oppressive ruling class.

Across from the Neue Wache is the:

9. Deutsche Staatsoper, rebuilt after World War II and a venue for opera, ballet, and concerts. Unter den Linden terminates at:

10. Marx-Engels-Brücke, formerly called Schlossbrücke (Palace Bridge), which was designed by Schinkel. Its eight statues are based on goddesses and warriors of Greek mythology.

A REFUELING STOP The **11. Operncafé,** Unter den Linden 5, is one of Berlin's most famous coffeehouses. Occupying part of a palace originally built in 1733 and faithfully restored after World War II, it offers both indoor and outdoor dining. Upstairs is a restaurant serving typical German fare.

MUSEUMSINSEL Instead of crossing Marx-Engels-Brücke, take a left on Kupfergraben and walk to the second bridge. This is the entrance to the:

12. Pergamon Museum, the most important and famous museum on Museumsinsel, developed through the 19th and early 20th centuries as a museum complex meant to rival those of other European capitals. The Pergamon Museum is its crowning achievement. Essentially a museum of architectural wonders, it's named after its most prized treasure, the Pergamon Altar, dating from 160–180 B.C. It also contains Asian, Near Eastern, and Islamic art, as well as German folk art.

Beside the Pergamon Museum is the:

13. Bode Museum, which contains the Egyptian Museum, the Early Christian and Byzantine Collection, the Museum for Primeval and Early History, the Sculpture Collection, and the Picture Gallery with art from the 14th to the 18th century. Behind the Pergamon is the:

14. Nationalgalerie (National Gallery), which features art from the 19th and 20th centuries.

From the Nationalgalerie, walk south on Museumsinsel in the direction of the huge church. That's the:

15. Berliner Dom (Berlin Cathedral), erected at the turn of the century in Italian Renaissance style. It faces a tree-lined square called the:

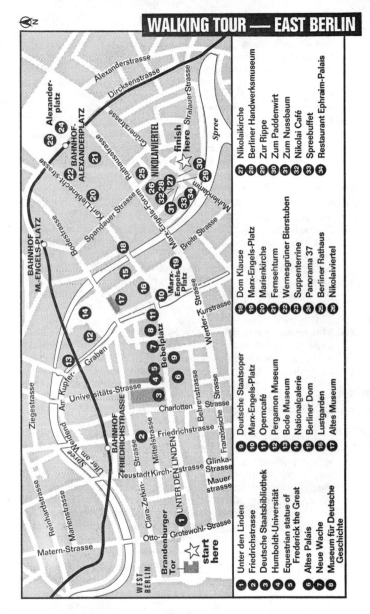

Nikolaikirche
Berliner Handwerksmuseum
Zur Rippe
Zum Paddenwirt
Zum Nussbaum
Nikolai Café
Spreebuffet
Restaurant Ephraim-Palais

27 28 29 31 32 33 34

Dom Klause
Marx-Engels-Platz
Marienkirche
Fernsehturm
Wernesgrüner Bierstuben
Suppenterrine
Panorama 37
Berliner Rathaus
Nikolaiviertel

18 19 20 21 22 23 24 25 26

Deutsche Staatsoper
Marx-Engels-Platz
Operncafé
Pergamon Museum
Bode Museum
Nationalgalerie
Berliner Dom
Lustgarden
Altes Museum

9 10 11 12 13 14 15 16 17

Unter den Linden
Friedrichstrasse
Deutsche Staatsbibliothek
Humboldt-Universität
Equestrian statue of Frederick the Great
Altes Palais
Neue Wache
Museum für Deutsche Geschichte

1 2 3 4 5 6 7 8

16. Lustgarten (Pleasure Garden), once the site of parades and rallies. Also facing the Lustgarten is the:

17. Altes Museum (Old Museum), which stages changing exhibitions devoted to art and objects of ancient times. Built from plans by Schinkel, it features 18 Ionic columns and resembles a Greek temple. (Incidentally, behind the Altes Museum is the Neues Museum [New Museum], which has supposedly been "under restoration" for decades but which has shown little signs of change. East Berliners have always joked that at the present rate of progress, restoration wouldn't be complete until well into the 21st century—if at all. Now that Berlin is united, maybe money for restoration will be made available at last.)

A REFUELING STOP   Behind the Berliner Dom and across the bridge is a pleasant German restaurant, **18. Dom Klause,** located in the Palasthotel at Karl-Liebknecht-Strasse 5. There's an English menu that lists traditional German fare, and in the summer you can sit outside beside the Spree River.

FROM MUSEUMSINSEL TO ALEXANDERPLATZ   Opposite the Lustgarten is the:
19. **Marx-Engels-Platz,** which has that no-nonsense and rather dull look characteristic of building by socialist regimes. It is the site of government buildings. With the Lustgarten on your left, walk past the Berliner Dom, cross the Spree River, and continue down Karl-Liebknecht-Strasse. After crossing Spandauer Strasse, you'll see a small brick church on your right, looking rather out of place with the huge Fernsehturm (Television Tower) behind it. This is the:
20. **Marienkirche** (Church of St. Mary), the second-oldest church in Berlin. First constructed in the 13th century and then added to through the centuries, it's noted for its marble baroque pulpit by Andreas Schlüter. Note, too, its *Dance of Death* mural in its tower hall; painted in the 15th century, the mural was subsequently covered up and wasn't rediscovered until 1860. The church is open Monday through Thursday from 10am to noon and 1 to 4pm, on Saturday from noon to 4pm.
  Behind the church sprawls Alexanderplatz with its landmark:
21. **Fernsehturm.** The 1,200-foot-high tower contains an observation platform and a revolving restaurant—with long lines waiting for both. Before the Wall fell, of course, this was one of the few opportunities East Germans had for a glimpse of the West. But even a reunited Germany has not dimmed its popularity. Of interest to visitors is the tourist office located at the base of the tower. If you're tired, you can take the S-Bahn from Alexanderplatz to Bahnhof Zoo and beyond.

REFUELING STOPS   The **22. Wernesgrüner Bierstuben,** located in a basement across from the Fernsehturm at Karl-Liebknecht-Strasse 11, is a typical workingman's pub. In addition to liters of beer, it also offers daily German specials, from Sauerbraten to lentil stew. If you're on a budget, you might wish to try the **23. Suppenterrine,** Alexanderplatz 2, which specializes in one-pot stews.

  For fine dining, head to the top of Hotel Stadt Berlin on Alexanderplatz, where there's the **24. Panorama 37** French restaurant. It's one of the best places in Berlin for dining with a view, and reservations are a must.

FROM ALEXANDERPLATZ THROUGH THE NIKOLAI QUARTER At the southwestern end of Alexanderplatz, on the corner of Rathausstrasse and Spandauer Strasse, is an imposing red-brick building topped with a tower. This is the:

25. **Berliner Rathaus** (City Hall), which served as the seat of Berlin's municipal administration after its construction in the 1860s. Note the frieze around the entire building—it's a stone chronicle of the history of Berlin.

      Walk past the Rathaus, cross Spandauer Strasse, and to your left you'll see a small side street leading to church spires. This is the beginning of the:

26. **Nikolaiviertel** (Nikolai Quarter), a re-created neighborhood of Berlin as it was centuries ago. In the center is the:

27. **Nikolaikirche** (St. Nicholas's Church), regarded as Berlin's oldest church even though it was destroyed during World War II and was largely rebuilt. Its history dates back to 1230, but the style of the church changed several times in the following centuries.

      The buildings you see around the church are all new, but many were built according to plans of earlier buildings that existed elsewhere. Facing the church, walk around it to the right and you'll see several shops selling handcrafted items. Take the first right (behind the church), which brings you to a busy street called Mühlendamm. Here, at Mühlendamm 5, you'll find the:

28. **Berliner Handwerksmuseum** (Berlin Crafts Museum), a tiny museum that features changing exhibitions of items produced in Berlin in the past. It's open daily except Monday from 10am to 6pm.

      Since the Nikolaiviertel is small and consists largely of apartment houses and bars, explore it at your leisure, stopping off for a beer or meal at one of the places below.

REFUELING STOPS Among the best-known Gaststätten in the Nikolaiviertel are **29. Zur Rippe,** on the corner of Mühlendamm and Poststrasse; **30. Zum Paddenwirt,** on Eiergasse; and **31. Zum Nussbaum,** on Propstrasse beside the Nikolaikirche. The **32. Nikolai Café,** across the street from the church at Am Nussbaum, is a good place for coffee and desserts. For an inexpensive meal, the **33. Spreebuffet,** on the Spreeufer (bank of the Spree River), is a cafeteria offering stews and soup. And if you really want to splurge, dine at the **34. Restaurant Ephraim-Palais,** a reconstruction of a rococo palace built for the court jeweler. If you want to dine here, however, be sure to make a reservation.

CHAPTER 8

BERLIN SHOPPING

1. THE SHOPPING SCENE
2. SHOPPING A TO Z

Shopping has always been an integral part of the Berlin scene. After all, the city's most famous and liveliest boulevard, the Ku'damm, is also its main shopping street. Add to that a myriad markets, department stores, specialty shops, art galleries, and antiques shops, and it soon becomes clear that Berlin has about everything anyone could possibly want. In fact, there's a saying that if it exists, it's available in Berlin. Just one trip through the KaDeWe department store made a believer of me.

1. THE SHOPPING SCENE

In case you haven't noticed, Germany is not a shopper's paradise in terms of cut-rate bargains. You won't find overwhelmingly cheaper prices here for German-made goods, primarily because the dollar is not as strong as it once was. In addition, Germany is one of the more expensive countries of Europe, far more expensive than countries to the south.

However, you will find a greater variety of European goods here than you would back home, including clothing, kitchenware, antiques, and artwork. Only you can judge whether your purchase is a true bargain, especially if it's a one-of-a-kind print or an antique. If you do plan on making a major purchase, be sure to comparison-shop before leaving home. It may not be worth it to buy that German comforter and pay the expense of shipping it home, only to find you've saved all of $5 for your efforts.

GREAT SHOPPING NAMES

Berlin and the **Kurfürstendamm** are synonymous. Two and a half miles long, the Kurfürstendamm, called Ku'damm by the locals, is the city's showcase—quite literally. Up and down its sidewalks you'll see freestanding display cases containing goods from the surrounding stores, just a little something to whet your appetite. There are boutiques and shops here selling clothing, accessories, porcelain, kitchenware, eyeglasses, and art. But don't neglect the side streets, since they're a virtual treasure trove of antiques shops, bookstores, and more clothing stores and art galleries. **Bleibtreustrasse,** for

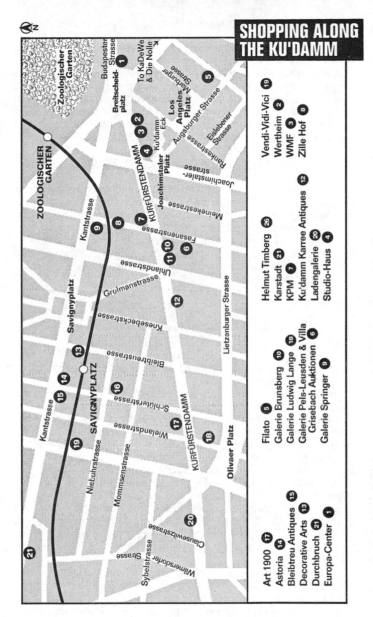

Vendi-Vidi-Vici **19**
Wertheim **2**
WMF **3**
Zille Hof **8**

Helmut Timberg **26**
Karstadt **21**
KPM **7**
Ku'damm Karree Antiques **12**
Ladengalerie **20**
Studio-Haus **4**

Filato **5**
Galerie Brunsberg **10**
Galerie Ludwig Lange **18**
Galerie Pels-Leusden & Villa Grisebach Auktionen **6**
Galerie Springer **9**

Art 1900 **17**
Astoria **14**
Bleibtreu Antiques **15**
Decorative Arts **13**
Durchbruch **21**
Europa-Center **1**

example, has a number of places specializing in art deco. **Tauentzienstrasse** is good for inexpensive and fun fashions.

The other big name in shopping streets is **Wilmersdorfer Strasse,** a pedestrians-only lane lined with department stores, boutiques, and restaurants. This is where the locals come to shop, both for essentials and such nonessential essentials as yet another skirt. Since there is a large concentration of stores here, you can cover a lot of ground in a short amount of time—simply take the U-Bahn to Wilmersdorfer Strasse.

Other places for concentrated shopping include the department stores and markets described under "Shopping A to Z." In fact, probably the best place to begin is **KaDeWe**, the largest department store on the European continent. Go there for everything from bedsheets, comforters, fabrics, and clothing to souvenirs and even sausages. After that it's an easy walk to the Ku'damm.

HOURS, TAXES & SHIPPING

Most shops and businesses are open Monday through Friday from 9 or 10am to 6 or 6:30pm and on Saturday from 9am to 2pm. On the first Saturday of the month (called *langer Samstag*), shops remain open until 6pm. In addition, some shops remain open longer on Thursday, until 8:30pm. Note, however, that some of the smaller establishments, especially art galleries and antiques shops, are open only in the afternoons. Be sure to check individual listings, therefore, to avoid disappointment.

If you purchase more than 60 DM ($36.35) worth of goods from any one store and you're taking your purchases out of the country, you're entitled to a recovery of the Value-Added Tax (VAT), in German, *Mehrwertsteuer*, which is 14% in Germany. Note, however, that you will not receive the total 14% refund. Rather, depending on the item you purchase, you will receive a refund of 6% to 11% of the purchase price. If you've purchased an object of considerable worth, even that can add up to a saving.

In any case, the procedure for obtaining the VAT refund is the same. All department stores and most major shops will issue a Tax-Free Cheque at the time of your purchase. Simply fill in the reverse side and, upon leaving Germany, present the Tax-Free Cheque, the receipt from the store, and the purchased goods to the German Customs official, who will stamp your cheque. If you're leaving Germany from Berlin's Tegel Airport, you can receive your cash refund immediately at the Berliner Bank counter in the Main Hall. In Frankfurt, you can receive an immediate refund at the International Departure Hall B Transit. Remember to show your purchases to the Customs officials before checking your luggage, unless you are hand-carrying your purchase. If you're leaving Germany by train, ask the Customs official who comes into your train to stamp your cheque.

You may wish to ship your purchases home, especially if you've gone overboard and can no longer carry everything with a reasonable semblance of dignity. Most shops used to dealing with tourists will ship your purchases home, which may be the easiest route to take. Your Tax-Free Cheque will indicate that the goods have already left the country; in some cases, you may even receive an immediate refund of the VAT at the store.

If you wish to send home a package yourself, you can do so at all major post offices. All you have to do is show up with your goods, since post offices sell boxes complete with string and tape. Boxes come in five sizes and range in price from 1.10 DM (65¢) to 3.60 DM ($2.20). If you're sending a purchase for which you are entitled to a

VAT refund, be sure to have an official at the post office stamp your Tax-Free Cheque (which you can then later present at the airport for an immediate refund).

Keep in mind, however, that there is a limit to the duty-free goods you can bring back with you to the United States. If you're sending a package, it will automatically go to Customs upon arrival in the United States. If the total value of goods acquired abroad is less than $50, the package is sent on to the post office and is delivered to you by your mail carrier. If the value is more than $50, the amount you owe will be collected by your mail carrier upon delivery of your package. Note that it is illegal to mail liquor to the United States.

As for hand-carried items, you are allowed to bring back free of duty $400 worth of personal and household goods obtained abroad. Anything above this $400 personal exemption is charged a flat 10% on the next $1,000. That means the most you will have to pay on purchases valued at $1,400 (your $400 personal exemption plus the next $1,000) is only $100.

BEST BUYS

If souvenirs make your heart beat faster, you'll delight in Berlin's stuffed toy bears (the city mascot), porcelain freedom bells (fashioned after the Freedom Bell hanging in Rathaus Schöneberg), and ashtrays and bowls picturing the Brandenburger Tor. If kitsch doesn't appeal to you, Germany is also known for kitchen gadgets and cutlery, beautiful linens, those luxuriously fluffy *Federbetten* (literally feather beds, or down comforters), binoculars and telescopes, cameras, and toys (including model trains, tin soldiers, and building blocks). If you like porcelain, brands to look for include Rosenthal, antique Meissen, and Berlin's own Königliche Porzellan-Manufaktur—assuming, of course, you have a Swiss bank account.

Another good purchase in Berlin is original artwork. There are so many galleries in the city that you could easily spend an entire lifetime making the rounds of changing exhibits. If you don't have the money for a major purchase, a good place to look for handmade arts and crafts is the weekend market on Strasse des 17. Juni, where young Berliners hawk their wares, including jewelry, sketches, and clothing.

Finally, antiques are also in abundant supply, as shown in the city's several flea markets and many antiques shops. Following a worldwide trend, shops dealing in art nouveau (Jugendstil) and art deco are also on the rise, appropriate for a city that was in the vanguard of the arts at the turn of the century and in the decades that followed.

2. SHOPPING A TO Z

In addition to the specialty stores listed below, the single best source for most needs is a large department store, several of which are listed above.

FROMMER'S SMART SHOPPER— BEST BUYS

VALUE-CONSCIOUS SHOPPERS SHOULD TAKE ADVANTAGE OF THE FOLLOWING:

1. Berlin's many department stores, which can often offer merchandise at prices cheaper than those of the smaller boutiques.
2. A return of the Value-Added Tax (VAT) on goods totaling more than 60 DM ($36.35) purchased in any one store.
3. Open-fronted clothing boutiques on Tauentzienstrasse, the Ku'damm, and Wilmersdorfer Strasse, offering cheap and fun fashions.
4. Berlin's many galleries dealing in local, German, and international art.
5. The city's many flea markets, which are fun entertainment even if you don't buy anything, though it would be hard to resist the bargains ranging from antiques and curios to handcrafted items.

QUESTIONS TO ASK IF YOU'RE ON A BUDGET

1. Does the store offer a VAT refund? You can receive a refund of up to 11% on goods purchased in Germany that you're taking out of the country.
2. How much does it cost to ship a package back home? Mail service is expensive in Germany; you may be much better off carrying your purchases home instead of shipping them.
3. Can you get it cheaper elsewhere? Ask yourself whether it's worthwhile shopping around. If you're at a market, try bargaining; some vendors are willing to lower their prices.
4. Is the item cheaper in Germany than back home? Do a little homework before beginning your trip, especially in regard to major purchases.

ANTIQUES

The best place to search for antiques and curios is at one of Berlin's several **flea markets.** Not only is the atmosphere festive, but the range of goods offered by the vendors is usually much more extensive than that offered by a single store. My favorite flea market is the one held every Saturday and Sunday on Strasse des 17. Juni, where vendors sell porcelain, coffee grinders, glassware, brass, door knockers, lamps, clothing, and a seemingly endless supply of junk, as well as handmade arts and crafts. Two indoor markets, open every day except Tuesday, can be found at the Ku'damm Karree, Kurfürstendamm 206-208, and on an upper platform of the Nollendorfplatz station. Check the "Markets" section for more information.

Otherwise, most of the stores below specialize in decorative objects from the turn of the century through the 1930s, a period that has enjoyed a resurgence in popularity the past few years. The shops here are all located on or near Bleibtreustrasse.

ART 1900, Kurfürstendamm 53. Tel. 881 56 27.

This ranks as one of the finest and most exclusive of Berlin's shops dealing in original Jugendstil (German art nouveau) and art deco pieces. The craftsmanship of its furniture, statues, glass, and porcelain is exquisite, with correspondingly high prices. If money is no object, you'll definitely want to stop by here. Art 1900 is located near the corner of Schlüterstrasse. Open: Mon–Fri 10am–6:30pm, Sat 10am–2pm (open to 6pm first Sat of the month). U-Bahn: Uhlandstrasse or Adenauerplatz, each a 5-minute walk.

ASTORIA, Bleibtreustrasse 50. Tel. 312 83 04.

Near the corner of Bleibtreustrasse and Kantstrasse, this art deco shop offers statues, jewelry, and some furniture, including mirrors, lamps, tables, and dressers. If the originals are too expensive but you like the sleek art deco look, you might be interested in some of the shop's replicas, which make up about 20% of the inventory. Open: Mon–Fri noon–6:30pm, Sat 11am–2pm (to 6pm first Sat of the month). S-Bahn: Savignyplatz, a 1-minute walk.

BLEIBTREU ANTIQUES, Bleibtreustrasse 5a. Tel. 313 46 25.

Owner Ingrid Vieregg Gülsen deals in decorative art from the Biedermeier (1816–48), Jugendstil, and art deco periods. Operating under the belief that pieces of various styles often complement one another, she specializes in Biedermeier furniture and in Jugendstil and art deco jewelry, lamps, and glassware. Open: Mon–Fri noon–6:30pm, Sat 11am–2pm. S-Bahn: Savignyplatz, a 1-minute walk.

DECORATIVE ARTS, Niebuhrstrasse 1. Tel. 882 73 73.

A small shop on the corner of Niebuhrstrasse and Bleibtreustrasse, Decorative Arts specializes in items from the Jugendstil period through the 1930s, including Thonet furniture and Gallé, Lutz, and Murano glass. Open: Mon–Fri noon–6:30pm, Sat 10:30am–2pm. S-Bahn: Savignyplatz, a 1-minute walk.

ZILLE HOF, Fasanenstrasse 14. Tel. 313 43 33.

Hard to believe that this quirky place exists near the exclusive Bristol Hotel Kempinski just off the Ku'damm—it looks like an abandoned junkyard. Occupying a little courtyard that spreads beside and under the elevated tracks of the S-Bahn, Zille Hof is a good place to browse through glasses, plates, rusted pots and pans, furniture, dusty books, clothing, and piles upon piles of junk. If nothing else, this place is worth a photograph. Open: Mon–Fri 8:30am–5:30pm, Sat 8:30am–1pm. U-Bahn: Uhlandstrasse, a 2-minute walk.

ART GALLERIES

There are so many art galleries in Berlin that it almost amounts to an epidemic—albeit a very nice one. One pamphlet lists more than 175 galleries; the city magazine *zitty* lists about 125. In any case, there are far too many to mention here. The ones below, all within easy walking distance of the Ku'damm, offer a varied assortment of contemporary art.

GALERIE BREMER, Fasanenstrasse 37. Tel. 881 49 08.

This is one of Berlin's established galleries, specializing in the works of such modern German artists as Laabs and Heiliger, as well as some of the up-and-comers. You will find it south of the Ku'damm, in the direction of Fasanenplatz. A gallery by day, in the evenings it reopens at 8pm as a bar serving pricey drinks in a very sophisticated atmosphere. Open: Tues–Fri noon–6pm, Sat 11am–1pm. U-Bahn: Uhlandstrasse, a 5-minute walk.

GALERIE BRUSBERG, Kurfürstendamm 213. Tel. 882 76 82.

Located on the second floor of a turn-of-the-century patrician home, this well-known gallery exhibits the works of Dali, Ernst, Miró, Picasso, and Bernhard Dörries, as well as lesser-known artists of considerable talent. These include East Berlin painters who continued to express themselves when their city was under Communist rule. The gallery is light and airy, with enough space to properly display the paintings and sculptures. With its museumlike quality, Galerie Brusberg is definitely worth a stop, and it doesn't cost anything to look. Open: Tues–Fri 10am–6:30pm, Sat 10am–2pm. U-Bahn: Uhlandstrasse, less than a 1-minute walk.

KUNSTHANDLUNG BANDOLY, Brandenburgische Strasse 27. Tel. 881 49 10.

This gallery deals in reproductions of famous paintings, small etchings of Berlin, and copperplate prints depicting the city's old architecture. Small etchings of such sights as the Brandenburger Tor are available for as little as 13 DM ($7.85), making this a good place to purchase a souvenir of Berlin. Open: Mon–Fri 10am–6pm, Sat 10am–1pm. U-Bahn: Adenauerplatz, a 3-minute walk.

LADENGALERIE, Kurfürstendamm 64. Tel. 881 42 14.

A one-room gallery specializing in one-person shows by contemporary German artists. One recent exhibition, for example, was Sarah Schumann's "Travels in the DDR." The displays are always interesting, making it worth a spin through. Open: Mon–Fri 10am–6:30pm, Sat 10am–2pm (to 6pm first Sat of the month). U-Bahn: Adenauerplatz, a 2-minute walk.

GALERIE LUDWIG LANGE, Wielandstrasse 26. Tel. 881 29 26.

On the ground floor of an ornate turn-of-the-century building, this beautiful gallery emphasizes German sculpture, including the works of Berliner Waldemar Grizmek. There is even a charming sculpture garden in the back, not to be missed. Open: Tues–Fri 11am–6pm, Sat 10am–2pm. U-Bahn: Adenauerplatz, a 6-minute walk.

GALERIE PELS-LEUSDEN AND VILLA GRISEBACH AUKTIONEN, Fasanenstrasse 25. Tel. 882 68 11.

Built a century ago as the home of architect Hans Grisebach, the beautiful Villa Grisebach has been restored and now serves as a gallery of contemporary art. (It stands next to the Käthe-Kollwitz-Museum.) Twice a year, in June and November, it also serves as the stage for the Villa Grisebach Auction, a sale of international painting, graphic art, and sculpture from the 19th and 20th centuries. Former auctions have dealt with works by Adolph von Menzel, Franz Marc, Erich Heckel, Paul Klee, Emil Nolde, Georg Kolbe, Jean Dubuffet, and Christo, drawing art dealers from around the world. Open: Mon–Fri 10am–6:30pm, Sat 10am–2pm. U-Bahn: Uhlandstrasse, a 1-minute walk.

GALERIE SPRINGER, Fasanenstrasse 13. Tel. 313 90 88.

Near the elevated tracks of the S-Bahn, Galerie Springer has none of the highbrow look of most other galleries, yet it has long remained on the crest of Berlin's artistic wave by recognizing young local talents and then sending them on to fame. Exhibitions range from avant-garde paintings to photography. Open: Tues–Fri 2–7pm, Sat 11am–2pm. U-Bahn: Uhlandstrasse, about a 3-minute walk.

CRAFTS

If you're looking for handmade arts and crafts, the best place to look is the **weekend market held on Strasse des 17. Juni,** just west of the Tiergarten S-Bahn station. Many young entrepreneurs and artisans set up shop here, selling sketches, jewelry, batik clothing, and other items they've made themselves. In addition, check with the Berlin tourist office to see whether any special crafts fairs are being held.

DEPARTMENT STORES & MALLS

THE EUROPA-CENTER AREA

EUROPA-CENTER, Tauentzienstrasse and Budapester Strasse.

Across the square from the Gedächtniskirche and easy to spot with the Mercedes-Benz star atop its roof, this is Berlin's largest indoor shopping center. In addition to its observation platform on the top floor, casino, hotel, thermal spa, and office space, it boasts approximately 70 shops on its first three floors, offering everything from records and cassettes to clothing, shoes, and accessories. A good place to explore on a cold or rainy day. There are also plenty of cafés, restaurants, and bars where you can stop for refreshment. Open: Shops, Mon–Fri 10am–6pm, Sat 10am–2pm (to 6pm first Sat of the month); Europa-Center itself stays open to 3am. U-Bahn: Kurfürstendamm or Bahnhof Zoologischer Garten, each a 2-minute walk.

KADEWE, Wittenbergplatz. Tel. 240171 or 21210.

Quite simply, the largest department store on the European continent. Officially known as Kaufhaus des Westens (which means "department store of the West") but popularly referred to as KaDeWe, it's just a 5-minute walk from the Ku'damm and the Gedächtniskirche. It occupies 51,600 square yards of selling space, has an inventory of 250,000 items, and employs a staff of 3,000. In addition to shopping its seven floors, customers can not only eat and buy theater tickets, but have their shoes repaired, their marriages and vacations planned, their hair done, their dogs shampooed, their money exchanged, their purchases wrapped and shipped abroad, their pictures taken, and—if necessary after all that—have first aid administered.

The many departments sell almost everything, and many leading designers have their own boutiques here. Especially good departments include those devoted to fabrics, linen and bedding (you'll ooh and ah over those goosedown comforters and all the colorful designer sheets that go with them), and glass and porcelain. Souvenirs are sold on the fourth floor, including beer steins and ash trays stamped with the motif of Berlin, the bear.

But by far the biggest attraction is the amazing sixth-floor food emporium. There are 1,000 different sorts of sausage, 500 different kinds of bread, 1,500 different types of cheese, and gourmet items from around the world. There are exotic teas, coffees, liquors, wines, jams, sweets, vegetables, fruits, spices, canned goods, and fresh seafood, including eels, lobster, and fish still swimming around in tanks. Since few people eat as much pork in so many different ways as the Germans, it's no wonder that KaDeWe's pork section is one of the world's largest. Throughout the sixth floor you'll find various sit-down counters where you can dine on everything from soup to seafood.

You could easily get lost and spend the rest of your days in the store—but there are certainly worse fates in life. Open: Mon–Fri 9am–6:30pm, Sat 9am–2pm (to 6pm first Sat of the month). U-Bahn: Wittenbergplatz, a 1-minute walk.

WERTHEIM, Kurfürstendamm 231. Tel. 88 20 61.

Conveniently situated at the eastern end of the Ku'damm, across from the Gedächtniskirche, Wertheim is good for basic needs such as shampoo, film, or picnic supplies. It also has fine clothing, porcelain, and housewares departments. Open: Mon–Fri 9am–6pm, Sat 9am–2pm (to 6pm first Sat of the month). U-Bahn: Kurfürstendamm, a 1-minute walk.

ON WILMERSDORFER STRASSE

HERTIE, Wilmersdorfer Strasse 118-119. Tel. 31 03 11.

Hertie department store, together with Quelle across the street, is a good medium-price store, serving the basic needs of families. Stop here for those traveling necessities. Open: Mon–Wed and Fri 9am–6:30pm, Thurs 9am–8:30pm, Sat 9am–2pm (to 6pm first Sat of the month). U-Bahn: Wilmersdorfer Strasse, a 1-minute walk.

KARSTADT, Wilmersdorfer Strasse 109-111. Tel. 31 891.

At the corner of Kantstrasse and Wilmersdorfer Strasse, this large department store is one of a chain that can be found all over Germany (and slightly more upscale than competing chains). A good place to look for clothing and accessories. Open: Mon–Wed and Fri 9am–6:30pm, Thurs 9am–8:30pm, Sat 9am–2pm (to 6pm first Sat of the month. U-Bahn: Wilmersdorfer Strasse, a 1-minute walk.

QUELLE, Wilmersdorfer Strasse 50. Tel. 31 51 11.

The last of the three big department stores on Wilmersdorfer Strasse, with much the same merchandise and comparable prices, Quelle is a good place to stock up on film. There's a good cafeteria on the second floor. Open: Mon–Wed and Fri 9am–6:30pm, Thurs 9am–8:30pm, Sat 9am–2pm (to 6pm first Sat of the month). U-Bahn: Wilmersdorfer Strasse, a 1-minute walk.

FASHIONS

The best places to check for clothing and accessories are the many department stores listed above, where there are various departments for men, women, children, and teenagers. In addition, there are many boutiques in the Europa-Center, as well as open-fronted shops along the Ku'damm, Tauentzienstrasse, and Wilmersdorfer Strasse selling young, fun fashions at inexpensive prices.

The following shops are just a few of the more specialized boutiques selling traditional clothing and Berlin-designed avant-garde fashions.

TRADITIONAL CLOTHING

RIEDL, Carl-Schurz-Strasse 60, Spandau. Tel. 333 99 94.

Less than five years old, this boutique in Spandau's Altstadt is proof that traditional German costumes are as much in fashion now as they were half a century ago. You'll find casual clothing for women, men, and children, including sweaters, skirts, scarves, and blouses, plus accessories to complete the outfit. Julius Lang, Euringer, Elch, Huber, Imperial, and Hagro are just some of the brands sold here, and there are also gift items such as pewter and ceramic tableware. Open: Mon–Fri 10am–6:30pm, Sat 10am–2pm (to 6pm first Sat of the month). U-Bahn: Altstadt Spandau, a 1-minute walk.

TRIEBEL, Schönwalder Strasse 12, Spandau. Tel. 335 50 01.

Also in Spandau, on a street that stretches north of the Altstadt, Triebel is more proof that traditional German clothing can look contemporary and even sophisticated. Come here if you're interested in those wonderful Geiger sweaters or jackets, or if you like styles that look appropriate whether you're dining in a country lodge or off on a fox hunt. In addition to Geiger, the shop stocks clothing by Admont, Lodenfrey, and Perry. And besides hunting and riding clothes, it also sells hiking boots. Open: Mon–Fri 10am–6pm, Sat 10am–2pm (to 6pm first Sat of the month). U-Bahn: Altstadt Spandau.

BERLIN-DESIGNED FASHIONS

DURCHBRUCH, Schlüterstrasse 54. Tel. 881 55 68.

Durchbruch means "breakthrough," a timely name for a shop in Berlin. But the shop, the logo for which is a brick wall sliced in half, preceded the crumbling of the Wall by about six years; thus, "breakthrough" could also apply to its influence on Berlin's fashion scene. For this is where those in the know come for women's clothing of unusual and original German design, usually one-of-a-kind items. If you don't want to show up at the next cocktail party wearing the same thing as everyone else, try Durchbruch, located north of the Ku'damm. Open: Mon–Fri noon–6:30pm, Sat 11am–2pm (to 6pm first Sat of the month). S-Bahn: Savignyplatz, about a 2-minute walk.

FILATO, Nürnberger Strasse 24a. Tel. 24 54 77.

Filato is the label of two Berlin designers, Andrea Schuricht and Jutta Meierling, who use only natural materials in their line of casual and dressy womenswear. The unusual cuts and unexpected twists of their fashions appeal to young professional women who desire well-tailored clothes but who don't want to look too conservative. The shop, which sells other labels besides Filato, is found one block south of Tauentzienstrasse and the Europa-Center. Open: Mon–Fri 11am–6pm, Sat 10am–2pm (to 6pm first Sat of the month). U-Bahn: Augsburger Strasse, a 1-minute walk.

VENDI-VIDI-VICI, Leibnizstrasse 40. Tel. 323 23 22.

Berliner Sabine Cordey, an up-and-coming young designer of menswear, began her career by cutting up old suits and coats and redesigning them in the style of the 1980s. She became so successful that she now imports material from Italy and employs a small team of seamstresses to realize her ideas. Her clothing, which combines the classic with a touch of the avant-garde, is appropriate for all ages, from bankers to pony-tailed artistic types. Open: Mon–Fri noon–8pm, Sat 10:30am–3pm. S-Bahn: Savignyplatz, about a 4-minute walk.

FOOD

Almost all department stores in Germany have food departments, usually in their basements. In Berlin the ultimate in food emporiums is the sixth floor of the **KaDeWe department store** on Wittenbergplatz, with an incredible stockpile of gourmet foods (see "Department Stores and Malls," above). If it's to be found anywhere in Berlin, KaDeWe is the place.

If your tastes run toward natural foods, across the square from KaDeWe is a small shop called **Einhorn,** Wittenbergplatz 5-6 (tel. 24 63 47). In addition to ready-made vegetarian dishes, the place also sells Muesli, breads, organic fruits and vegetables, nuts, and more. It's open Monday through Friday from 10am to 6pm and on Saturday from 10am to 2pm. A second Einhorn is located at Mommsenstrasse 2 (tel. 881 42 41), a minute's walk north of the Ku'damm, with the same open hours.

GIFTS/SOUVENIRS

The largest selection of gifts and souvenirs can be found in Berlin's department stores, particularly **KaDeWe** and **Wertheim,** which are used to a steady flow of tourist traffic. Other places to look for unique gifts include the **weekend crafts market on Strasse des 17.**

Juni, where young entrepreneurs sell their own creations; **Kunsthandlung Bandoly,** described above under "Art Galleries," where etchings of Berlin are sold at inexpensive prices; **Harry Lehmann,** listed below, which has been selling perfume for 65 years; and **Studio-Haus** and **WMF,** described below under "Kitchenwares."

KITCHENWARES

STUDIO-HAUS, Kurfürstendamm 226. Tel. 881 7051.

This smart-looking shop sells a wide range of decorative and functional items for the home, including Rosenthal porcelain, Boda glass, tableware, and chrome kitchenware. Prices are high, but if you're looking for a wedding gift, this is a good place to start. Open: Mon–Fri 9am–6:30pm, Sat 9am–2pm (to 6pm first Sat of the month). U-Bahn: Kurfürstendamm, less than a 1-minute walk.

WMF, Kurfürstendamm 229. Tel. 882 39 41.

As many people know, the Germans make some of the best and most sought-after kitchen gadgets around. WMF, a chain found all over Germany, specializes in both tableware and cookingware, from chrome eggcups to pots and pans—sleek, functional, and sturdy. But WMF also has all those useful gadgets, from bottle stoppers to hardboiled-egg slicers. Open: Mon–Wed and Fri 9:30am–6:30pm, Thurs 9:30am–8:30pm, Sat 9am–2pm (to 6pm first Sat of the month). U-Bahn: Kurfürstendamm, a 1-minute walk.

MARKETS

Some of Berlin's best buys can be found at its many and various markets. Some are indoor and are held almost daily. Others are outdoor and are open only one or two days a week. Below are some of the best.

DIE NOLLE, above Nollendorfplatz station, Nollendorfplatz. Tel. 216 75 46.

This is a rather unusual antiques market—it spreads along the upper platform of a defunct railway station, with shops and stalls in old converted train compartments. Here you'll find second-hand books, old and new jewelry, model cars, porcelain, stamps and coins, glass, lighters, brass, and odds and ends. Prices aren't cheap, but the atmosphere is fun and there's a cheerful pub with a sunny terrace at one end of the platform. At the opposite end you can board an old-fashioned Berliner streetcar for a short ride to the next station, home of a small Turkish bazaar. Open: Wed–Mon 11am–7pm. U-Bahn: Nollendorfplatz, above the station.

KU'DAMM KARREE ANTIQUES MARKET, Kurfürstendamm 206-208. Tel. 881 41 71.

Located right on the Ku'damm is the Ku'damm Karree, an indoor shopping mall. Take the escalator up to the first floor, where you'll find an antiques flea market with various booths selling jewelry, clothing, furniture, old records, books, glassware, and typewriters. There's a lot of junk in among the treasures. If shopping makes you tired, be sure to drop in on the adjoining pub, Museumskneipe— well named, since it is crammed with all kinds of junk and curios, some items suspended from the ceiling. Open: Wed–Mon 3–10pm. U-Bahn: Uhlandstrasse, about a 2-minute walk.

MARKET AT STRASSE DES 17. JUNI, Strasse des 17. Juni. Tel. 322 81 99.

My favorite market, and one I never miss when I'm in Berlin. Stretching just west of the Tiergarten S-Bahn station, this weekend market offers a staggering variety of antiques, including silverware, books, china, glass, jewelry, clothing, kitchenware— and junk. Don't miss the second half of the market (past the stone portal and on the other side of the bridge), which features such original arts and crafts as funky and ethnic jewelry, clothing, hats, sketches, and innovative artwork. It's a good place to hunt for gifts, and prices are very reasonable. Don't miss it. Open: Sat and Sun 10am–5pm. S-Bahn: Tiergarten, a 1-minute walk.

TURKISH MARKET, bank of the Maybachufer River, Kreuzberg. Tel. 6809 29 26.

Kreuzberg is home to much of the city's Turkish population, so it's little wonder that you'll also find Berlin's best Turkish market here, spread along the bank of a river. This is also the city's most fascinating market, with both German and Turkish vendors selling vegetables, noodles, spices, clothing, and Turkish fast food. Try a Turkish pizza, a donner kebab, or falafel. If you like color, activity, the smell of exotic spices, and being outdoors, you'll love this place. Open: Tues and Fri noon–6:30pm. U-Bahn: Kottbusser Tor, about a 5-minute walk.

WEIHNACHTSMARKT, Breitscheidplatz and from Nürnberger Strasse to Joachimstaler Strasse.

Every December from the beginning of the month to Christmas Eve, there's a traditional Christmas market in the inner city. It radiates out from the Gedächtniskirche on Breitscheidplatz to Wittenbergplatz, particularly on Nürnberger Strasse and Joachimstaler Strasse. Colorful stalls sell those wonderful German Christmas ornaments, as well as candies, cookies, sausages, and other goodies, including Glühwein (spiced mulled wine). (Incidentally, there are other Christmas markets in Berlin—for example, in Spandau's Altstadt and on Alexanderplatz in East Berlin.) Open: Dec 1–24 daily 11am–9pm. U-Bahn: Kurfürstendamm, Bahnhof Zoologischer Garten, or Wittenbergplatz, each a 1-minute walk.

WINTERFELDPLATZ MARKET, Winterfeldplatz, Schöneberg.

Berlin's largest weekly market selling fruits, vegetables, meat, flowers, clothing, and accessories is just a 5-minute walk south of Nollendorfplatz. This is where Berliners come to do their shopping, whether it's for cabbage, olives, basil, mozzarella, or flowers. And of course, they also come to meet their friends and exchange the latest gossip. After making their purchases, many of the younger shoppers retire to Slumberland or Café Sidney, two bars on Winterfeldplatz. Open: Wed and Sat dawn–1pm. U-Bahn: Nollendorfplatz, a 5-minute walk.

PERFUME

For the big names in perfume from around the world, head for the ground floor of **KaDeWe,** described above in the department store section.

However, if you're looking for a scent unique to Berlin or an inexpensive and unusual gift, try **Harry Lehmann,** Kantstrasse 106 (tel. 324 35 82). This tiny family-owned shop has been selling its own concoctions since 1926, with approximately 50 scents now available (made from flowers, leaves, and grasses). They are sold by weight, starting at 2.50 DM ($1.50) for 10 grams. You can either bring your own perfume bottle or purchase one of the inexpensive vials available, a concept begun by Harry Lehmann, who decided it was a shame that pretty bottles had to be discarded when the perfume ran out. In addition to its scents, the shop—now in its third generation of owners—also sells Kölnisch Wasser and other colognes, as well as after-shave lotion for men. Don't be put off by the fake flowers; they're just one of the idiosyncrasies of this charming little establishment. It's found just a stone's throw west of the Wilmersdorfer Strasse pedestrian lane. Open Mon–Fri 9am–6:30pm, Sat 9am–2pm (to 6pm the first Sat of the month). U-Bahn: Wilmersdorfer Strasse, about 2 minutes away.

PORCELAIN

HELMUT TIMBERG, Kurfürstendamm 214. Tel. 881 91 58.

Meissen and Dresden porcelain are sold at this small place on the Ku'damm, where customers can shop for place settings, figurines, candlestick holders, and coffee or tea sets. Prices are high, and the atmosphere is subdued and hushed, as though the slightest noise would crack these fragile-looking pieces. Open: Mon–Fri 9am–6:30pm, Sat 9am–2pm (to 6pm first Sat of the month). U-Bahn: Uhlandstrasse, less than a 1-minute walk.

KPM, Kurfürstendamm 26a. Tel. 881 18 02.

The Königliche Porzellan-Manufaktur (KPM) is a Berlin tradition stretching back more than 225 years. In 1763 Frederick the Great acquired a preexisting porcelain company, renamed it the Königliche Porzellan-Manufaktur, and gave it royal-purveyor status. Since then, monarchs and heads of state from around the world have owned KPM porcelain, including Catherine II of Russia, Louis XVI of France, Elizabeth II of England, Princess Diana, Margaret Thatcher, Henry Kissinger, and Ed Koch. Although the firm's official name was changed in 1918 to Staatliche Porzellan-Manufaktur, its pieces are still identified with the KPM mark and everyone simply calls it KPM.

KPM today makes table settings, vases, baskets, figurines, and art pieces. All decorations and floral designs are hand-painted. The most popular items with tourists include reproductions of the Freedom Bell in Rathaus Schöneberg, white statues of the Berlin bear, and Christmas plates issued each year.

Although not as centrally located, the main shop of KPM is at Wegelystrasse 1 (tel. 39 00 90). Open: Ku'damm branch, Mon–Wed and Fri 9:30am–6:30pm, Thurs 9:30am–8:30pm, Sat 9am–2pm (to 6pm first Sat of the month); main shop, Mon–Fri 9am–6pm. U-Bahn for Ku'damm branch: Uhlandstrasse, a 1-minute walk. S-Bahn for main shop: Tiergarten, a few minutes' walk.

CHAPTER 9

BERLIN NIGHTS

1. THE PERFORMING ARTS

2. THE CLUB & MUSIC SCENE

3. THE BAR SCENE

4. MORE ENTERTAINMENT

Aside from the diversity and quality of its museums, the one thing that sets Berlin apart from all other German cities is its nightlife. When the streets of Munich and Hamburg are being rolled up at 1am, the Berliners are just getting started. The city never sleeps, simply because it doesn't have to. There are no closing hours for nightclubs, discos, and bars, so a few establishments stay open round the clock, while others call it quits at 3am or as late as 6am.

Little wonder that Berlin enjoys a popularity among Europe's younger generation of travelers comparable to that of Copenhagen or Amsterdam. One native Berliner once told me, "The reason everyone comes to Berlin is its nightlife," and he was serious. When I pointed out that people might come also because of the city's excellent museums, he seemed never to have considered the possibility. But the action starts late—you'll never see anything if you're in bed by 11pm. I suspect that more than a few travelers have remained unaware of the city's nighttime transformation, perhaps blissfully so. There's something to be said for early curfews.

On the other hand, it would be hard to remain completely unaware of Berlin's darker nighttime side, because there are signs of it everywhere and the city doesn't hide it. Everything exists side by side—the wicked beside the innocent, the tawdry beside the sophisticated. One single street near the Ku'damm may contain a first-class hotel, a strip joint and peep show, an Italian pizzeria, a pornography shop, and a restaurant serving French haute cuisine. The Ku'damm itself, by day Berlin's most popular shopping street, is by night the domain of dolled-up prostitutes; they are as much an accepted part of the boulevard as the display cases. It's this diversity that makes the city interesting. It's this tolerance that has made the city what it is today.

But you don't have to be a night owl to enjoy evenings in Berlin. There are cabarets, wine cellars, live-music houses, and a gambling casino. More refined tastes can indulge in opera, chamber music, the playing of two world-renowned orchestras, and classical and contemporary theater.

To find out what's going on in the traditional performing arts, pick up a copy of *Berlin Programm*. It gives a day-by-day account of events in all the city's opera houses, theaters, and concert halls. Rock concerts, experimental theater, and avant-garde happenings are covered in the city magazines *tip* and *zitty*.

If you don't mind paying a commission, convenient ticket outlets can be found at **Centrum,** Meinekestrasse 25 (tel. 882 76 11); the **Europa-Center,** Tauentzienstrasse 9 (tel. 261 70 51); the **KaDeWe** department store, Wittenbergplatz (tel. 24 80 36); and the **Wertheim department store,** Kurfürstendamm 231 (tel. 882 25 00).

You'll save money, however, by buying your ticket directly from the theater or concert hall during box-office hours or an hour before the performance begins. Some theaters give students discounts for unused tickets on the night of the performance. At the renowned Schiller-Theater, for example, students can get a 50% reduction on unsold tickets that regularly cost 18 DM ($10.90), and more by showing their student card on the night of the performance.

1. THE PERFORMING ARTS

CLASSICAL MUSIC

PHILHARMONIE, Mattäikirchstrasse 1. Tel. 25 48 80 or 261 43 83.

Without a doubt, this is Berlin's most famous concert hall, in part because it's the home of the world-renowned **Berlin Philharmonic Orchestra.** Situated on the southern edge of the Tiergarten district, the Philharmonie was designed by architect Hans Scharoun in 1963. It's an asymmetrical structure with a tentlike roof. The main auditorium seats more than 2,200, with conductor and orchestra placed at the very center and no concert-goer more than 100 feet from the podium. The acoustics are said to be nearly perfect.

 MAJOR CONCERT & PERFORMANCE HALLS

Berliner Ensemble, Am Bertolt-Brecht-Platz, tel. 282 3160
Deutschlandhalle, Messedamm 26, tel. 3 03 81
Deutsche Oper Berlin, Bismarckstrasse 35, tel. 34 381
Deutsche Staatsoper, Unter der Linden, tel. 207 18 28 or 205 45 56
Internationales Congress-Centrum (ICC), Am Messedamm, tel. 30 381
Philharmonie, Mattäikirchstrasse 1, tel. 25 48 80 or 261 43 83
Schiller-Theater, Bismarckstrasse 110, tel. 319 52 36
Waldbühne, Ruhleben, Charlottenburg, tel 852 40 80

The Berlin Philharmonic Orchestra, founded in 1882, has been led by some of the world's greatest conductors. It gained acclaim under the baton of the late Herbert von Karajan, acclaim that now continues unabated for his successor, Claudio Abbado. Leading guest conductors and soloists regularly join the Berlin Philharmonic, including such notables as Sir Yehudi Menuhin, Zubin Mehta, Christoph von Dohnányi, Sir Georg Solti, Daniel Barenboim, and Seiji Ozawa.

The Philharmonic performs approximately 100 times in Berlin during its August-through-June season, attracting more than 220,000 people annually. Each year it also performs 20 to 30 concerts worldwide. Because the orchestra is so popular, tickets often sell out two months in advance. If you're able to procure one, consider yourself very lucky.

The Philharmonie is also the venue of the **Radio Symphony Orchestra,** guest orchestras, and ensembles. The famous **Berlin Jazz Festival** also takes place here.

In addition to the main hall, there's also a smaller **Kammer-musiksaal** (Chamber Music Hall).

Open: Box office Mon–Fri 3:30–6pm, Sat and Sun and holidays 11am–2pm. Bus: 24, 29, 48, or 83.

OPERA, OPERETTA & BALLET

DEUTSCHE OPER BERLIN, Bismarckstrasse 35. Tel. 34 381 (information), 341 02 49 (tickets).

Whereas most of Europe's opera houses are grand and ornate edifices dating from another era, the Deutsche Oper Berlin was rebuilt after World War II in an intentionally plain and modern style, made even plainer by the stark street-side wall designed to shut out traffic noise. Seating 1,900, it features performances of opera almost every night, except when there's ballet. The Deutsche Oper Berlin attained worldwide success in the 1920s under such great conductors as Richard Strauss, Bruno Walter, Leo Blech, Wilhelm Furtwängler, Erich Kleiber, and Otto Klemperer.

Prices: 10–125 DM ($6.05–$75.75); student reductions available before performances begin.

Open: Box office Mon–Fri 2–8pm, Sat and Sun 10am–2pm; performances daily at 7:30 or 8pm. **U-Bahn:** Deutsche Oper.

DEUTSCHE STAATSOPER, Unter den Linden 7, East Berlin. Tel. 207 18 28 or 205 45 56.

Located on the famous Unter den Linden, the Deutsche Staatsoper (German State Opera) has long been one of Berlin's premier opera houses. Although the present building dates only from the 1950s, its facade faithfully copies that of the preexisting structure, first erected in the 1740s by Knobelsdorff and renovated in 1927. The schedule features opera, ballet, and concerts.

Prices: Telephone for latest ticket prices.

Open: Box office Mon–Sat noon–6pm, Sun and holidays 4–

6pm; performances most evenings except Mon at 7 or 8pm. **S-Bahn:** Friedrichstrasse.

THEATER DES WESTENS, Kantstrasse 12. Tel. 319 03 193.

Built in 1896 and occupying a prime spot near the Ku'damm and Bahnhof Zoo, this is the place to go for operettas, musicals, and popular productions.
Prices: 13–68 DM ($7.85–$41.20).
Open: Box office Mon–Sat 10am–6pm, Sun 3–6pm; performances usually nightly at 8pm. **U-Bahn** and **S-Bahn:** Bahnhof Zoologischer Garten.

KOMISCHE OPER, Behrenstrasse 55, tel. 229 25 55

The Comic Opera presents a varied program of orchestra concerts, light opera, and operetta.
Prices: 3–45 DM ($1.85–$28).
Open: Box office Tues.–Fri noon–6pm, Sat 10am–6pm, Sun and holidays 1 hr before the performance. **S-Bahn:** Friedrichstrasse.

THEATER

With a long tradition behind it, Berlin has played a leading role in the history and development of the theater in Germany. Hauptmann, Ibsen, Strindberg, and Brecht all left their mark on Berlin's stages, as did such well-known directors as Max Reinhardt, Erwin Piscator, and Gustaf Gründgens.

Today the theater in Berlin is still going strong. You'll be at a disadvantage if you don't speak German, but if you do, you're in for a treat.

SCHILLER-THEATER, Bismarckstrasse 110. Tel. 319 52 36.

Of Berlin's many theaters, this is the best known. Germans come from all over the country to watch its performances of classical and modern drama, both German and foreign. Built in 1951 from the ruins of an older theater destroyed in World War II, it has 1,065 seats. A smaller stage, called the Schiller-Theater Werkstatt (Workshop), is used for experimental pieces.
Prices: 8–53 DM ($4.85–$32); 50% reduction for students on unsold tickets regularly costing 18 DM ($10.90) and up, available the night of performance.
Open: Box office Mon–Fri 2–8pm, Sat and Sun 10am–2pm; performances usually daily at 7 or 8pm. **U-Bahn:** Ernst-Reuter-Platz.

SCHLOSSPARK-THEATER, Schlossstrasse 48, Steglitz. Tel. 791 15 15.

The Schlosspark-Theater, built in 1920 as part of the Schloss Steglitz, is a state-owned theater known for its classical and modern productions.
Prices: 7–50 DM ($4.25–$30.30); student reduction of 50% for unsold tickets regularly costing 15 DM ($9.10) and up, available 30 minutes before each performance.

Open: Box office daily from 10am to performance time; performances usually daily at 8pm. **U-Bahn:** Rathaus Steglitz.

SCHAUBÜHNE AM LEHNINER PLATZ, Kurfürstendamm 153. Tel. 89 00 23.

One of Berlin's leading venues for experimental drama, located toward the eastern end of the Ku'damm near Lehniner Platz, it occupies what used to be a former theater. Although the original 1920s facade has been preserved, the inside has the latest in modern theatrical technology, including three stages where plays can be given simultaneously.

Prices: 18–48 DM ($10.90–$29.10).

Open: Box office Mon–Sat 10am–7pm, Sun and holidays 10am–2pm and 5–7pm; performances usually Tues–Sun 8 or 8:30pm. **U-Bahn:** Adenauerplatz.

BERLINER ENSEMBLE, Am Bertolt-Brecht-Platz, East Berlin. Tel. 282 31 60.

Bertolt Brecht and Helene Weigel founded this remarkable theater in 1945, and it has been staging his works ever since. Even when the Wall cut off the Berliner Ensemble from Western eyes, it maintained a reputation in West Germany as one of the best places in the world to see Brecht. It also features works by guest playwrights.

Prices: From 6 DM ($3.65).

Open: Box office Mon–Fri 11am–1:30pm and 2–6pm (Mon to 5pm only); performances usually Tues–Sun at 7pm. **S-Bahn:** Friedrichstrasse.

ROCK CONCERTS & OTHER SHOWS

WALDBÜHNE, Ruhleben, Charlottenburg. Tel. 852 40 80.

Beautifully situated in a wooded ravine near the Olympiastadion (Olympic Stadium), the Waldbühne is Germany's largest open-air arena. It's Berlin's best-loved spot for rock, pop, and folklore concerts held in summer. Although such performers as Joe Cocker, Tina Turner, and Prince are usually featured, the Berlin Philharmonic Orchestra has been known to give concerts here as well. Be sure to pack a picnic and a warm blanket, and bring along raingear just in case.

Open: Performances May to October. **U-Bahn:** Ruhleben, then a 20-minute walk through a park.

DEUTSCHLANDHALLE, Messedamm 26. Tel. 3 03 81.

With 14,000 seats, the Deutschlandhalle is Berlin's largest arena.

IMPRESSIONS

He said that in Berlin, if you wanted to make a scandal in the theater, you had to have a mother committing incest with two sons; one wasn't enough.
—ARNOLD BENNETT, quoting Rudolf Kommer, 1925

The place is used for occasional rock concerts—Simply Red and Tears for Fears have played here—as well as for conventions, horse shows, and other events with mass attendance. It's located on the grounds of the city's largest conference and convention center, the Internationales Congress-Centrum (ICC).

Open: Box office Mon–Fri noon–6pm, Sat 10am–2pm. **Bus:** 4, 66, or 69.

INTERNATIONALES CONGRESS-CENTRUM (ICC), Am Messedamm. Tel. 30 38 1.

The massive ICC, right next to the Funkturm (Radio Tower), opened in 1979. Besides some 80 lecture halls and meeting rooms, it boasts two main halls (one seating 2,000, the other 5,000) used for both conferences and concerts. Past performers here have included Johnny Cash, Harry Belafonte, Falco, and Laurie Anderson.

Open: Box office Mon–Fri noon–6pm, Sat 10am–2pm. **Bus:** 4, 66, or 69.

METROPOL, Nollendorfplatz 5. Tel. 216 41 22.

A disco on weekends, the Metropol offers some of the best music around during its weekday-evening concerts. Though the space is too small to accommodate the big names, you can catch your favorite lesser-known artists here before they do make it big; Johnny Clegg and Savuka played here on one of my last visits. A smaller, separate stage called Loft provides a more intimate setting for concerts ranging from punk rock to rhythm and blues.

Open: Phone for ticket and concert information. **U-Bahn:** Nollendorfplatz.

TEMPODROM, Tiergarten. Tel. 394 40 45 or 612 41 07.

Tempodrom is a huge tent right in the middle of the city, erected in an effort to provide alternative performances at a permanent site. The programs include circus shows, theater, music, and revues. Consult *tip, zitty,* or the *Berlin Programm* for current attractions. The tent is located near the Kongresshalle at the north end of the Tiergarten, not far from the Reichstag building.

Open: Performances May to October. **Bus:** 69 from Bahnhof Zoologischer Garten to Kongresshalle stop.

---

2. THE CLUB & MUSIC SCENE

CABARET

As Liza Minnelli sang, "Life is a cabaret, old chum," and nowhere is that more true than in Berlin. Granted, the old days of stinging political satires are long gone, which in any case required an excellent command of the German language to understand. Some nightclubs do offer political commentary, but mostly you'll find music and dance, including transvestite shows.

DIE STACHELSCHWEINE, basement of Europa-Center, Tauentzienstrasse and Budapester Strasse. Tel. 261 47 95.

This is one of Berlin's old-timers, a cabaret with more than 40 years under its belt. Its name means "porcupine," and it carries on the pre-Nazi tradition of political commentary—which means that you have to understand German to appreciate it.

Prices: 20–38 DM ($12.10–$23.05).

Open: Performances Mon–Sat 7:30 or 8:30pm. **U-Bahn:** Bahnhof Zoologischer Garten or Kurfürstendamm, each a few minutes' walk.

CHEZ NOUS, Marburger Strasse 14. Tel. 213 18 10.

Cabaret of a different sort, the transvestite show put on here has been titillating Berliners and visitors for more than 30 years with its elaborate costumes, its singing, dancing, and parodies. A Berlin institution, it's found just a minute's walk from the Europa-Center.

Prices: Obligatory drink minimum 35 DM ($21.20); long drinks average 25 DM ($15.15). **Admission:** 10 DM ($6.05).

Open: Box office daily 10am–1pm and from 1:30pm to performance time; performances daily 8:30pm and 11pm. **U-Bahn:** Kurfürstendamm or Augsburger Strasse, each about a 4-minute walk.

DOLLYWOOD, Kurfürstenstrasse 116. Tel. 24 89 50.

Another cabaret specializing in transvestite variety shows, the Dollywood is located beside the Hotel Sylter Hof. Because performers come from around the world, many of the songs and performances are in English.

Prices: Obligatory drink minimum 20 DM ($12.10). **Admission:** 15 DM ($9.10).

Open: Sun and Tues–Thurs shows at 8:30pm, 10pm, and midnight; Fri and Sat shows at 8pm, 11pm, 12:30am, and 2am. **U-Bahn:** Wittenbergplatz, about a 5-minute walk.

LIVE MUSIC HOUSES

FOLK MUSIC

GO-IN, Bleibtreustrasse 17. Tel. 881 72 18.

The Go-In was my introduction to Berlin nightlife when I first visited the city as a student in the early 1970s, and I'm happy to report that the place is still going strong. The clientele seems to have grown older along with the Go-In, which attracts an audience appreciative of folk music from around the world. It offers jazz, blues, bluegrass, Spanish flamenco, and Greek, German, and international folk songs, to name only some of the music heard here during the past two decades. (The place opened in 1968.) A few minutes' walk north of the Ku'damm.

Prices: Beer from 4 DM ($2.40). **Admission:** Usually free Sun–Thurs; cover Fri, Sat, and special concerts 6–12 DM ($3.65–$7.25).

Open: 8pm to 3am daily; music begins at 9pm. **S-Bahn:** Savignyplatz, about a 2-minute walk.

TROPICAL BRASIL, Kaiser-Friedrich-Strasse 40. Tel. 313 45 62.

This small, laid-back, and friendly establishment is the best place in town to hear Brazilian music. Popular with Berlin's Latin crowd, it can get quite lively and crowded, making for a great evening. Try a caipirinha, Brazil's national drink made with a sugar schnapps and lime.

Prices: Beer from 4 DM ($2.40). **Admission:** Free.

Open: Daily 7pm–2 or 3am; live music from 10pm. **U-Bahn:** Bismarckstrasse or Wilmersdorfer Strasse, each about a 5-minute walk.

ROCK, JAZZ & BLUES

QUASIMODO, Kantstrasse 12a. Tel. 312 80 86.

In a small building dwarfed by the Theater des Westens next door, Quasimodo features contemporary jazz and rock groups. It ranks as one of the best places in town to hear live music. Check *tip* or *zitty* for concert information.

Prices: Admission 10–25 DM ($6.05–$15.15), depending on the band.

Open: Concerts usually start around 10pm. **U-Bahn:** Bahnhof Zoologischer Garten.

LOFT, Nollendorfplatz 5. Tel. 216 10 20.

Located in the massive building that also houses the Metropol disco, Loft serves as a smaller arena for everything from punk rock and experimental music to rhythm and blues. Musicians come from around the world, including many bands from the United States and Great Britain. If there's an opening act as well, the band is likely to be one of Berlin's own.

Prices: Admission usually 10–20 DM ($6.05–$12.10), depending on the group.

Open: Concerts 2 to 4 times weekly, at 8:30pm. **U-Bahn:** Nollendorfplatz, a 1-minute walk.

EIERSCHALE, Rankestrasse 1. Tel. 882 53 05.

Conveniently situated just off the Ku'damm across the street from the Gedächtniskirche, this popular music house and bar offers live music nightly, primarily traditional jazz and blues. With outdoor sidewalk seating in the summer, it also makes a good place to come for breakfast, especially on Sunday, when there's live music all day long.

Prices: Beer from 4.10 DM ($2.50). **Admission:** 4 DM ($2.40) when there's live music, which goes toward first drink.

Open: Sun–Thurs 8am–2am, Fri and Sat 8am–4am. Live music from 9:30pm. **U-Bahn:** Kurfürstendamm, a 1-minute walk.

MUSEUMSKNEIPE, Ku'damm Karree, Kurfürstendamm 206-208. Tel. 881 41 71.

Located in a mall called Ku'damm Karree, up on the first floor next to an antiques flea market, this interesting bar features live music every night at 9pm and on Sunday afternoon beginning around noon. Appropriately enough, it's decorated like a junk and curio shop, with old musical instruments, a bicycle, a baby carriage, and old lamps hanging from the ceiling and walls. The action keeps going until the manager decides he's had enough, usually in the wee hours of the morning.

Prices: Beer 4.50 DM ($2.70). **Admission:** Free Sun–Thurs; cover Fri and Sat 5 DM ($3.05).

Open: Mon and Wed–Fri 2pm–?, Tues 5pm–?, Sat and Sun 11am–? **U-Bahn:** Uhlandstrasse, a few minutes' walk.

DANCE CLUBS & DISCOS

METROPOL, Nollendorfplatz 5. Tel. 216 41 22.

For several years now the Metropol, housed in a colossal, striking building converted from a former theater, has managed to remain on top as one of the most popular and innovative establishments on the Berlin scene, due in part to the many diversions it offers (including a laser show). On weekends it's strictly a disco; during the week it features live concerts with bands from around the world. In addition, a separate and smaller arena called the Loft presents live concerts two to four times a week. The disco crowd tends to be people in their 20s.

Prices: Drinks from 4 DM ($2.40). **Admission:** Cover 10 DM ($6.05), 3 DM of which goes toward first drink.

Open: Disco Fri and Sat only, 10pm–6am. **U-Bahn:** Nollendorfplatz, a 1-minute walk.

BIG EDEN, Kurfürstendamm 202. Tel. 882 61 20.

Right on the Ku'damm, Big Eden has been around seemingly forever. Opened in 1968, the disco proudly displays photographs of celebrities who have passed through its doors in the years that followed, including Klaus Kinski, Roman Polanski, Telly Savalas, and a very young-looking Paul McCartney. Those days when the Big

---

IMPRESSIONS

Public courtesans are more numerous here than in any town in Europe. . . . They appear openly at windows in the day time, beckon to passengers as they walk in the streets, and ply for employment in any way they please, without disturbance from the magistrate.
—JOHN MOORE, 1779

Eden was the hottest thing in town have long gone, but it still attracts young visitors of every nationality. Teenagers crowd the dance floor until midnight; after they catch the last subway home, an older generation of revelers in their 20s takes over. In addition to a large dance floor, the place also has pool tables and pinball machines. It maintains a strict front-door policy: No one admitted who even looks drunk.

Prices: Beer from 6 DM, long drinks and cocktails from 7.50 DM ($4.55). **Admission:** Cover Mon–Thurs 4 DM ($2.40), Fri and Sat 8 DM ($4.85), Sun 6 DM ($3.65), which includes ticket good for 4 DM ($2.40) toward first drink; unaccompanied women admitted free.

Open: Sun–Thurs 7pm–4am, Fri and Sat 7pm–7am. **U-Bahn:** Uhlandstrasse, about a 3-minute walk.

CHA CHA, Nürnberger Strasse 50. Tel. 24 24 47.

This disco is smaller than those listed above and caters largely to an older, 25- to 35-year-old market. A mellow and civilized place with dimly lit murals of dancing Latin Americans, it is at its most crowded at 2 or 3am. About a 5-minute walk from the Ku'Damm or the Europa-Center.

Prices: Drinks from 6 DM ($3.65). **Admission:** Cover Sun, Tues–Thurs 5 DM ($3.05); Fri and Sat 10 DM ($6.05).

Open: Tues–Sun 11pm–6am. **U-Bahn:** Augsburger Strasse, a 1-minute walk.

FIRST, Joachimstaler Strasse 26. Tel. 882 26 86.

The name says it all—First considers itself Berlin's number one disco for the well-heeled yuppie and business crowd. The music ranges from pop and disco tunes to jazz and swing. A small place not far from the Ku'damm, it has a long-drink menu and even accepts credit cards.

Prices: Beer from 7 DM ($4.25), cocktails and long drinks 10–20 DM ($6.05–$12.10). **Admission:** Free.

Open: Wed–Sun 11pm–5am. **U-Bahn:** Kurfürstendamm, about a 3-minute walk.

CAFÉ KEESE, Bismarckstrasse 108. Tel. 312 91 11.

A Berlin institution, and a unique one at that. For in contrast to most dance halls, it's the women who choose partners here (except for the hourly "Men's Choice," when the green light goes on). Seating 700, the place is popular with the middle-aged set, though some of the curious include visitors in their 30s and 40s. It opened in 1966, a sister to the Café Keese that's been in operation in Hamburg since 1948; both establishments claim that in the past 40-odd years more than 95,000 couples have met on their dance floors and subsequently married. Who knows, maybe this will be your lucky night. No jeans or tennis shoes are allowed; most men are in coat and tie, and the women dress up. A live band plays most evenings. If you're over 30, you'll probably get a kick out of Café Keese, about a 15-minute walk north of the Ku'damm.

Prices: No cover charge, but obligatory minimum drink charge of 6 DM ($3.65).

Open: Mon–Thurs 8pm–3am, Fri and Sat 8pm–4am, Sun 4pm–1am. **U-Bahn:** Ernst-Reuter-Platz.

3. THE BAR SCENE

Before setting out for one of Berlin's many bars, there are a couple of things you should know. First of all, absolutely the worst thing you can do in a German *Kneipe,* or bar, is to sit at a table marked *Stammtisch*—it's reserved for privileged regulars. In addition, it's considered bad manners to drink without raising your glass to your fellow drinkers (the clinking was thought to scare away bad spirits in medieval times). Unless otherwise stated, there is no cover charge or admission to the following bars. Prost!

ON OR NEAR THE KU'DAMM

BEIZ, Schlüterstrasse 38. Tel. 883 89 57.

One of the best places in town to sample German wines from the Rheingau, Pfalz, Franken, Württemberg, and other wine regions of the country. A simple, cloisterlike establishment with starkly white walls, vaulted ceilings, a plank floor, and wooden tables, it serves German food in addition to its wines and is popular with an older, sophisticated crowd. Try a Himmelsleiter ("Ladder to Heaven") for 20 DM ($12.10), which allows you to sample seven different German wines. Beiz is found just north of the Ku'damm.

Prices: Wine from 6 DM ($3.65) for a small glass.

Open: Daily 6pm–2am. **U-Bahn:** Uhlandstrasse or Adenauerplatz, each about a 5-minute walk.

NEW YORK, Olivaer Platz 15. Tel. 883 62 58.

Casual yet trendy, New York is one of the "in" spots for those in their 20s and 30s. Even in the middle of the day people hang out here, read the newspaper, and shoot pool—making it a good place to go if you're in search of an afternoon drink. Resembling a café by day, after midnight it looks more like a bar; breakfast is served from 2am on Friday and Saturday. The place is located on a square south of the Ku'damm, near Adenauerplatz.

Prices: Beer from 3.50 DM ($2.10), wine from 5.50 DM ($3.30).

Open: Sun–Thurs 10am–4am, Fri and Sat 10am–6am. **U-Bahn:** Adenauerplatz.

TASTY, Kurfürstendamm 53. Tel. 883 94 44.

Right on the Ku'damm near Schlüterstrasse, this upmarket and chic bar offers "snacks for gourmets," which turn out to be a few changing daily specials that can range from chili con carne or French onion soup to Welsh rarebit or smoked salmon. Sleekly decorated with marble-topped tables, black furniture, and artwork on the walls, Tasty is a good place for a pre-dinner drink or an afternoon snack, since it closes shockingly early.

Prices: Beer and wine from 3.50 DM ($2.10).

Open: Summers, Mon–Sat 11am–10pm; winters, Mon–Sat 11am–8pm. **U-Bahn:** Uhlandstrasse or Adenauerplatz, each about a 5-minute walk.

KU'DORF, Joachimstaler Strasse 15. Tel. 883 66 66.

Located in a basement, the Ku'Dorf is a sprawling underground "village" consisting of several "lanes" lined with one tiny bar after another. In fact, there are 18 different bars here, each decorated in a different theme, so customers simply walk around until they find one that fits their fancy. At one end of the village is a disco; at the other end is the Klostergarten, looking like the inner courtyard of a cloister—some of the seats even resemble headstones. Popular with the middle-aged generation, the Klostergarten features candles on the tables and live piano music after 9pm. Note, however, that everyone in the Ku'Dorf is likely to be a tourist, perhaps because the place is so conveniently situated. If you want to be among Berliners, go someplace else.

Prices: Half liter of beer 6.70 DM ($4.05). **Admission:** Cover 3 DM ($1.80).

Open: Mon–Thurs 8pm–2am, Fri and Sat 8pm–4am. **U-Bahn:** Kurfürstendamm, about a 2-minute walk.

WIRTSHAUS ZUM LÖWEN, Hardenbergstrasse 29. Tel. 262 10 20.

This beer hall recalls those in Munich and even serves Bavarian beer, Löwenbräu. There's outdoor seating in summer, but even in winter you can drink inside and still pretend you're in a beer garden—the interior is ingeniously constructed to resemble a tree-filled Bavarian plaza. As with most beer halls, hearty platters of German food are also available, and there's traditional Bavarian music beginning at 7pm. Just north of the Gedächtniskirche.

Prices: Half liter of beer 4.50 DM ($2.70) in the day, 6 DM ($3.65) at night.

Open: Sun–Thurs 10am–midnight, Fri and Sat 10am–2am. **U-Bahn:** Kurfürstendamm or Bahnhof Zoologischer Garten, each a 1-minute walk.

NEAR SAVIGNYPLATZ

Savignyplatz is a small square just a 5-minute walk north of the Ku'damm, easily reached by strolling north on Knesebeckstrasse. There are a number of bars and restaurants here, making it a good place to bar hop.

AX BAX, Leibnizstrasse 34. Tel. 313 85 94.

For a thirtysomething Berliner out on the town, Ax Bax is likely to be on the agenda. Everyone who's anyone puts in an appearance at this popular watering hole, including writers and personalities in the film industry, and the average age of customers here is a comfortable 35 to 40. Founded by a transplant from Vienna, this combination restaurant/bar offers a changing selection of Viennese specialties, which may include a meat-and-vegetable Strudel, a Viennese salad, or marinated beef. Early in the evening, people come to eat; after 10pm they usually come for the more serious business of drinking, though food is served until a late 1am. A few minutes' walk west of Savignyplatz, off Kantstrasse.

Prices: Cocktails from 10 DM ($6.05).

Open: Sun–Fri 7pm–2am. **S-Bahn:** Savignyplatz, less than a 4-minute walk.

CAFÉ BLEIBTREU, Bleibtreustrasse 45. Tel. 881 47 56.

This is one of my favorite cafés, day or night. I like the atmosphere, the clientele, and the background music. One of the first so-called café/bars to open in 1972, it has a warm, pleasant feel to it, with plants, ceiling fans, and large front windows. Popular with the 30-ish crowd, it serves breakfast until 2pm.

Prices: Half liter of beer 3.70 DM ($2.25); wine from 4.50 DM ($2.70).

Open: Sun–Thurs 9:30am–1am, Fri and Sat 9:30am–2:30am. **S-Bahn:** Savignyplatz.

CAFÉ UNTREU, Bleibtreustrasse 13. Tel. 883 71 31.

The walls of this small bar have murals of bubbles rising in water, as though the whole place were slowly sinking. Café Untreu's name (which means "unfaithful") is a cheeky reference to the street's name, *Bleibtreu,* which means "to remain faithful." In any case, the customers here tend to be in their early 20s, and music from the sound system ranges from jazz to the latest disco tunes.

Prices: Beer 3.30 DM ($2), wine 4.90 DM ($2.95), mixed drinks 7.50 DM ($4.55).

Open: Daily 7pm–3am. **S-Bahn:** Savignyplatz, a 2-minute walk.

COUR CARRÉE, Savignyplatz 5. Tel. 312 52 38.

There's nothing special about this place except that it occupies a prime spot on Savignyplatz and offers outdoor seating beneath a canopy of spreading vines. Come in the summertime and watch the world go by.

Prices: Beer from 3.30 DM ($2), mixed drinks from 6 DM ($3.65).

Open: Daily noon–2am. **S-Bahn:** Savignyplatz, about a two-minute walk.

DICKE WIRTIN, Carmerstrasse 9. Tel. 312 49 52.

The days when this was the hottest bar around have long passed, but it still has a faithful and devoted clientele. I've never been here in the wee hours of the night, but judging from the serious beer drinkers who are already here by early evening, things can only get rowdier. Named after the rather large barmaid who used to run the place, it's an old-style German pub known for its stews costing 4 DM ($2.40) a bowlful. For years it's been worth coming here for the building alone (Dicke Wirtin occupies only a small part of it on the ground floor)—bullet-ridden, ancient, and beautiful but neglected. Now it's been earmarked for renovation and a facelift.

Prices: Half liter beer 3.90 DM ($2.35).

Open: Daily noon–4am. **S-Bahn:** Savignyplatz, about a 3-minute walk.

DIENER, Grolmanstrasse 47. Tel. 881 53 29.

This is a typical German Kneipe, or bar, except for the fact that it's been here for decades and is named after former champion boxer Franz Diener. Filling the walls are photographs of famous people who have dropped in, including theater and film stars. Otherwise, it's an unpretentious-looking place, the service is friendly, and German soups and snacks are served.

Prices: Beer from 4.20 DM ($2.55), wine from 5.80 DM ($3.50).
Open: Wed–Mon 6pm–1am. **S-Bahn** and **U-Bahn:** Savignyplatz and Uhlandstrasse, both about a 3-minute walk.

SCHWARZES CAFÉ, Kantstrasse 148. Tel. 313 80 38.

The trademark here is unconventionality, with some of the strangest open hours in town. *Schwarz* means "black," and true to its name, the café has its front room painted black. If you find black rooms depressing, head upstairs for brighter and more cheerful surroundings, where the only black in sight is the furniture. Breakfasts are a specialty, available anytime and ranging from 6 DM ($3.65) for a Continental to 14.50 DM ($8.75) for the works. There is also a large selection of coffees, including concoctions with alcohol, plus ice cream.

Prices: Coffee from 2.70 DM ($1.65) a cup; spiked coffee from 7.50 DM ($4.55).
Open: Round the clock, except Tues 3am–9pm. **S-Bahn** and **U-Bahn:** Savignyplatz and Uhlandstrasse, both about a three-minute walk.

TIMES BAR, Savoy Hotel, Fasanenstrasse 9-10. Tel. 31 10 30.

A great place for a quiet drink, this hotel bar is also convenient if you're visiting the nearby Theater des Westens. The small, wood-paneled room offers a selection of international newspapers for the unhurried perusal of its customers, including the *Financial Times,* the London *Times, Herald Tribune,* and *USA Today.*

Prices: Beer from 5.50 DM ($3.30), cocktails from 15 DM ($9.10).
Open: Daily 5pm–1am. **U-Bahn:** Bahnhof Zoologischer Garten, a 3-minute walk; Kurfürstendamm, a 4-minute walk.

WIRTSHAUS WUPPKE, Schlüterstrasse 21. Tel. 313 81 62.

Though most people come just to drink at this plain and unrefined worker's neighborhood pub, there are daily specials written on a blackboard, including hearty stews and salads. For entertainment, there's a pinball machine. The owner, Harold, speaks English.

Prices: Beer from 3.50 DM ($2.10), wine from 3.80 DM ($2.30).
Open: Summer, daily 9am–3am; winter, noon–3am. **S-Bahn:** Savignyplatz, about a 1-minute walk.

ZILLEMARKT, Bleibtreustrasse 48a. Tel. 881 70 40.

On the same street as the cafés Bleibtreu and Untreu and the music house Go-In, this pleasant and airy establishment is named after an antiques-and-curios market that used to take place here. The building goes back to the turn of the century and features a brick-and-cement floor, grillwork, and plants. In summer there's a garden out back with outdoor seating. Breakfast is served until a late 4pm.

Prices: Beer from 4.20 DM ($2.55), Berliner Weisse 5.50 DM ($3.30), wine from 4.90 DM ($2.95).
Open: Daily 8am–2am. **S-Bahn:** Savignyplatz, a 1-minute walk.

ZWIEBELFISCH, Savignyplatz 7-8. Tel. 31 73 63.

An old-timer, the Zwiebelfisch has been around for more than 20 years and still enjoys great popularity. Because it stays open later than other bars in the area, everyone ends up here. It can be at its most crowded at 4am.

Prices: Wine from 3.30 DM ($2), a tiny beer 2 DM ($1.20).

Open: Daily noon–6am. **S-Bahn:** Savignyplatz, less than a 3-minute walk.

NEAR WILMERSDORFER STRASSE

If you find yourself on Wilmersdorfer Strasse after a hard day's shopping, you might wish to reward yourself with a stop at one of these two places.

EXTRA DRY, Mommsenstrasse 34. Tel. 324 60 38.

This café *for women only,* is certainly one of the best of its kind in Berlin. Clean, modern, and nicely furnished, it maintains a strict policy against alcoholic drinks, offering instead milkshakes, fruit cocktails, and light snacks. It serves as a meeting place for various women's groups, including those involving battered women and women who have been drug-dependent and need a clean environment in which to socialize. It's also a good place for women traveling alone or tired of the usual bar scene—somewhere to simply sit and write letters if that's what you feel like doing. The service is friendly.

Prices: Drinks around 3 DM ($1.80).

Open: Tues–Thurs noon–11pm, Fri noon–midnight, Sat 11am–midnight, Sun 11am–11pm. **U-Bahn:** Wilmersdorfer Strasse. **S-Bahn:** Charlottenburg.

WILHELM HOECK, Wilmersdorfer Strasse 149. Tel. 341 31 10.

You'll find two doors at this address. The door on the left leads to a simple family-style restaurant; the one on the right leads to the bar, which has been around since 1892. The decor features old wooden beer barrels against one wall, as well as long-ago photographs that illustrate the history of the place. If you're hungry, a menu offers home-cooked dishes "from Grandmother's kitchen," including Kasseler Braten (smoked pork chops) with cabbage and potatoes, Schnitzel with vegetables and potatoes, and fried liver with apples, onions, and potatoes; most platters are priced between 8 and 18 DM ($4.85 and $10.90).

Prices: Half liter of beer 4 DM ($2.40).

Open: Mon–Sat 8am–midnight. **Closed:** Sun and holidays. **U-Bahn:** Bismarckstrasse, a few minutes' walk.

NEAR NOLLENDORFPLATZ

HARRY'S NEW YORK BAR, Hotel Grand Esplanade, Lützowufer 15. Tel. 26 10 11.

Harry's New York Bar first opened in Paris in 1911 and gained fame as the favorite watering hole of F. Scott Fitzgerald, Ernest Hemingway, and Gertrude Stein. Berlin's rendition is as popular as its Paris namesake. Very sophisticated with its red-leather sofas and incredibly long bar (emphasized by slick back lighting), it attracts visiting business professionals from around the world. There's live piano music nightly after 8pm, and everything is under the watchful eyes of all the U.S. presidents, whose portraits line one entire wall.

Prices: Beer from 3.30 DM ($2), cocktails from 14 DM ($8.50).
Open: Daily noon–1am or later. **U-Bahn:** Nollendorfplatz, a 5-minute walk.

CAFÉ SIDNEY, Winterfeldstrasse 40. Tel. 216 52 53.

This modern and breezy café/bar stands on a square called Winterfeldplatz, famous for its morning market on Wednesdays and Saturdays. Breakfast is available at any time, and there are two pool tables.

Prices: Half liter of beer 5.50 DM ($3.30), cocktails 9–13 DM ($5.45–$7.85).
Open: Daily 9am–4am. **U-Bahn:** Nollendorfplatz, about a 5-minute walk.

SLUMBERLAND, Winterfeldplatz. Tel. 216 53 49.

Everyone seems to drop by here after visiting the Saturday market on Winterfeldplatz. But Slumberland is at its most crowded in the very late hours, after other bars have closed down. It plays African, Caribbean, reggae, and calypso music, and even has a real sand floor—along with fake banana trees and palms—to set the mood.

Prices: Beer from 3.80 DM ($2.30), wine from 4.50 DM ($2.70).
Open: Sun–Fri 9:30pm–4am, Sat 11am–5pm and 9:30pm–4am.
U-Bahn: Nollendorfplatz, about a 5-minute walk.

CAFÉ SWING, Nollendorfplatz 3-4. Tel. 216 61 37.

Popular with a young and slightly radical crowd, the Swing is about as informal and casual as you can get. A bit run-down, it offers outdoor seating in summer, and on Monday and Thursday evenings there's free live music from 1am.

Prices: Beer from 3.30 DM ($2), wine from 3.50 DM ($2.10).
Open: Summer, daily 8:30am–4am; winter, daily 10:30am–4am.
U-Bahn: Nollendorfplatz, a 1-minute walk.

IN EAST BERLIN

East Berlin is changing rapidly, with more and more restaurants, bars, and entertainment facilities opening daily. You may, therefore, wish to do a little scouting on your own, since it's impossible for a guide book to keep up with the latest developments.

NEAR UNTER DEN LINDEN

BAR AM PFAUENAUGE, Grand Hotel, Friedrichstrasse 158-164. Tel. 209 23253.

This elegant bar is probably the most sophisticated in all East Berlin. Located up on the first floor of the Grand Hotel, it can be reached via a magnificent sweeping staircase. Wonder of wonders, the place never closes, and there's live music in the evenings.

Prices: Cocktails 16–22 DM ($9.70–$13.35).
Open: 24 hours. **S-Bahn:** Friedrichstrasse, about a 6-minute walk.

IN THE NIKOLAIVIERTEL

The three bars listed here are located just off Alexanderplatz, in a reconstructed neighborhood known as the Nikolaiviertel (Nikolai Quarter). There's little difference between the establishments, so your best bet is simply to look for an empty seat. They're very popular with visiting tourists.

ZUM NUSSBAUM, Propstrasse. Tel. 2171 33 28.

A reconstruction of a famous inn built in 1571 but destroyed during World War II, Zum Nussbaum is a tiny, pleasant, and cozy place with wood-paneled walls and minuscule rooms. There are a few tables outside, where you have a view of the Nikolaikirche (St. Nicholas's Church), after which the quarter was named.

Prices: Beer from 2.10 DM ($1.25).
Open: Daily 11am–midnight. **Closed:** Second Tues of the month. **U-Bahn:** Alexanderplatz or Klosterstrasse.

ZUM PADDENWIRT, Eiergasse. Tel. 2171 32 31.

Another lively drinking place, simply decorated like taverns of former centuries. Located behind the Nikolaikirche, it also dishes out platters of German fare.

Prices: Beer from 2.10 DM ($1.25).
Open: Mon–Sat noon–midnight. **U-Bahn:** Alexanderplatz or Klosterstrasse.

ZUR RIPPE, Mühlendamm and Poststrasse. Tel. 2171 32 35.

This tavern was named after a medieval inn first mentioned in documents dated 1672. Although it offers daily specials of German cuisine, most people come here to drink.

Prices: Beer from 2.10 DM ($1.25).
Open: Tues–Sun 11am–11pm. **U-Bahn:** Alexanderplatz or Klosterstrasse.

NEAR SCHÖNHAUSER ALLEE

Schönhauser Allee is a large thoroughfare north of Alexanderplatz and in recent years has gained a reputation for its several bars.

ALTBERLINER BIERSTUBEN, Saarbrucker Strasse 17. Tel. 282 89 33.

So popular is this place that it's difficult to wade through the crowd to order a drink at the bar, let alone find a seat. It's decorated in the old Berliner style, with a front room where people drink standing at counters, and a back room where they can sit at tables. Popular with students of all ages, the bar is one of my Berlin favorites. You'll find it on the corner of Saarbrucker Strasse and Schönhauser Allee.

Prices: Beer from 2 DM ($1.20).
Open: Mon–Thurs 11am–1am, Fri–Sun 11am–2am. **Closed:** Fourth Wed of every month. **U-Bahn:** Senefelderplatz, a 1-minute walk (take the Saarbrucker Strasse exit).

CAFÉ LOTOS, Schönhauser Allee 46. Tel. 448 35 62.

A modern and trendy café/bar with innovative lighting—a good example of the new East Berlin—it serves both mixed drinks and ice cream and closes very late.

Prices: Drinks from 3 DM ($1.80).

Open: Mon–Thurs 2pm–2am, Fri 2pm–4am, Sat 4pm–4am, Sun 4pm–8pm. **Closed:** First Tues of every month. **U-Bahn:** Dimitroffstrasse.

WIENER CAFÉ, Schönhauser Allee 68. Tel. 448 57 22.

This simple café is popular with young Germans out on a date. There's outdoor seating in summer, and it offers ice cream and various spiked coffees.

Prices: Mixed drinks 4.50–9 DM ($2.70–$5.45).

Open: Summer, daily 10am–10pm; winter, Mon–Fri 11am–midnight, Sat and Sun 2pm–midnight.

---

4. MORE ENTERTAINMENT

MOVIES

You won't have any trouble finding a cinema showing the latest movies from Hollywood. However, Berlin's main cinematic attraction lies in its "Off-Ku'damm" cinemas, those specializing in film classics and in new releases by independent German and international filmmakers. Check *tip* or *zitty* for listings of current films. (*OF*) means that the film is in the original language; (*OmU*), that it has German subtitles. The following are two well-known cinemas.

ARSENAL, Welserstrasse 25. Tel. 24 68 48.

The original Off-Ku'damm cinema, since the 1970s it has been paving the way for alternative programming; retrospectives, series, and experimental and avant-garde films from around the world.

Prices: Tickets 8 DM ($4.85). **U-Bahn:** Wittenbergplatz.

ODEON, Hauptstrasse 116. Tel. 781 5667.

This is the place to go if you want to see the latest Hollywood flick, since it specializes in recent English-language releases.

Prices: Tickets 10 DM ($6.05). **U-Bahn:** Innsbrucker Platz.

GAMBLING

If you wish to try your luck at the gambling tables, head toward the Europa-Center on Budapester Strasse, where you'll find the **Spielbank Berlin** (tel. 250 08 90). Since opening in 1975, it has witnessed an average of 1,000 guests a day, who come to play French and American roulette, blackjack, baccarat, and the one-arm bandits. Admission is 5 DM ($3.05), and a coat and tie are required of men in the winter. The Spielbank Berlin is open daily from 3pm to 3am, and the nearest U-Bahn stations are Kurfürstendamm and Bahnhof Zoologisher Garten, both just a couple of minutes away.

CHAPTER 10

DAY TRIPS AROUND BERLIN

1. POTSDAM
2. KÖPENICK
3. SPANDAU
4. LÜBARS
5. PFAUENINSEL
6. THE SPREEWALD

Some of the day trips described below are within Greater Berlin, and attest to the city's size and variety: Köpenick with its almost intact Altstadt, Spandau with its citadel and old city center, the ancient farm village of Lübars, and the nature-reserve island of Pfaueninsel.

Southeast of Berlin, the Spreewald offers boat trips through a unique landscape of waterways. However, if you take only one excursion, it should be to Potsdam and Frederick the Great's palace of Sanssouci.

1. POTSDAM

Situated less than 15 miles southwest of Berlin, Potsdam was once Germany's most important baroque town, serving both as a garrison and as the residence of Prussia's kings and royal families throughout the 18th and 19th centuries. It was from here that Frederick the Great built his empire. And to rule more ably, he built a delightful rococo palace where he could escape on occasion to maintain his sanity. Although much of Potsdam was destroyed during World War II, his palace still stands, surrounded by a 750-acre estate containing several other magnificent structures.

ORIENTATION

The easiest way to reach Potsdam is by bus 99, which departs approximately every 10 minutes from Wannsee S-Bahn station, reaching Potsdam's city center in about half an hour. Cost of the bus is 2.70 DM ($1.65) one way. It would be prudent, however, to check both the bus number and place of departure before setting out, since Berlin's transportation system has been undergoing change in the face of the city's reunification.

You may prefer to visit Potsdam in the comfort of a guided tour. In the crowded summer months you may even be better off joining one, since tours offered to the general public at Schloss Sanssouci (Sanssouci Palace) are often sold out by noon. For more information, refer to the "Organized Tours" section in Chapter 6.

If you come on your own by bus, you'll arrive at Potsdam's bus center in the middle of the city. From there it's an easy walk to Schloss Sanssouci and its surrounding park grounds. You probably won't be able to find a map of Potsdam unless the situation changes dramatically—printers simply cannot keep up with the demand as West Germans descend upon new destinations in the East in ever greater numbers. The best thing to do is ask along the way for directions, though it's fairly easy to find your way to Sanssouci park.

Start with a walk through the old Holländisches Viertel (Dutch Quarter), located right next to the bus center. The 134 homes of gabled brick, built in the mid-1700s for settlers from the Low Countries, represent the largest concentration of Dutch-style homes outside Holland; they are slowly being renovated. Nearby is a pedestrian shopping lane, marked by a large portal called **Brandenburger Tor** (Berlin isn't the only city with a Brandenburg Gate). The gate marks the beginning of the royal estate. Near the estate you'll also find the palace of Cecilienhof, about a 30-minute walk from the bus center.

WHAT TO SEE & DO

THE PALACE & PARK OF SANSSOUCI

Although Potsdam was first mentioned in documents in 993 and became the second residence of the Great Elector of Brandenburg in 1660, it was under Friedrich Wilhelm I (Frederick William I) that the city blossomed into a garrison town. Credited with building the great Prussian army, Friedrich Wilhelm I was succeeded by a rather reluctant son, Friedrich II, who first tried to shirk his responsibilities by fleeing to England with his friend, Lieutenant von Kette. They were caught and tried as deserters and Friedrich was forced to witness the beheading of his friend (some said lover) as punishment. Friedrich II thereafter conformed to his father's wishes, married, and became the third king of Prussia, more popularly known as Friedrich der Grosse (Frederick the Great). He doubled the size of the Prussian army and went on to make Prussia the greatest military power on the Continent.

It was Frederick the Great who built much of Sanssouci as we know it today, in part to satisfy his artistic and intellectual passions. For instead of being able to devote himself fully to literature and to issues of the Enlightenment, as he would have liked, Frederick became involved in one war after another, including the Silesian Wars and the Seven Years War. He retreated to Sanssouci to meditate,

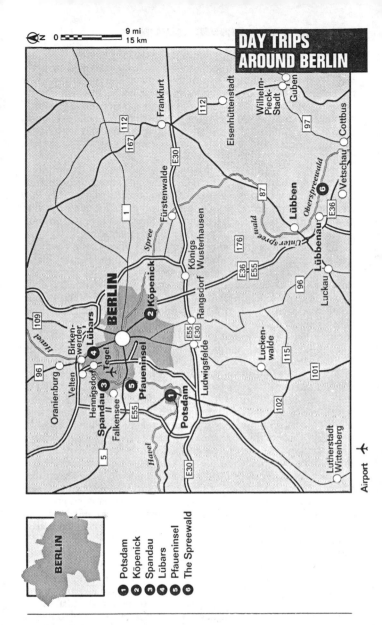

DAY TRIPS AROUND BERLIN

1. Potsdam
2. Köpenick
3. Spandau
4. Lübars
5. Pfaueninsel
6. The Spreewald

pursue philosophy, and forget the worries of life. In fact, *sans souci* means "without worry." Among the guests who came to Sanssouci was Voltaire, the great French philosopher. He stayed in Potsdam for three years, during which time he and the king spent many an evening together.

Schloss Sanssouci (Sanssouci Palace), the summer residence of Frederick the Great, was designed by Georg von Knobelsdorff in the 1740s according to plans drawn up by the king himself. Although it looks comparatively modest and ordinary if approached from the main road and entrance, it is breathtaking if viewed from the park on the other side. For the palace sits atop six grassy terraces, cut into the side of a hill like steps in a pyramid. The terraces were once vineyards, and seem to overwhelm the much smaller one-story palace. It's only after you've climbed the staircases leading up through the terraces that the cheerful and airy palace finally reveals itself, like a surprise package.

Frederick the Great must have liked wine, because the motifs of grapes and wine are carried from the vineyards into the palace itself. Note the figures supporting the roof facing the vineyards—they look a bit tipsy, as though they've just indulged in the fruits of the vine. Inside are statues of Bacchus, god of wine, as well as pictures and reliefs of grapes, vines, and people enjoying themselves.

Yet Frederick led a rather austere life, preferring to sleep in a soldier's camp bed rather than a royal bed. Even the Festival Hall is modestly small, noted for its inlaid marble floor in the pattern of a vineyard. The Concert Room is exquisite with a stucco ceiling in the pattern of a spider web, creating a light and airy illusion. The Voltaire Room boasts hand-carved wooden reliefs painted in bright yellows, blues, reds, and other colors, as well as a chandelier with delicate porcelain and brass flowers.

Schloss Sanssouci is open only for guided tours, which are conducted exclusively in German (hopefully this will change someday). Since the tours fill up quickly, especially on weekends, try to get here before noon. Tours, which leave every 20 minutes, cost 1.05 DM (65¢) and last 40 minutes. The palace is open April through September from 9am to 5pm; October, February, and March from 9am to 4pm; and November through January from 9am to 3pm. It's closed the first and third Mondays of every month. If you're worried about getting into the palace and wish to have a tour in English, you're better off joining an organized sightseeing tour from Berlin.

Sanssouci Park is huge, containing a wide range of gardens, ponds, streams, and statues of Greek and mythological figures. There are, for example, the Dutch, Sicilian, and Nordic gardens, as well as the Östlicher Lustgarten (Eastern Pleasure Garden) and Nestlicher Lustgarden (Western Pleasure Garden). In the Östicher Lustgarten you'll find the **Bildergalerie** (Picture Gallery), built between 1755 and 1763 to house Frederick the Great's collection. It still contains works by Italian Renaissance, Dutch, and Flemish old masters.

The **Orangerie,** located in the Westlicher Lustgarten and reached via pathways through the Sicilian and Nordic gardens, was built in Italian Renaissance style to house tropical plants, later being turned into rather elaborate guest accommodations. Here, too, is the Chinesisches Teehaus (Chinese Teahouse), constructed in the shape of a clover and featuring gilded statues of mandarins. The largest building in the park is the **Neues Palais** (New Palace), built 20 years after Schloss Sanssouci as a show of Prussian strength after the devastation of the Seven Years War and used as a residence for members of the royal family. You can visit the Neues Palais on your own without joining a tour, and the hours and admission are the same as for Schloss Sanssouci.

CECILIENHOF

Cecilienhof looks like an English country lodge instead of a German palace, and intentionally so. The newest palace in Potsdam, it was built between 1913 and 1916 in mock-Tudor style by Kaiser Wilhelm II and served as a royal residence of the last German crown prince until the end of World War II. Its 176 rooms now contain a museum, a hotel, and a restaurant. It also boasts 55 chimneys, each one different.

Cecilienhof gained everlasting fame in 1945 when it served as headquarters for the Potsdam Conference. It was here that Truman, Stalin, and Churchill (and later Atlee) met to discuss the disarmament and future of a divided Germany. There's a museum here showing the conference room and the round table where the Big Three sat. The museum, which costs 50 pfennigs (30¢) admission, is open May through October from 9am to 5:15pm and November through April from 9am to 4:15pm. It's closed the second and fourth Mondays of each month.

WHERE TO DINE

HOTEL SCHLOSS CECILIENHOF, Neuer Garten. Tel. 231 41.
    Cuisine: GERMAN/INTERNATIONAL   **Reservations:** Imperative.   **Directions:** A 30-minute walk from city bus center or Schloss Sanssouci.
$ Prices: Appetizers 10–14 DM ($6.05–$8.50), entrées 14–35 DM ($8.50–$21.20). AE, DC, MC, V.
    Open: Daily 11:30am–11pm.

Although considered one of the finest dining establishments in Potsdam, it cannot compare to restaurants in Berlin. However, it is conveniently located in Cecilienhof, the former royal residence now partly converted into a hotel. Its menu includes Ukrainian soljanka soup, calves' steak, pepper steak, chicken fricassee, and beef roulade.

MINSK, Am Brauhausberg, Max-Planck-Strasse 10. Tel. 2 36 36.
    Cuisine: GERMAN   **Reservations:** Recommended.
    Streetcar: 1 or 6 to Schwimmhalle am Brauhausberg stop.
$ Prices: Appetizers and soups 2.50–9 DM ($1.50–$5.45), entrées 14–18 DM ($8.50–$10.90). Cash only.
    Open: Daily 11am–6pm and 7pm–midnight.

Named after Potsdam's sister city in Russia, this modern, well-known restaurant is often used by tour groups. The adequate food includes daily specials, duck, and pork dishes. The best thing about this place is its terrace with outdoor seating, where you have a view of the city. In the evenings there's music and a small dance floor, where you can trip the light fantastic.

JAGDHAUS, Zur Historischen Mühle, Sanssouci Park. Tel. 23 110.
    Cuisine: GERMAN SNACKS
$ Prices: 2–5 DM ($1.20–$3.05). Cash only.
    Open: Wed–Mon 10am–4pm.

This snack bar is located near Schloss Sanssouci, across the road from the Old Mill. It offers beer, coffee, soft drinks, and Bockwurst with bread, and may be your best bet if restaurants are full. However, even here you'll probably have to queue.

2. KÖPENICK

Although a part of Berlin since 1920 (and, more recently, East Berlin), Köpenick has an ancient history longer than Berlin itself. There's been a settlement here since the 9th century, and in the 17th century Schloss Köpenick was constructed on an island in the Dahme River; the palace now houses the Kunstgewerbemuseum (Museum of Applied Arts). As for Köpenick today, it's a pleasant and charming community with a fairly intact Altstadt (Old Town), also on an island at the confluence of the Spree and Dahme rivers. Its rural and provincial atmosphere contrasts completely with the hustle and bustle of Berlin's city center. An important industrial area, Köpenick is primarily working class. Even the fall of the Wall has not brought much change here, although that may be only a matter of time. If you want a clearer picture of what Berlin was like 10 or 20 years ago, this is a good place for a half day's stroll.

ORIENTATION

Köpenick is easily reached by taking the S-Bahn from Alexanderplatz in the direction of Erkner and getting off approximately 30 minutes later at Köpenick station. From there follow signs that read *Bahnhofstrasse* and *Schlossinsel* (Castle Island). Although you could take streetcar 83 or 86 three stops to the Altstadt, I recommend that you walk. It's less than a 30-minute stroll from the train station to Schloss Köpenick.

WHAT TO SEE & DO

From the train station, walk about 10 minutes along Bahnhofstrasse, Köpenick's main shopping street, until you reach **Mecklenburger Dorf** on your left. This is an outdoor dining and drinking establishment, with thatched stalls selling curry Wurst, chicken, beer, and other German snacks. Weave your way through (or stop for a beer or meal), and then follow the Spree River to the left. Along the water you'll see small garden plots, popular with Germans who live in the city but yearn for a bit of earth of their own. Cross the bridge, and then follow the tram tracks to the right, in the direction of the steeples. This is the **Altstadt,** which is actually an island in the Spree River. On Alt-Köpenick Strasse you'll pass the **Rathaus** at no. 21, a turreted and ornate brick building. If you haven't eaten, try the Ratskeller restaurant in its basement. In the Altstadt are also a few old fishermen's homes on Böttcher-, Laurenz- and Rosengasse, testimony to the importance the fishing industry played in the development of this riverside community.

If you continue walking past the Rathaus, you'll soon come to Schlossplatz with its many streetcar stops. Across this square is the **Schloss Köpenick** (tel. 657 26 51 or 657 15 04), approached by a wooden bridge.

There's been a fortress on this island in the river ever since the 12th century. In the 16th century it was remodeled into a hunting lodge for Elector Joachim II, but in the mid-17th century it was once again changed, under the direction of a Dutch architect, into the baroque palace it is today. It was here that Friedrich II (Frederick the Great) was court-martialed in 1730, along with his friend Lieutenant von Katte, for trying to flee the country and kingly responsibilities.

In addition to the palace, the island contains a small garden, pleasant for a stroll. But of course the most important thing to do here is to visit the **Kunstgewerbemusem** (Museum of Applied Arts), located in the palace itself. It contains glass, ceramics, jewelry, tapestries, furniture, and silver and gold objects, from the Middle Ages through the 20th century. What makes the contemporary collection particularly interesting is the presence of artists from East Berlin, Dresden, Leipzig, Erfurt, Weimar, and other cities formerly of East Germany, thus providing insight into the DDR art scene during the existence of the Wall. Another highlight of the palace, which still has its baroque stucco ceilings, is the **Wappensaal** (Coat of Arms Hall), the most ornate room in Schloss Köpenick and site of Friedrich II's court-martial; above the fireplace is the coat of arms of the Prussian Brandenburg State.

The palace is open Wednesday through Sunday from 10am to 6pm, and there is an admission fee of 1.05 DM (65¢) for adults and 50 pfennigs (30¢) for students and children. If you choose not to walk, take streetcar 83 or 86 to Schlossinsel.

WHERE TO DINE

RATSKELLER KÖPENICK, Rathaus, Alt-Köpenick Strasse 21. Tel. 657 20 35.

Cuisine: GERMAN. **Reservations:** Recommended; necessary on weekends. **Directions:** About a 15-minute walk from Schloss Köpenick or the S-Bahn Köpenick station.

$ Prices: Entrées 7–14 DM ($4.25–$8.50). Cash only.

Open: Sun–Thurs 10am–11pm, Fri and Sat 10am–1am.

Located in the basement of the Rathaus, this Ratskeller is rather small and simple compared to many town-hall restaurants in Germany. Still, with its vaulted ceiling and stained-glass windows, it makes a pleasant choice for dining. It seats only 130 persons, so most likely you'll sit at a table with other people. The menu includes such traditional German foods as chicken fricassee with mushrooms, Gulasch, Kasslerbraten, Berliner Eisbein, roast duck, and grilled liver.

MECKLENBURGER DORF, Platz des 23. April and Bahnhofstrasse.

Cuisine: GERMAN SNACKS **S-Bahn:** A 10-minute walk from Köpenick station.

$ Prices: 2–5 DM ($1.20–$3.05). Cash only.

Open: June–Aug daily 10am–8pm, Sept–May Wed–Sun 10am–6pm.

In pleasant weather, this beer garden on the banks of the Spree makes a great place for a snack: perhaps Würst or grilled chicken, plus a beer. Vendors sell food from thatch-roofed stalls. Mecklenburger Dorf is packed with families and visitors, providing plenty of opportunity for people-watching.

3. SPANDAU

Köpenick and Spandau have much in common, so much so that it's difficult to believe they are at opposite ends of Berlin and were once on opposite sides of the Wall. For example, Spandau is proud that it's older than Berlin—even if by only five years. And just like Köpenick, Spandau owes its existence to the convergence of two rivers, in this case the Spree and the Havel. During the decades of the Wall, Köpenick served as East Berlin's largest industrial area and its most important water recreational destination, a role mirrored by Spandau in the West. Both towns have important nature reserves and both have old city centers. And finally, both towns remained independent cities right up until 1920, when they were incorporated into Greater Berlin. Even today, people of Spandau talk of "going to Berlin" whenever they're heading for the city center.

But whereas Köpenick remains the domain of the working class, Spandau is thriving and conspicuously more wealthy. Although heavily bombed during World War, it fared better than many other parts of Berlin, and its Altstadt is still fairly intact, with pedestrians-only lanes giving it a small-town atmosphere. By far the most famous structure is the Spandauer Zitadelle (Spandau Citadel). First constructed as a frontier fortress in the 12th century, the present Zitadelle stems from the 16th century and is considered the best example of Italian military architecture in Germany. In addition to a museum of local history, the Zitadelle houses a restaurant that is about as close as you can get to dining in medieval times.

ORIENTATION

Spandau is most easily reached by taking U-Bahn 7 from Berlin's city center to the Altstadt Spandau stop, a trip of about 20 minutes. The main shopping streets in the Altstadt are Carl-Schurz-Strasse and Breite Strasse. From the Altstadt, the Juliusturmbrücke bridge leads over the Havel to the Zitadelle. If you wish to go only to the fortress, get off at the Zitadelle U-Bahn station.

WHAT TO SEE & DO

If you're interested in shopping, you'll want to stroll up and down **Carl-Schurz-Strasse** and **Breite Strasse,** two parallel shopping streets. At Breite Strasse 20 you'll see the impressive facade of a patrician home dating from 1800, while at Breite Strasse 32 you'll find Spandau's oldest home, first built in the 15th century in Gothic style. Two of the prettiest streets are **Behnitz** and **Kolk,** both of which have homes dating from the 18th century mixed in with newer structures. Other important buildings in the Altstadt are the **Rathaus,** completed in 1913 on the optimistic assumption that Spandau would remain independent of Berlin, and the **Nikolaikirche** (St. Nicholas's Church), in the middle of the Altstadt on Reformationsplatz. First built in the 15th century, it was later converted to baroque and neo-Gothic styles.

The **Spandauer Zitadelle** can be approached on foot only via a long, narrow bridge. Although a fortress was first erected at this site in the 12th century, today's Zitadelle dates from the 16th century. Constructed according to the Italian preference for acute-angled bastion walls rather than the more ordinary round ones, it was intended to protect Spandau from the ever-growing threat imposed by an expanding Berlin. The Zitadelle is entirely surrounded by a moat. Although considered impregnable, it was twice occupied by foreign forces without a struggle—first by Sweden during the Thirty Years War and then by Napoleon's forces in 1806. Getting the French forces out, however, was another matter, and it was only after a bitter struggle that the 3,000 troops were rooted out.

After crossing the bridge, you'll come to the former command post. Here, to the right, is the **Heimatmuseum Spandau** (Museum of Local History) (tel. 330 33 834). Open Tuesday through Friday from 9am to 4:30pm and on Saturday and Sunday from 10am to 4:30pm, it displays archeological finds relating to Spandau's history, including pots and tools used by early tribes, armor and weapons, and special changing exhibitions. Be sure, too, to visit the **Juliusturm,** the oldest existing part of the Zitadelle. Built as the castle keep in the 14th century, it was used for the safekeeping of gold marks until 1919. In the Juliusturm you'll also find the dungeon restaurant described below.

WHERE TO DINE

ZITADELLE, Am Juliusturm. Tel. 334 21 06.
    Cuisine: GERMAN   **Reservations:** Recommended, especially weekends.   **U-Bahn:** Zitadelle.
$ Prices: Entrées 20–40 DM ($12.10–$24.25); fixed-price meal 65.50 DM ($39.65). AE, DC, MC, V.
    Open: Tues–Fri 6–11pm, Sat and Sun 11:30am–11pm.

    This restaurant is the best reason for coming to Spandau. The idea behind the place is to imitate as closely as possible the eating style of the Middle Ages—made easy by the fact that the restaurant actually lies within the Spandauer Zitadelle. Guests are requested to use only a special knife and their fingers (they didn't have forks back in medieval times). With brick vaulted ceilings, stone walls, wooden tables, and an open fireplace, this fortress restaurant offers an à la carte menu on weekdays, but the real fun is on Friday, Saturday, and Sunday evenings, when there's a medieval banquet with ballad singing and special entertainment.

On weekdays Zitadelle offers an à la carte menu with typical German fare such as pork cutlet or trout, but the real fun is on Friday, Saturday, and Sunday evenings, when there's a medieval banquet with ballad singing and special entertainment. The fixed-price meal includes a welcoming drink served in a bull's horn, bread, appetizer, a main course such as Spiessbraten, and several other dishes. Highly recommended.

4. LÜBARS

Located on the northern edge of Berlin in Reinickendorf precinct, Lübars is a rural farming community that has somehow escaped modernization. First mentioned in documents in 1247, its old village is built around a grassy square and a church. Lübars is a pleasant place for a stroll, both in the village and in the surrounding area.

ORIENTATION

To reach the old village of Lübars, take S-Bahn 2 to Waidmannslust, a trip of about 30 minutes from the center of Berlin, followed by bus 20 to the end of the line. On the bus ride you'll pass the controversial high-rise housing projects of Märkisches Viertel, which holds 50,000 people. For years it's been considered a cultural and urban wasteland, without enough restaurants, shops, and public facilities to make the place viable. Although some efforts have been made to improve the quality of life here, it's still considered the most objectionable housing project in West Berlin.

Before reaching Lübars, your bus will pass fields and then modern houses before pulling in at a final stop near the old village center of Alt-Lübars (old Lübars).

WHAT TO SEE & DO

As mentioned above, the best thing to do in Lübars is walk around and recuperate from hectic city life. Back when West Berlin was contained by the Wall, West Berliners used to come here for a taste of rural life. Families would show their children animals like cows and chickens, as well as working farms that raised wheat and barley—rare sights for city kids unable to take trips to the East German countryside. The Wall used to pass right outside Lübars, visible from the town square. Now, of course, the Wall is gone and you can walk as far as you like. Buildings of note include the village church, built in baroque style in 1793; the village school; and the many one-story farmhouses. One of the oldest structures in Berlin is here, a thatch-roofed farmhouse at Alt-Lübars 22, which is still inhabited and therefore not open to the public.

WHERE TO DINE

DORFKRUG ZUM LUSTIGEN FINKEN, Alt-Lübars 20. Tel. 402 78 45.
    Cuisine: GERMAN.   **S-Bahn:** Waidmannslust, then bus 20 to Alt-Lübars.
$ Prices: 13.50–20 DM ($8.20–$12.10). Cash only.

Open: Sat–Wed 11am–7pm.

This country-style restaurant would be reason enough to come to Lübars—and is indeed the reason many do. A small house that dates back to 1682, it was originally built as a shepherd's home, becoming a restaurant in 1870. Its dining room is a bit corny, with old-fashioned furniture and fake flowers—and I wouldn't want it any other way. Be sure to take a peek at the back room, a dance hall that was added in 1874. Packed with antlers and mounted animals, lamps, and more fake flowers—and with a stage that still sports a piano—it has to be seen to be believed. Definitely from another era. As for the food, it ranges from Eisbein and Schnitzel to Kasslerbraten and Sauerbraten, with huge and hearty portions. The place is known for its bread. In summer there's a garden where you can sit outside, a perfect spot to eat lunch or while away an afternoon.

5. PFAUENINSEL

Pfaueninsel (Peacock Island) is the largest island in the Havel and has long been one of the most popular destinations for day-trippers from Berlin. A nature reserve with many rare trees and birds, it also boasts an amusing 18-century palace built in imitation of a ruin, plus several other historic buildings. The island gets its name from a flock of 60 or so peacocks that has roamed freely since 1795. There used to be a menagerie of other animals as well, including monkeys and bears, which in the mid-1800s formed the basis of the Berlin Zoo. Closed to cars, the island lends itself perfectly to strolls.

ORIENTATION

The only way to get to Pfaueninsel is by ferry, which you can reach by taking bus 6 or 18 to Pfaueninselchaussee and then walking to the end of Nikolskoer Weg. The ferry costs 2 DM ($1.20) one way. Excursion boats are also available from Wannsee station. Admission is free to the island, which in summer can be visited from 8am to 8pm and in winter from 10am to 4pm. The castle ruin, however, is open only from April through October. For more information on ferry timetables, consult the Berlin Tourist Information Office.

WHAT TO SEE & DO

With an area of 185 acres, Pfaueninsel is perfect for exploring on foot. It takes about an hour or two to walk around the island, though you'll probably want to make several stops along the way.

Almost directly in front of the ferry landing is **Schloss Pfaueninsel** (tel. 805 30 42), a fake ruin built in the 1790s by Friedrich Wilhelm II for his mistress, the Countess Lichtenau. In contrast to his uncle, Frederick the Great, who spent much of his life waging wars and building empires, Friedrich Wilhelm II apparently preferred to spend his time building architectural fantasies—a much milder Prussian version of Bavaria's Ludwig II. The castle, later used by Friedrich Wilhelm III and Queen Luise as a summer residence, consists of two floors, with four rooms on each level. Originally constructed of wood, it has been reinforced with concrete. It contains a small museum with furnishings and artworks dating from 1795 to 1830, including valuable carpets and portraits of the former royal inhabitants. The castle is open only from April through October, Tuesday through Sunday from 10am to 5pm. Admission is 2.50 DM ($1.50) for adults and 1.50 DM (90¢) for students and children.

As you walk around the island, note the many rare trees and shrubs that were planted here, including Weymouth and Arolla pines, sequoias, ginkgos, and cedars. Other items of interest include the **Schweizerhaus** (Swiss Cottage), designed by Karl Friedrich Schinkel in 1825; the **Kavaliershaus,** built in 1804 and renovated by Schinkel in 1826, when he added the facade of a late-Gothic patrician home from Danzig; and the **Meierei** (Dairy Farm), located on the north end of the island and also built in the style of a ruin.

WHERE TO DINE

This is the perfect place for a picnic lunch. Refer to the dining chapter's "Picnic Fare and Where to Eat It" for information on where you can purchase your supplies.

6. THE SPREEWALD

Approximately 60 miles southeast of Berlin, the Spreewald forms one of middle Europe's unique landscapes. This is where the Spree spreads out into countless streams and ponds, a labyrinth of waterways through woodlands—a bayou. Little wonder that for decades it's been a lure for city dwellers, who come here for a ride in a hand-poled boat, the German version of the gondola.

ORIENTATION

The best jumping-off spots for trips through the Spreewald are Lübbenau and Lübben, the most important centers for boat rentals. Both can be reached by train from Berlin (inquire at the Berlin Tourist Information Office for the latest information on how to get there, plus schedules). You should plan on at least a few hours for your boat ride; there are several routes, of varying lengths, to choose from. The best time to visit the Spreewald is from May to October, though even in winter you can still find a boater willing to pole you through the woods. For information about boats and prices, telephone Lübbenau at 22 25 (again, check for the latest information on the area code).

WHAT TO SEE & DO

If you understand German and you hire a gregarious boatman, you'll probably be regaled with tales about the Spreewald and the people who live here. As you glide along the canals, you'll pass rounded haystacks as tall as houses; weeping willows, poplars and ashes, and farmhouses made of logs and brick and surrounded by neat gardens. The **upper Spreewald,** the area you'll cover if you leave from Lübbenau, contains about 300 miles of tree-lined canals winding through a flat countryside of meadows. Almost none of the canals are open to motorized boats, with the result that barges laden with vegetables bound for market are also hand-poled. If you leave from Lübben, you'll travel through the **lower Spreewald,** which has more woods than canals and is broken up by small valleys and dunes created in the last ice age.

In addition to taking a boat ride, you can also walk through the Spreewald. True, many a path ends abruptly at one of the hundreds of canals, but that shouldn't deter you from hiking. It's only on foot that you'll have the chance to inspect more closely the flora and fauna as well as the many water birds that inhabit this special bayou.

WHERE TO DINE

By all means pack a lunch to bring with you, since this is an idyllic spot for a picnic. Refer to the dining chapter's "Picnic Fare and Where to Eat It" for information on where to buy your goodies.

APPENDIX

A. VOCABULARY

German is not a difficult language to learn, especially pronunciation. Unlike English or French, it contains no hidden surprises and everything is pronounced exactly as it's written—according, of course, to German rules. *Ei* is always pronounced as a long *i;* thus, *nein* (which means "no") is pronounced *nine*. A *w* is pronounced *v;* a *v* is pronounced as *f.* As for those two dots over vowels, they signal a slight change in pronunciation.

ENGLISH	GERMAN	PRONUNCIATION
Hello	**Guten Tag**	goo-ten tahk
Goodbye	**Auf Wiedersehen**	owf vee-der-zay-en
How are you?	**Wie geht es Ihnen?**	vee gayt ess ee-nen
Very well	**Sehr gut**	zayr goot
Please	**Bitte**	bit-tuh
Thank you	**Danke schön**	dahn-keh shern
Excuse me	**Entschuldigen Sie**	en-shool-d-gen zee
You're welcome	**Gern geschehen**	gehrn geshai'en
Yes	**Ja**	yah
No	**Nein**	nine
Mr./Mrs.	**Herr/Frau**	hehr/vrow
I don't understand	**Ich verstehe nicht**	ish fer-steh-he nisht
I understand	**Ich verstehe**	ish fer-steh-he
Where is . . . ?	**Wo ist . . . ?**	voh eest
the station	**der Bahnhof**	deyr bahn-hohf
a hotel	**ein Hotel**	ain hotel
a restaurant	**ein Restaurant**	ain res-tow-rahng
the toilet	**die Toilette**	dee twah-let-tah
a bank	**ein Bank**	ain bahnk
a post office	**ein Postamt**	ain postahmt
the bus stop	**die Bus haltestelle**	dee bus haltestelle
the tourist information office	**das Verkehr-samt**	dass fer-kerr-samt
To the right	**Nach rechts**	nakh reshts
To the left	**Nach links**	nakh leenks
Straight ahead	**Geradeaus**	geh-rah-deh-ous
Ladies/Gentlemen	**Damen/Herren**	dahmen/hehren
How much does it cost?	**Wieviel kostet es?**	vee-feel kah-stet ess
Expensive	**Teuer**	toyer

Cheap	**Billig**	bil-lich
The check, please	**Die Rechnung, bitte**	dee rekh-noong, bit-tuh
I would like . . .	**Ich möchte . . .**	ikh mersh-ta
stamps	**Briefmarken**	breef-mahr-ken
to eat	**essen**	ess-en
a room	**ein Zimmer**	ain tzim-mer
for one night	**für eine Nacht**	feer ai-neh nakht
Breakfast	**Frühstück**	free-shtick
Lunch	**Mittagessen**	mi-tahg-gess-en
Dinner	**Abendessen**	ah-bend-ess-en
Free (vacant)/occupied	**Frei/besetzt**	Frahy/besets
When?	**Wann?**	vahn
Yesterday	**Gestern**	geh-stern
Today	**Heute**	hoy-tuh
Tomorrow	**Morgen**	more-gen
Sunday	**Sonntag**	zohn-tahk
Monday	**Montag**	mon-tahk
Tuesday	**Dienstag**	deen-stahk
Wednesday	**Mittwoch**	mitt-voch
Thursday	**Donnerstag**	donner-stahk
Friday	**Freitag**	frahy-tahk
Saturday	**Samstag**	zahmz-tahk

NUMBERS

0 **Null** (nool)	16 **Sechszehn** (zex-tzayn)	70 **Siebzig** (zeeb-tzik)
1 **Eins** (aintz)	17 **Siebzehn** (zeeb-tzayn)	80 **Achtzig** (akht-tzik)
2 **Zwei** (tzvai)	18 **Achtzehn** (akh-tzayn)	90 **Neunzig** (noyn-tzik)
3 **Drei** (dry)	19 **Neunzehn** (noyn-tzayn)	100 **Hundert** (hoon-dert)
4 **Vier** (feer)	20 **Zwanzig** (tzvahn-tzik)	101 **Hunderteins** (hoon-dert-ahyns)
5 **Fünf** (fewnf)	25 **Fünf-und-Zwanzig**	200 **Zweihundert** (tzvai-hoon-dert)
6 **Sechs** (zex)	30 **Dreissig** (dry-sik)	1,000 **Ein tausend** (ahyn-tau-zent)
7 **Sieben** (zee-ben)	40 **Vierzig** (feer-tzik)	
8 **Acht** (ahkht)	50 **Fünfzig** (fewnf-tzik)	
9 **Neun** (noyn)	60 **Sechzig** (zex-tzik)	
10 **Zehn** (tzayn)		
11 **Elf** (ellf)		
12 **Zwölf** (tzvuhlf)		
13 **Dreizehn** (dry-tzayn)		
14 **Vierzehn** (feer-tzayn)		
15 **Fünfzehn** (fewnf-tzayn)		

MENU TRANSLATIONS
Condiments and Table Items

Brot Bread   **Butter** Butter
Brötchen Rolls   **Eis** Ice

Essig Vinegar
Pfeffer Pepper
Salz Salt

Senf Mustard
Zitrone Lemon
Zucker Sugar

Soups

Erbsensuppe Pea soup
Gemüsesuppe Vegetable soup
Gulaschsuppe Spicy Hungarian beef soup
Hühnerbrühe Chicken soup
Kartoffelsuppe Potato soup

Leberknödelsuppe beef-liver dumpling soup
Linsensuppe lentil soup
Nudelsuppe noodle soup
Ochsenschwanzsuppe oxtail soup
Schildkrötensuppe turtle soup

Salads

Gemischter Salat Mixed salad
Gurkensalat Cucumber salad

Kopfsalat/Grünsalat Lettuce salad
Tomatensalat Tomato salad

Sandwiches

Käsebrot Cheese sandwich
Schinkenbrot Ham sandwich

Wurstbrot Sausage sandwich

Eggs

Eier in Schale Boiled eggs
Mit Speck With bacon
Rühreier Scrambled eggs
Spiegeleier Fried eggs

Verlorene Eier Poached eggs
Soleier Pickled eggs

Vegetables and Side Dishes

Artischocken Artichokes
Blumenkohl Cauliflower
Bohnen Beans
Bratkartoffeln Fried potatoes
Erbsen Peas
Grüne Bohnen Green beans
Gurken Cucumbers
Karotten Carrots
Kartoffeln Potatoes
Kartoffelsalat Potato salad

Knödel Dumplings
Kohl Cabbage
Reis Rice
Rote Rüben Red beets
Rotkraut Red cabbage
Salat Lettuce
Salzkartoffeln Boiled potatoes
Sauerkraut Sauerkraut
Spargel Asparagus
Spinat Spinach
Tomaten Tomatoes

Meats

Aufschnitt Cold cuts
Bockwurst Berlin sausage
Boulette Meatball
Brathuhn Roast chicken
Bratwurst Grilled sausage
Eisbein Pig's knuckle

Ente Duck
Gans Goose
Gefüllte Kalbsbrust Stuffed breast of veal
Hammel Mutton
Hirn Brains

Kalb Veal
Kaltes Geflügel Cold poultry
Kassler Rippchen/ Rippenspeer Pork chops
Lamm Lamb
Leber Liver
Leberkäs German meatloaf
Nieren Kidneys
Ragout Stew
Rinderbraten Roast beef
Rindfleisch Beef
Sauerbraten Marinated beef
Schinken Ham
Schlachteplatte Platter of blood sausage, liverwurst, kidneys, and boiled pork
Schweinebraten/ Schweinsbraten Roast pork
Schweinshaxen Grilled knuckle of pork
Spanferkel Suckling pig
Sülze Jellied meat
Tafelspitz Boiled beef with vegetables
Taube Pigeon
Truthahn Turkey
Wiener Schnitzel veal cutlet
Wurst Sausage

Fish

Aal Eel
Brathering Grilled herring
Forelle Trout
Hecht Pike
Karpfen Carp
Krebs Crawfish
Lachs Salmon
Makrele Mackerel
Schellfisch Haddock
Seezunge Sole

Desserts

Blatterteiggebäck Puff pastry
Bratapfel Baked apple
Eis Ice cream
Käse Cheese
Kompott Stewed fruit
Obstkuchen Fruit tart
Obstsalat Fruit salad
Pfannkuchen Sugared pancakes
Pflaumenkompott Stewed plums
Teegebäck Tea cakes
Torten Pastries

Fruits

Ananas Pineapple
Apfel Apple
Apfelsinen Oranges
Bananen Bananas
Birnen Pears
Erdbeeren Strawberries
Kirschen Cherries
Pfirsiche Peaches
Weintrauben Grapes
Zitronen Lemons

Beverages

Bier Beer
Berliner Weisse Draft wheat beer with a shot of raspberry or green woodruff syrup
Bier vom Fass Draft beer
Bock Bier Dark and rich beer
Ein Dunkles A dark beer
Ein Helles A light beer
Pils Light and bitter beer
Milch Milk
Saft Juice
Apfelsaft Apple juice
Sahne Cream
Schokolade Chocolate
Eine Tasse Kaffee A cup of coffee
Eine Tasse Tee A cup of tea
Tomatensaft Tomato juice
Wasser Water
Wein Wine
Sekt Champagne

Rotwein Red wine   **Weinbrand** Brandy
Weisswein White wine

GLOSSARY

Altstadt old town (traditional part of town or city)
Apotheke pharmacy
Art deco stylized art and architecture in the 1920s and 1930s
Art nouveau highly decorative form of art, objects, and interior design with twining, flowing motifs, late 19th and early 20th centuries
Bahn railway, train
    Bahnhof railway station
    Hauptbahnhof main railway station
    Stadtbahn (S-Bahn) commuter railway
    Untergrundbahn (U-Bahn) subway, city underground system
Baroque ornate, decorated style of architecture in the 18th century, characterized by use of elaborate ornamentation and gilding. Also applied to art of the same period.
Bauhaus style of functional design for architecture and objects, originating in early 20th century in Germany
Biedermeier Solid, bourgeois style of furniture design and interior decoration in the middle 19th century
Der Blaue Reiter group of nonfigurative painters, founded in Munich in 1911 by Franz Marc and Wassily Kandinsky
Die Brücke group of avant-garde expressionist painters originating in Dresden around 1905
Burg fortified castle
Dom cathedral
Drogerie shop selling cosmetics and sundries
Expressionism style of painting in early 20th century Germany characterized by strong use of form and color
Gothic medieval architectural style characterized by arches, soaring spaces, and ribbed vaulting, lasting into the 16th century; also applied to painting of the period
Jugendstil German form of art nouveau
Kaufhaus department store
Kirche church
Kneipe bar, mostly for drinking
Konditorei café for coffee and pastries
Kunst art
Oper opera/opera house
Rathaus town or city hall
Schauspielhaus theater for plays
Schloss palace, castle
Secession modernist movement in German art that strongly disavowed expressionism.
Stadt town, city
Tor gateway
Turm tower
Verkehrsamt tourist office
Zitadelle fortress

B. CLIMATE & CONVERSION TABLES

BERLIN'S AVERAGE DAYTIME TEMPERATURE AND RAINFALL

Temperature

	Jan	Feb	Mar	Apr	May	June	July	Aug	Sept	Oct	Nov	Dec
Temp. °F	30	32	40	48	53	60	64	62	56	49	40	34
°C	−1	0	4	9	12	16	18	17	13	9	4	1

Rainfall

Inches	2.2	1.6	1.2	1.6	2.3	2.9	3.2	2.7	2.2	1.6	2.4	1.9

MILEAGE TABLE
Distances from Berlin

Bonn	375 miles	Koblenz	379
Bremen	243	Lübeck	200
Cologne	357	Munich	363
Constance	200	Nürnberg	272
Düsseldorf	350	Stuttgart	392
Frankfurt	343	Trier	450
Hamburg	184	Wiesbaden	361
Kiel	226	Würzburg	309

CURRENCY EXCHANGE TABLE

At this writing, U.S. $1 = approximately 1.65 DM (or 1 DM = 61¢), and this was the rate of exchange used to calculate the dollar values given in this book (rounded to the nearest nickel). This rate fluctuates from time to time and may not be the same when you travel to Berlin. Therefore, the following table should be used only as a rough guide.

DM	U.S. $	DM	U.S. $	DM	U.S. $
1	.61	9	5.49	45	27.45
2	1.22	10	6.10	50	30.50
3	1.83	15	9.15	60	36.60
4	2.44	20	12.20	70	42.70
5	3.05	25	15.25	80	48.80
6	3.66	30	18.30	90	54.90
7	4.27	35	21.35	100	61.00
8	4.88	40	24.40	500	305.00

THE METRIC SYSTEM

LENGTH

1 millimeter (mm)	=	.04 inches (*or* less than 1/16 in.)
1 centimeter (cm	=	.39 inches (*or* just under ½ in.)
1 meter (m)	=	39 inches (*or* about 1.1 yards)
1 kilometer (km)	=	.62 miles (*or* about ⅔ of a mile)

To convert kilometers to miles, multiply the number of kilometers by .62. Also use to convert kilometers per hour (kmph) to miles per hours (m.p.h.)

To convert miles to kilometers, multiply the number of miles by 1.61. Also use to convert speeds from m.p.h. to kmph.

CAPACITY

1 liter (l)	=	33.92 fluid ounces	=	2.1 pints	=	1.06 quarts
	=	.26 U.S. gallons				
1 Imperial gallon	=	1.2 U.S. gallons				

To convert liters to U.S. gallons, multiply the number of liters by .26.

To convert U.S. gallons to liters, multiply the number of gallons by 3.79.

To convert Imperial gallons to U.S. gallons, multiply the number of Imperial gallons by 1.2.

To convert U.S. gallons to Imperial gallons, multiply the number of U.S. gallons by .83.

WEIGHT

1 gram (g)	=	.035 ounces (*or* about a paperclip's weight)
1 kilogram (kg)	=	35.2 ounces
	=	2.2 pounds
1 metric ton	=	2,205 pounds = 1.1 short ton

To convert kilograms to pounds, multiply the number of kilograms by 2.2

To convert pounds to kilograms, multiply the pounds by .45.

TEMPERATURE

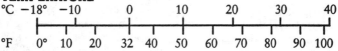

°C	−18°	−10		0		10		20		30		40
°F	0°	10	20	32	40	50	60	70	80	90	100	

To convert degrees Celsius to degrees Fahrenheit, multiply °C by 9, divide by 5, and add 32 (example: 20°C × 9/5 + 32 = 68°F).

To convert degrees Fahrenheit to degrees Celsius, subtract 32 from °F, multiply by 5, then divide by 9 (example: 85°F − 32 × 5/9 = 29.4°C).

INDEX

GENERAL INFORMATION

SIGHTS AND ATTRACTIONS

EAST BERLIN

Note: Asterisks indicate author's favorites

WEST BERLIN

DAY-TRIP AREAS

ACCOMMODATIONS

EAST BERLIN

WEST BERLIN

Key to Abbreviations: B = Budget; D = Deluxe; E = Expensive; I = Inexpensive; M = Moderately priced; asterisks indicate author's favorites

RESTAURANTS

EAST BERLIN

Key to Abbreviations: *B* = Budget; *E* = Expensive; *I* = Inexpensive; *M* = Moderate; *VE* = Very Expensive; asterisks indicate author's favorites

WEST BERLIN

DAY-TRIP AREAS

NOW, SAVE MONEY ON ALL
YOUR TRAVELS!
Join Frommer's™ Dollarwise® Travel Club

Saving money while traveling is never a simple matter, which is why the **Dollarwise Travel Club** was formed 31 years ago. Developed in response to requests from Frommer's Travel Guide readers, the Club provides cost-cutting travel strategies, up-to-date travel information, and a sense of community for value-conscious travelers from all over the world.

In keeping with the money-saving concept, the annual membership fee is low—$20 for U.S. residents or $25 for residents of Canada, Mexico, and other countries—and is immediately exceeded by the value of your benefits, which include:

1. Any TWO books listed on the following pages.
2. Plus any ONE Frommer's City Guide.
3. A subscription to our quarterly newspaper, *The Dollarwise Traveler*.
4. A membership card that entitles you to purchase through the Club all Frommer's publications for 33% to 40% off their retail price.

The eight-page *Dollarwise Traveler* tells you about the latest developments in good-value travel worldwide and includes the following columns: **Hospitality Exchange** (for those offering and seeking hospitality In cities all over the world); **Share-a-Trip** (for those looking for travel companions to share costs); and **Readers Ask . . . Readers Reply** (for those with travel questions that other members can answer).

Aside from the Frommer's Guides and the Gault Millau Guides, you can also choose from our Special Editions. These include such titles as *California with Kids* (a compendium of the best of California's accommodations, restaurants, and sightseeing attractions appropriate for those traveling with toddlers through teens); *Candy Apple: New York with Kids* (a spirited guide to the Big Apple by a savvy New York grandmother that's perfect for both visitors and residents); *Caribbean Hideaways* (the 100 most romantic places to stay in the Islands, all rated on ambience, food, sports opportunities, and price); *Honeymoon Destinations* (a guide to planning and choosing just the right destination from hundreds of possibilities in the U.S., Mexico, and the Caribbean); *Marilyn Wood's Wonderful Weekends* (a selection of the best mini-vacations within a 200-mile radius of New York City, including descriptions of country inns and other accommodations, restaurants, picnic spots, sights, and activities); and *Paris Rendez-Vous* (a delightful guide to the best places to meet in Paris whether for power breakfasts or dancing till dawn).

To join this Club, simply send the appropriate membership fee with your name and address to: Frommer's Dollarwise Travel Club, 15 Columbus Circle, New York, NY 10023. Remember to specify which single city guide and which two other guides you wish to receive in your initial package of member's benefits. Or tear out the next page, check off your choices, and send the page to us with your membership fee.

FROMMER BOOKS
PRENTICE HALL PRESS
15 COLUMBUS CIRCLE
NEW YORK, NY 10023
212/373-8125

Date_____

Friends:

Please send me the books checked below.

FROMMER'S™ GUIDES

(Guides to sightseeing and tourist accommodations and facilities from budget to deluxe, with emphasis on the medium-priced.)

☐ Alaska $14.95		☐ Germany $14.95
☐ Australia $14.95		☐ Italy $14.95
☐ Austria & Hungary $14.95		☐ Japan & Hong Kong $14.95
☐ Belgium, Holland & Lux-		☐ Mid-Atlantic States $14.95
embourg $14.95		☐ New England $14.95
☐ Bermuda & The Bahamas . . . $14.95		☐ New Mexico (avail. June '91) $12.95
☐ Brazil $14.95		☐ New York State $14.95
☐ Canada $14.95		☐ Northwest $15.95
☐ Caribbean $14.95		☐ Portugal, Madeira & the Azores $14.95
☐ Cruises (incl. Alaska, Carib, Mex, Ha-		☐ Scandinavia (avail. May '91) $15.95
waii, Panama, Canada & US) . . $14.95		☐ South Pacific $14.95
☐ California & Las Vegas $14.95		☐ Southeast Asia $14.95
☐ Egypt $14.95		☐ Southern Atlantic States $14.95
☐ England & Scotland $14.95		☐ Southwest $14.95
☐ Florida $14.95		☐ Switzerland & Liechtenstein $14.95
☐ France $14.95		☐ USA $16.95

FROMMER'S $-A-DAY® GUIDES

(In-depth guides to sightseeing and low-cost tourist accommodations and facilities.)

☐ Europe on $40 a Day $15.95		☐ Israel on $40 a Day $13.95
☐ Australia on $40 a Day $13.95		☐ Mexico on $35 a Day $14.95
☐ Costa Rica, Guatemala & Belize		☐ New York on $60 a Day $13.95
on $35 a Day (avail. Mar. '91) $15.95		☐ New Zealand on $45 a Day $13.95
☐ Eastern Europe on $25 a Day $15.95		☐ Scotland & Wales on $40 a Day $13.95
☐ England on $50 a Day $13.95		☐ South America on $40 a Day $15.95
☐ Greece on $35 a Day $13.95		☐ Spain on $50 a Day $15.95
☐ Hawaii on $60 a Day $14.95		☐ Turkey on $30 a Day $13.95
☐ India on $25 a Day $12.95		☐ Washington, D.C. & Historic Va. on
☐ Ireland on $40 a Day $14.95		$40 a Day $13.95

FROMMER'S TOURING GUIDES

(Color illustrated guides that include walking tours, cultural and historic sites, and other vital travel information.)

☐ Amsterdam $10.95		☐ New York $10.95
☐ Australia $10.95		☐ Paris $8.95
☐ Brazil $10.95		☐ Rome $10.95
☐ Egypt $8.95		☐ Scotland $9.95
☐ Florence $8.95		☐ Thailand $10.95
☐ Hong Kong $10.95		☐ Turkey $10.95
☐ London $10.95		☐ Venice $8.95

(TURN PAGE FOR ADDITONAL BOOKS AND ORDER FORM)

1290

FROMMER'S CITY GUIDES

(Pocket-size guides to sightseeing and tourist accommodations and facilities in all price ranges.)

☐ Amsterdam/Holland	$8.95	☐ Minneapolis/St. Paul	$8.95
☐ Athens	$8.95	☐ Montréal/Québec City	$8.95
☐ Atlanta	$8.95	☐ New Orleans	$8.95
☐ Atlantic City/Cape May	$8.95	☐ New York	$8.95
☐ Barcelona	$7.95	☐ Orlando	$8.95
☐ Belgium	$7.95	☐ Paris	$8.95
☐ Berlin (avail. Mar. '91)	$8.95	☐ Philadelphia	$8.95
☐ Boston	$8.95	☐ Rio	$8.95
☐ Cancún/Cozumel/Yucatán	$8.95	☐ Rome	$8.95
☐ Chicago	$8.95	☐ Salt Lake City	$8.95
☐ Denver/Boulder/Colorado		☐ San Diego	$8.95
Springs	$7.95	☐ San Francisco	$8.95
☐ Dublin/Ireland	$8.95	☐ Santa Fe/Taos/Albuquerque	$8.95
☐ Hawaii	$8.95	☐ Seattle/Portland	$7.95
☐ Hong Kong	$7.95	☐ St. Louis/Kansas City (avail. May '91)	$8.95
☐ Las Vegas	$8.95	☐ Sydney	$8.95
☐ Lisbon/Madrid/Costa del Sol	$8.95	☐ Tampa/St. Petersburg	$8.95
☐ London	$8.95	☐ Tokyo	$7.95
☐ Los Angeles	$8.95	☐ Toronto	$8.95
☐ Mexico City/Acapulco	$8.95	☐ Vancouver/Victoria	$7.95
☐ Miami	$8.95	☐ Washington, D.C.	$8.95

SPECIAL EDITIONS

☐ Beat the High Cost of Travel	$6.95	☐ Motorist's Phrase Book (Fr/Ger/Sp)	$4.95
☐ Bed & Breakfast—N. America	$14.95	☐ Paris Rendez-Vous	$10.95
☐ California with Kids	$15.95	☐ Swap and Go (Home Exchanging)	$10.95
☐ Caribbean Hideaways	$14.95	☐ The Candy Apple (NY with Kids)	$12.95
☐ Manhattan's Outdoor		☐ Travel Diary and Record Book	$5.95
Sculpture	$15.95		

☐ Honeymoon Destinations (US, Mex & Carib) $14.95

☐ Where to Stay USA (From $3 to $30 a night) $13.95

☐ Marilyn Wood's Wonderful Weekends (CT, DE, MA, NH, NJ, NY, PA, RI, VT) $11.95

☐ The New World of Travel (Annual sourcebook by Arthur Frommer for savvy travelers) . . $16.95

GAULT MILLAU

(The only guides that distinguish the truly superlative from the merely overrated.)

☐ The Best of Chicago	$15.95	☐ The Best of Los Angeles	$16.95
☐ The Best of France	$16.95	☐ The Best of New England	$15.95
☐ The Best of Hawaii	$16.95	☐ The Best of New Orleans	$16.95
☐ The Best of Hong Kong	$16.95	☐ The Best of New York	$16.95
☐ The Best of Italy	$16.95	☐ The Best of Paris	$16.95
☐ The Best of London	$16.95	☐ The Best of San Francisco	$16.95

☐ The Best of Washington, D.C. $16.95

ORDER NOW!

In U.S. include $2 shipping UPS for 1st book; $1 ea. add'l book. Outside U.S. $3 and $1, respectively.
Allow four to six weeks for delivery in U.S., longer outside U.S.

Enclosed is my check or money order for $_____

NAME_____

ADDRESS_____

CITY_____ STATE_____ ZIP_____

1290